T0354949

Endorsements:

This is a great book that explains the new life called truth which comes from heaven above. John 18:37 — *"You say rightly that I am a king. For this cause I was born, and for this cause I have come into the world, that I should bear witness to the truth. Everyone who is of the truth hears My voice."* The now generation has an ear to hear Father. The Spirit of the Son can awaken all who read this book. Thanks for friends in high places, — Pastor Jim Chiddix

It is an honor to know Randy and his family. Their character represents the character of God.

It is my privilege to have the opportunity to recommend this book to all who will take time to dive into its pages. I am confident that as you read this a fresh yearning for intimacy with God will be birthed. This book is full of present day truth revealed through the Holy Spirit. This truth will set you free. Within the pages of this book is but just the beginning of a new depth of understanding about God and his perfect love. God is love! — Connie Boyer

'Seeing From Heaven' is well written and a must read for everyone. The simple yet profound message found throughout this book has given me new insights in how to approach God's word and apply it to my life. I enjoyed this book and want to read it again and again. I recommend it to everyone as it can help those who have been turned off by "religion" as well as Christians who have been struggling with various issues like guilt and judgmental attitudes. — Janet Jenkins

SEEING *from* HEAVEN

RANDY FINLAY

iUniverse, Inc.
Bloomington

Seeing from Heaven

iUniverse books may be ordered through booksellers or by contacting:

iUniverse
1663 Liberty Drive
Bloomington, IN 47403
www.iuniverse.com
1-800-Authors (1-800-288-4677)

ISBN: 978-1-4502-7759-4 (sc)
ISBN: 978-1-4502-7761-7 (dj)
ISBN: 978-1-4502-7760-0 (ebk)

Printed in the United States of America

iUniverse rev. date: 11/29/2010

TABLE OF CONTENTS

Part 1: Who Is God

Chapter 1: Jesus Is The Chief Cornerstone 7

Chapter 2: Jesus Is The Lamb of God 55

Chapter 3: Jesus Is The King of Kings 91

Chapter 4: God Is Love 128

Chapter 5: God is Good 145

Chapter 6: Who Is God 183

Part 2: The Finished Work

Chapter 1: An End To The Law 201

Chapter 2: Jesus Finished What He Came To Do 218

Chapter 3: God's Judgment And Wrath 239

Chapter 4: Redemption Is A Finished Work 253

Chapter 5: Jesue Reconciled The Whole World 261

Chapter 6: The Kingdom Of Heaven Is At Hand 274

Chapter 7: The I AM 281

SEEING FROM HEAVEN

Introduction

'SEEING FROM HEAVEN' is a book with a God given purpose of renewing the mind or getting a mind-set so we can have God's perspective rather than our own earth bound or traditional view. It is not written for the purpose of destroying anyone's true hope or beliefs, but it may very well cause us to see differently from the Highest point of view, His! So it is not an attempt to get people to believe my way or the way of Pentecost, or Baptist, or Methodist, or the faith movement, or Kingdom, or anything else. It is about seeing God and then seeing through His eyes, which will surely give us greater hope and beliefs than what we might have had before.

If it is truly, I no longer live, but Christ that lives in me[1], then it's not about my religion, or traditional teachings, or my own beliefs. It is all about who He is, and His expression of life in and through me. At this point my life is absorbed into His and my believing comes out of that oneness.

We would naturally think that what God believes is right, and He has the right belief, but that is not true. Nowhere in the Bible does it say, God believes this, that, and another thing. God doesn't have

---

1   Gal. 2:20

a set of beliefs that He follows. That in itself would limit God and place Him under His own laws of a belief system. He only believes His word that comes out of His life-giving spirit of love. There are no rules, no laws, no set of beliefs, and no need for restraint because His life is pure, holy, and good without any variation or shadow of turning. Jesus never stated that, "I believe God to be such and such." He knows his Father and is one with the Father. He was God and a partaker of that life.

Jesus expressed Himself as knowing the Father personally; therefore, He was not governed by the laws of Moses or even Jewish customs. Jesus had no need to live by such things when He had the life of God dwelling in Him. It was Jesus' custom to go into the synagogue, but not as a Jew under the law, but as a Son having intimate relations with the Father! He was born a Jew, but He knew He was the Son. And the Son is of a higher order of life (zoe) than that of the Jew under the law. He is from above, but the Jews and Gentiles alike are from below, if they still have an unrighteous conscience. But, we are from above if we are in Christ, for our citizenship is in heaven.

Knowing this, Jesus saw the law as not a set of rules to follow in order to please His Father. He saw the law as a revelation of who the Father is and who He is. God does not steal, but He gives. God does not bear false witness, but He is the truth. God does not commit adultery, but He is the faithful marriage partner who will never leave us nor forsake us, even if while in darkness, we forsake Him. As a Son, Jesus fulfilled the law and the prophets, not as a Jew observing the law and under the law, but as a Son. So Jesus lived His life as a divine expression of the Father's life in Him, and not by certain beliefs established by the law. So, it is not by our beliefs that we are to live by, but as Christ Jesus lived by the life of God in Him, so do we.

Our beliefs should only draw us closer to God and reassure us of His love and goodness He has toward us. Our beliefs should cause us to see Him more clearly so we might freely partake of His life. Then it is according to that impression of His life in us that we live and move and have our being. By this life-giving impression we can say as Jesus said, "I only speak what I hear my Father speak, and I only do what I see my Father do."[2] Why? As He is, so are we in this world. Jesus saw the Father and then saw Himself. How so? He knew He was sent from His Father in His likeness and image as his Son. Whose image does the word of God say you are made in? Whose son are you? Not the son of the first Adam, because he died on the cross, but you are the son of the resurrected Christ man from heaven manifest in the earth![3] You are the risen Christ![4] For you are a member of His body, and He is the head![5]

Did Jesus have certain beliefs? Yes, He believed what the Father told Him and showed Him, but not as a hard rule of law to obey or follow, but as an expression of His greater life at that time called the I AM. Really what Jesus was saying in Jn. 14 is that if you want to see the Father, I AM! Jesus ate always from the tree of life and not from the tree of the knowledge of good and evil. Adam ate of that tree in Gen. 2 and that sin of separation of thought from oneness with the Spirit brought death. Jesus never lived or judged by the knowledge of knowing good and evil. He was tempted in the wilderness by such thoughts, but He never succumbed to those thoughts.

As one eating from the tree of life, we cannot be a hard-nosed, stiff-necked people who stress our differences in beliefs. There is no partaking of the tree of life when we do such things, only the eating of the tree of the knowledge of good and evil. Stating our differences must be as an expression of His indwelling life, or we are only offering to others to eat of the fruit of the knowledge of good and evil. If we think or express ourselves that our beliefs are better than your beliefs, then this is an

---

2 Jn. 8:26, 8:28, 8:38, 12:50, 5:36, 10:25, 14:10

3 Rom. 8:15, 6:4 & 5

4 1 Cor. 15:21, Php. 3:10

5 1 Cor. 6:19, Eph. 5:23, Col. 1:18

expression of the law without the Spirit. Even if they truly are better or greater beliefs, they have no power to deliver or help because they did not contain His life of love when we declare them. Declaring the truth as a revelation of who He is will cause wrong beliefs to disappear in the sight of His glory and grace. The same with sin, we should not preach against sin; but by preaching righteousness that comes through what Jesus did alone will remove even the desire to sin. The life of Christ in us is far better than the short temporal pleasures of sin. Sure, temptations will come just as they came to Jesus; but just like Jesus, our oneness with our Father is of a greater and more satisfying way of life.

We have all been at the place where we unknowingly honor and even esteem our own personal beliefs above that of the life and nature of God dwelling in us. It is our pride in our beliefs and traditions that we have that caused us to express ourselves with an attitude that declares: I have my own beliefs, so don't try to change what I believe! This seems to be the response of most church going people today. Why is it such a mystery to us who believe in the <u>One</u> Lord Jesus Christ, as to the way God sees and views things? If He is the Head of the Church, let us see with His eyes. Let's put on the head of Christ rather than the head of Adam (the unrenewed mind). Is it the body that has eyes or the head? Jesus is the Head of the body of believers. Our Head can be speaking to us in our spirit, but the head of religious Adam is saying something else. So let us honor the life of Christ in us above our beliefs. Then we will begin to truly see as He sees. Now we are open for change; and a greater awareness and revelation awaits us!

Pride in our set of beliefs seems to be more valuable to us than loving one another. We take pride in being able to defend our beliefs without expressing His life in whom we believe. (Selah) We train up others, even our own children, so that they can defend our beliefs. In doing so, there may be the absence of the presence of God and His love; and therefore, no expression of His higher life is experienced in such training. 'Seeing From Heaven' is all about God, and thus seeing all things from God's heavenly perspective, so that He may indeed be all and in all.[6] It is my hope and the dream of my heart to reveal the life of Christ in us so we might see His point of view from the throne in heaven as our expression of His life.

Our beliefs are extremely important. Our beliefs form our God! If there is something we believe that is untrue about God and what He is saying in His written word, then that untruth forms an image of God in our minds. That particular belief has just made an idol or man-made image of God. That image affects us and how we see ourselves and others. That false image is powerless and speechless to help. It is powerless, because it is a deception. It is speechless, because it doesn't speak by the Spirit, but only by our lying imaginations. It will also turn us away from the true and living God. So what we believe is of utmost importance because what we believe is what we will partake of and express in this life.

A good close look at the Chief Cornerstone is the foundational stone for seeing from heaven's viewpoint.[7] That point of view is literally the life of Christ, which is the highest expression of life. It is impossible to lay another foundation of truth because the foundation is already laid in Christ Jesus. Christ is the unchangeable foundation. Therefore, we will only be taking a close look at that which is already laid so we might see Him. The right view of God should always point to or reflect Christ Jesus, the Chief Cornerstone of our foundation. If it does not, we should ask ourselves and God what is this view of what was spoken pointing me to? The truth, the kingdom of heaven, the scriptures, and the gospel is not of any man's private interpretations of the word of God that might intrigue us or fit our concept of what we believe. But it is seeing God so that we may see all things from within that life revealed to us.

No one shall see God and live is a wonderful and glorious scripture that tells us when we see God, Adam or the man of the sinful flesh dies

---

6   Mat. 4:6
7   1 Cor. 3:11, Eph. 2:20, 1 Pet. 2:6

having seen Him who died as us. Seeing God also changes our Adamic thinking so our mind is renewed.[8] No flesh having sin (Adam) can stand in the presence of God. Yet, we can boldly come into the presence of God as one not born of flesh and blood only, but born of God and still having a flesh and blood body! With the death of Adam, then must come the death of the old Adamic thinking. Unless we see Him as He truly is today, how can we be married to Him today? How can we be married to a stranger? No, when we see Him, we are drawn to Him; and His appearing to us draws us into oneness with Him. It produces the death of our old Adamic thinking.

We are raised with Him as a new creation in this life having the thoughts of God![9] When we see God clearly, our lower perspective is changed by the greater light dawning in us! That's a glorious changing! The death of Adam and our old Adamic thinking is a good thing; the temporal now is the temple of the eternal and the corruptible mind has put on the incorruptible! Unless the (old) husband dies, we are not free to marry another, who is Christ. But, the only thing powerful enough to bring about that death and change of mind is seeing God! Every time we truly see God without religion or tradition, we become partakers of His divine life, and are changed from glory to glory!

This book, though inspired of God, is not the whole book that could be and yet shall be written of Him. Neither do I attempt to cover in depth everything that could be written and yet shall be. The Lord has total rights to take away from this book or add to it as the knowledge of Him increases to you by His Spirit. So as you read and study this book, do not allow religious differences, opinions, or old teachings to sway you one way or another, but allow only the Holy Spirit to lead and guide you into all truth, and we all shall be changed according to His image.

---

8   Rom. 12:2
9   2 Cor. 5:17, 1 Cor. 2:16

SEEING FROM HEAVEN

PART 1

WHO IS GOD

Chapter 1

JESUS IS THE CHIEF CORNERSTONE

How can looking at a foundation give anyone a view from heaven? Jesus Christ was from heaven, and He is the foundation of heaven by which the earth was made. That foundation came in the flesh as the Chief Cornerstone for all our lives to be built and formed on. So, looking at Him is not looking at earthly things, but heavenly things manifest in the earth. Jesus totally meant it when He said, "The kingdom of heaven is near," and "The kingdom of God is within you."[10] Heaven is as near to you as your inner man, your spirit. Heaven is the atmosphere/aurora of the kingdom of God that is within you. Now, for an earth dweller to see from Heaven, he most likely cannot physically go there to look and see. He must see from that same heaven that dwells in us all. That heaven within us does not need to be developed, for it is already complete. It

---

10   Mat. 3:2, Lk. 17:21

is after all heaven, the dwelling place of God, the presence of God, and the kingdom of God.

All we need is to look at and understand the Chief Cornerstone. He is the Son of man from heaven and He brought heaven with Him; therefore, seeing Jesus the Christ is seeing heaven. This reality causes us to come into Christ as one in Him. Being in Him who is seated at the right hand of the Father is looking out from within heaven.[11] We are seated in heavenly places in Christ Jesus.[12] It is a spiritual place that is pure and much higher than our natural minds or what our five senses can comprehend alone. But, the Christ in us, being unveiled to us is our hope of dwelling in such a place called Heaven.

You are not a physical house trying to become spiritual. You have a physical body wherein the living Spirit of God now dwells. You are a spiritual house! You have been given a physical body in which you are able to manifest the presence of God in and through that body. It is really the presence of God that keeps the physical body, not the other way around. What is the presence of God? Is it not heaven? We do not need to die first in order to experience heaven. Heaven is in you, and if you can see from God's perspective, heaven is all around you.

If God was to move the spiritual life out of the physical body, the physical body would become as dead. The spiritual life is eternal, but the physical house is temporal. So, it is the physical body that depends on the spiritual life for its existence. It is the owner that lives in the house that does all the maintenance on the house that keeps the house from collapsing. Most of us spend too much of our time looking at the appearance of the house, outer man, the body of flesh. We dress it up to make it look good, and exercise to make it look healthy. While all this time and effort is good for the body, we seem to forget that it is the Christ in us that holds all things together. We can dress up Adam all we want and heaven is not impressed one bit. It is when we put on the inner man,

11   Eph. 1:20
12   Eph. 2:6

and clothe ourselves with the life and love of God, that all of heaven takes notice. The joy of the Lord empowers or strengthens our natural body.[13] It is a good idea to dress up Adam, the natural earthy man needs it; but putting on the new man is far more valuable and beneficial to all.

It is when we put on the Christ man, that people have a tendency not to notice our outward appearance as much. The Chief Cornerstone reveals the Christ in you. It is a spiritual awakening and revelation, not a physical one that can manifest the Cornerstone to us; therefore, any interpretation of the scriptures that points us to some future physical event in time falls way short of the greater view from heaven and a spiritual understanding. A true spiritual revelation reveals to us the hidden man of the heart, our hope of glory.

No more does God see us as having filthy rags since we have come into this grace of His. He now sees the glory of Himself living in us! If we could just see what He sees, then look out world! For a man of God will truly be walking the earth! And you are that man! Not the physical man, but that spiritual man that comes from heaven! If you can see from heaven, then you can come from heaven with your thoughts, presence, and life giving power.

This place called heaven is also described as a city whose maker and builder is God. It is not a physical location, but a spiritual knowing and understanding. Heaven is a spiritual place, and the foundation of that city lies within you and all who have believed! Looking at the foundation and looking from that place of the foundation gives us a view from that city that God has built. Within that city dwells all who now believe on the Lord Jesus Christ which is why there is such a wonderful manifestation of the presence of God when we meet together. It's not because we are such great and wonderful people in and of ourselves, but because the Living Stone of the foundation makes us all lively stones. We are the expression of the life of God which comes from heaven or from His life giving Spirit.

---

13   Neh. 8:10

Seeing the Chief Cornerstone, the Lord Jesus Christ, His life, His character, and His accomplishments will change our thinking and renew our minds. If you do not desire a further change of mind, stop here and read no farther. But, if you still desire more of God and to know Him more intimately, then you must also desire change, a change of mind. It's been quoted, "If you always do what you've always done, you'll always have what you've always had." Thinking the same way and doing the same thing but expecting different results just doesn't add up. But, if you desire more of God, then seeing God will shake your heavens and your earth thus bringing change in both realms. That desire is from God; and you are a prime candidate for seeing God through the eyes of a little child and understanding the simplicity of His word. Even the most mature sons of God must remain as little children in their own eyes before they can live like manifested sons of God. When Jesus said, "God is My Father"; He was also saying that He sees Himself as a little child. A little child desires and clings to love, relationships, guidance, knowledge of the truth, and is thrilled about discovering who his family is. In this manner the child discovers who they are. Children are easily encouraged and empowered. Seeing God and partaking of His life freely gives us all these things.

All that may be gleaned from 'Seeing From Heaven' is up to each individual or group of people who study the Cornerstone and yield to the great teacher, the Holy Spirit. It is my sincere prayer that in every person there be a hunger to know Christ in a greater light of knowledge and understanding by His Spirit. We may be looking into a mirror today and seeing ourselves from an earthly perspective, which is seeing dimly, but then face to face. When is the 'then' going to come so we can see Him face to face? When we come to an understanding that we are today as He is, which is according to the word of God. We <u>are</u> the light of the world and not just a reflection of the light, because the light of His life is in us. Our spirit is face to face with the Spirit of God, which is where the light comes from.[14] True Christianity is not an attempt to

---

14   Rom. 8:16

imitate Christ, or Jesus, or Paul or anyone else, but a reality of knowing and experiencing oneness with Christ. The first is an imitation, the latter is <u>being</u> who you were created to be.

Our being face to face with God is not like a Moses view of the backside of God with the understanding that comes from a works mentality. Nor does seeing God face to face include what we have done or are doing. Nor does it identify God by the experience of what we think He's done in response to our failure to keep the law. But Christ, the very presence of God, is already laid in us as a living stone separate from the law by which we are already in His image and likeness. A further unveiling of Christ in us causes us to see Him as He is, as one who is face to face. Never in the Old Testament scriptures did it say, "You are the light of the world." It is Jesus Christ, the foundation laid in us that makes us lights, for He is the light of every man that comes into the world.[15] That light causes us to see Him face to face. If we are looking into the light, we are looking into His face. God is light.[16]

Have you ever asked yourself; how do I see God face to face when God is a Spirit? How do you see a spirit? By faith in His living word, and by the life of Christ that dwells in us. <u>Seeing God face to face is knowing what God is about to do before He does something, not after He does it.</u> Looking into the face of God creates in us corresponding action that expresses His life. Looking at the Chief Cornerstone, which is not a thing but a description of a person, the Lord Jesus Christ, is seeing the Father face to face. Looking at Him is looking into the eyes of God. It reveals the character, thoughts and intents of the heart of God, and the finished works of Jesus Christ. Too often we have in the past looked at our own flesh, which reveals only the man of the flesh, sinful flesh. God has instructed us to look at no man after the flesh, and that includes ourselves.[17] But looking at Christ reveals only the new

---

15   Jn. 1:9
16   1 Jn. 1:5
17   2 Cor. 5:16

man hidden in that body of flesh. He is the pearl of great price in the field, and you are that field.

Looking at one another after the flesh is having an earthly perspective. That is Adam's view point or opinion which none of us are interested in.

> **2 Cor. 5:16 — *Therefore, from now on, we regard no one according to the flesh. Even though we have known Christ according to the flesh, yet now we know Him thus no longer.***

The word regard means to see, know, behold, look upon, consider, or understand. We even knew Christ according to the flesh. In other words, we judged Him by what He did. We used to judge one another by what they did. But now, we know or see no one according to the works of the flesh but according to the Christ that dwells in them. If you see someone do wrong, how are we who are spiritual supposed to restore them? By ripping them apart with words that condemn in hope that they learned their lesson? No! In the spirit of meekness, we remind them of who they really are. You are not the person of the flesh but of the new creation in the image and likeness of God. We have a tendency to forget who we really are; and therefore, we need reminded that we are of God little children and have overcome them that are in the world.[18] Our flesh is of this world, but our spirit is of God. It is our mind that needs a true image of who we came from and who we are and to whom we are going.

Training ourselves to look from the <u>living</u> Corner<u>stone</u> as our perspective will cause us to look anew into a mirror and see only the Christ in us. This is how the corruptible puts on incorruption and the mortal man puts on immortality. It is then that we are seeing face to face and know that we are loved. Then we are able to love

---

18   1 Jn. 4:4

others as He has loved us. We can only love one another as we love ourselves.[19] When we are loved by our Lord Jesus Christ, we cannot help but love who He has made us to be. We actually love who we are because He loves us! We are able to love others with the same love He loves us with.

In the same way we can only minister as we have been ministered to. Jesus ministered many times after being in prayer all night long. Jesus was being ministered to by the Father. Now He was able to minister to others even as He was ministered to. To the same measure that Jesus was loved by His Father, He was able to love others.

We can only truly live as we see His life in us. The Chief Cornerstone gives us such a view from heaven, the throne of God. It causes us to see ourselves as God sees us, which has no condemnation and is without fault finding. Now the Church will have a much greater impact in this world. Instead of calling themselves Christians, others will call them Christians because they see the real Christ in them.

'Cause and Effect' — 'Cause I see greater things than these earthly, natural, and limited things, I have greater effect. Just as Jesus came from heaven, so are we coming from heaven because His life is giving us His view from heaven. I'm not talking about knowing a bunch of stuff about Him that we have learned along the way. Those things might be good, but I'm talking about recognizing the Christ in you as your life source that then gives you the mind of Christ. Christ making impressions from within you upon your mind is the light of your life. If our citizenship is (now present tense) in heaven where God is light, we ought to be seeing the light of heaven now! Amen?

> **Php. 3:20, 21 —** *For our citizenship is in heaven, from which we also eagerly wait for the Savior, the Lord Jesus Christ, who will transform our lowly* **(earthly image)** *body that it may be conformed to*

19   Eph. 5:28, 33, Jn. 13:34

13

***His glorious body, according to the working by which
He is able even to subdue all things to Himself.***

From our dwelling place in heaven, we wait, look for, and expect fully the Savior, the Lord Jesus Christ. Too often we put off into the future what we can have now. Our citizenship is now in heaven, not just after we die. If the U.S.A. sent an ambassador to China, the American is taken out of the U.S.A.; but the U.S.A. cannot be taken out of the American. He is free on the inside and expresses himself not as a Chinese citizen, but as one from the U.S.A. He may for a short time live in China, but He lives according to his raising, training, and heritage he received while in the U.S.A. This ambassador still sees from the perspective of the U.S.A. and ministers from that point of view.

We do not live according to the lower earth life, but we look for His appearing as the Christ in us from heaven. That communion with Him will transform or change our earthly lower perspective so we might live according to the higher life as a citizen from heaven. Now the lowly body has put on Christ, incorruption, and immortality. This is how we are changed from glory to glory and are conformed to His glorious body. It's not just a futuristic hope of receiving a new body like that of Jesus Christ after He rose from the dead; it includes that. But, it is a present hope for a glorious mortal body that is now being further clothed with immortality and living according to what we see from heaven right now.

Was the appearing of Jesus on the earth in a mortal body glorious? Absolutely! Jesus did have a mortal body. But how could He walk through the crowd that was about to cast Him off a cliff? How could that mortal body walk on water? How could that mortal body be transfigured? The mortal body put on immortality by having the Father's perspective from heaven. As long as we think we are nothing but a corrupt, weak, frail, mortal human being, that is all we will be able to live in and manifest. That is nothing more than weak humanity putting on more of the same.

14

Whatever a man thinks in his heart, so is he.[20] But we desire to be further clothed with immortality.[21] Then put on Christ!

That's what God sees when He looks at us. Why? He looks upon the heart or the spirit of man, not the flesh. God sees the fullness of Christ in you! How would you live if you saw yourself every minute of the day the same way God sees you and that is having the fullness of Christ dwelling in you? We are on earth now so that we might manifest heaven on earth. Without us, Christ's body transformed and seeing from heaven, there is no manifestation of God in the earth. We need God, and God needs us to be all that He has created us to be in Christ Jesus. So, He joined us together with Himself in Christ Jesus as One. God never declared He would do anything without us but with us. We are joined to His living word.[22] Seeing as God sees is a must if we are to represent Him fully and correctly as His ambassadors.

The ambassador from the U.S.A. must see from the view point of the U.S.A. if he is to represent the U.S.A. correctly. He is not there to represent or manifest himself as though he is self-centered and self-seeking having another purpose in mind. While he is there, he is a transformed person in the image of the U.S.A. for as long as he sees correctly from that view. While in China, if he forgets who he is, then the spirit of the U.S.A will not be manifest. If he fails in representing the U.S.A. and that view, he is brought home and his view is corrected. He is further equipped by the President himself and then sent again. No condemnation, just a better understanding or view of what you are, an American! This parable is not about being an American, for every natural country has its strengths and weaknesses. But, we have a country or city whose builder and maker is God! It is a dwelling place that has no weaknesses, but is manifest in our weakness now so that we might see His appearing to us from heaven. When I am weak, then

---

20   Pro. 23:7

21   2 Cor. 5 2–5

22   Mat. 16:20

I am strong![23] Why? Seeing from heaven is seeing the grace of God working in my weakness. God's weakness is stronger than my strength by myself.

We are Christ's ambassadors and have been given His word of reconciliation, reconciling the world to Himself. We all have had our own view of what the Bible says, but His view, His heavenly view might just change our own present view. Our own view from any particular mind-set is our own opinion. We do not live out of a mind or mind-set, but a spiritual union as one with the Father. For if we have His view, that view is not our own, because we know where that view came from. So, how could we say; "I have my own beliefs or my own view of what the Bible says?" We may be on the same Ferris-Wheel, but the view at the top is much better than that from the bottom. He is always causing you to arise, for the glory of the Lord is risen upon you.[24]

No prophecy (inspired speaking) of the scripture is of any private (own self) interpretation.[25] If you easily get offended because someone says something contrary to your view or beliefs of the Bible, you are clinging to your own opinionated doctrines and beliefs, and not to His life in you. (Remember, we live by His life and not by our beliefs. Our beliefs are to lead us to Him so we might be able to identify Him.) It doesn't matter if those interpretations and beliefs were handed down from a hundred generations or came from the most famous preacher you know. If that belief doesn't come from a view as seeing from the Chief Cornerstone that is laid in you from heaven, it's not unshakable. Those beliefs will not stand the test of time. Those beliefs will die with you if you continue to see from a lower perspective. You can believe it is going to work, and believe, and believe some more, but if it is not working, then it does not work!

---

23   2 Cor. 12:10
24   Isa. 60:1
25   2 Pet. 1:20

On the other hand, if you are seeing from heaven and someone says something contrary to that of your heavenly view, then you are still at peace and not offended. You are able to speak greater things than those if prompted to. Don't bother trying to correct or share a heavenly view of the life of Christ with a hard hearted Scribe who knows it all. It is like casting your pearls before swine. Just keep your peace and keep on loving them. If they love the muddy existence they're in, clean water is not what they want to drink. It just isn't going to accomplish anything. Seed grows best in a cultivated field, not a field that is all grown up (so they think).

So, it is not my view or your view that's anything, but the view that heaven has given us, Christ's view. Then it's no longer I that speaks, but Christ in me speaking volumes.[26] If my view is of my own, only from an earthy physical one side of the mountain-view, then it's really not the greatest view that comes from being seated in heavenly places. It may be the only view I have at that time, but God is not done showing me His view! It is not the fallen man of earth trying to make his way up one side of the mountain that has the greatest position to help someone, but the risen man that comes from the top does. The Most High place founded on the Rock is positioned with great grace and power to help.

The rock that Moses struck and water came out of it was located on top of the mountain, not on one side of the mountain. That's what we all should be drinking! If you have died with Him, then are you raised with Him to the top, seated on the throne with Him. You are now that man from heaven ready to minister. He has made you the head and not the tail.[27] He has made you to be above and not beneath. Can you see it? Then believe it, and be perfectly joined together to Him as one.

Have you ever been to the mountains and stopped at a lookout point to view the beautiful scenery? I remember my wife, Cindy, and I had stopped to do just that. There were several cars at this lookout point and

---

26   2 Cor. 4:13

27   Deut. 28:13

one person had a spotting scope. Well, we were looking at the beautiful valley surrounded by mountains, and then we gazed at the mountains across the valley. We thought we were pretty much seeing everything that was worth seeing, until the man with the spotting scope said he was looking at some mountain goats on a mountain across the valley. We squinted and saw maybe a few spots of white on the mountain he was looking at but wasn't sure. I had some binoculars in the car that could zoom in up to fifteen times. With the binoculars we could see the mountain goats clearly as they made their way across the mountain side. Everybody had the same viewpoint but saw different things. Seeing from a lower view point wouldn't have revealed such a marvelous sight. The higher the better! Some saw the beauty of the valley, others the mountains and trees, another saw a small stream, another saw the small lake, and yet another spotted mountain goats.

But without this other man pointing out the mountain goats to us, we would have missed it. We would have never known and experienced the beauty and life that was there all along if he had not shared what He saw. The greater view was there, but we hadn't seen it!

What would have happened if we had responded with a, "I don't believe it!" We would have never seen those mountain goats or the mountain terrain like we did. We had to make the effort to gaze through an equal viewing glass that had the power to magnify before we could see the same thing. It really didn't take that much effort, but we wanted to see it all! Are you the same way?

This is how it is concerning Christ in us. He is wondrous to behold. Sometimes we can spot some of those hidden things of Christ on our own, and then sometimes someone else points us to something we had not quite seen before. Eventually, we would have discovered the mountain goats on our own with our binoculars if we would have stayed at that lookout point long enough, maybe. But, it came quicker with his help. The greatest point of view of all things is from heaven. It is the highest point by which we are able to see all things clearly.

I know in my walk with the Lord I had too often looked at things from a natural one-side of the mountain perspective which is cloudy and confusing at best. Trying to see heavenly things from a natural perspective is even more confusing. Then the next thing you know, I now believe things because that's the way I see it from where I'm standing. In my eyes I'm seeing right, but then I read a scripture in the Bible that doesn't exactly line up with my thinking and my present beliefs. So, I either skip it because that's the easiest thing to do, or I begin to doubt what I have believed while still not knowing the truth. Most of the time, I had leaned on what I've been told about that scripture by someone else, which still might be confusing. By now, I might be thinking that I'd be better off just quitting the whole thing, and living the best I can in a natural world, and letting whatever will be will be. Ah! But I know that's not right either.

So, with a new hunger for the truth, we dive into the word of God and discover something that's been hidden, a greater revelation of Jesus Christ coming from the Chief Cornerstone, heaven's view already laid in us. The Holy Spirit is faithful to bring us out of darkness by showing us the Light. He is the Spirit of truth.[28] Because of our true hunger for the truth, we are willing even to be proven wrong, if that's what it takes to discover the truth. It's all part of growing as we remain as little children in our own eyes. It is my hope and prayer that this book will help you come to the lookout point of the Chief Cornerstone and see all things from His heavenly view. All these things cannot be taught, or revealed, or seen with words only, but He will make all things clear to us by His Spirit as we walk out our life's journey.

The word of God is seed, imperishable seed, everlasting seed, and an incorruptible seed. It is therefore not of this world. Everything we naturally see around us is temporal. But the word of God is eternal. Knowing this, I ask myself: Is it right that I only interpret the word of God from my natural earthly, temporal, and corruptible dwelling

---

28   Jn. 16:13, 15:26

place that I see most easily from? Would not this way of interpreting the Bible actually degrade, diminish, and lower the standard by which it was fully intended to be understood? How can I correctly interpret the word of God that is imperishable, everlasting, and incorruptible, if I only see myself standing in the place of a natural corrupted world? I conclude that I cannot.

We know that the word of God is incorruptible. If I am only understanding from my natural point of view, which is from the corruptible natural realm, then I am seeing from that place of corruption. I believe that what I am seeing is incorruptible, but the eye of my understanding is blurred by the place from where I am standing. I can't see the forest through the trees! I'm trying to understand and live according to the incorruptible from a place that is corrupted. But the corruptible must put on the incorruptible, and then the mortal is able to put on immortality.[29] How can I?

Immortality is the clothing that the mortal must put on to walk in His glorious body. It covers up the weaknesses of the mortal with strength that comes from knowing and experiencing His life. A solid foundation in our knowledge of Jesus Christ is the basis for receiving the life of Christ and putting it on. If our foundation is weakened or corrupted by human reasoning and traditions, then our foundation will be weak as well. In this condition, immortality seems like a long ways off. So, let's put it off into the future we reason. Unless our foundation is without fault, that kind of glorious body doesn't even seem possible. So again, let's put it off to sometime in the future and in the natural only after we physically die. Then we can get a new body we reason. But don't reason too much, or we might wonder why nobody that has died, except Jesus, and has yet received such a body. Maybe those who have died have to put that somewhere into the future too. If my only hope is in my future, let's skip the present and go on home now! No, this same confusion is what brings people to suicide. Your greatest time of being further clothed with the

29   1 Cor. 15:53

glory of God is right now! First clothe yourself with the incorruptible word by putting on the mind of Christ. Then as you believe what the Lord is speaking to you and are responding to His word, you are now being further clothed with immortality. The mortal isn't removed or dead, but further clothed with His greater life! This is the life of the true believer.

If the scriptures that bring hope are meant to be put off into some future time, then what good are they now? If this is the way we are to handle the word of God, then we don't need to grow and increase in the knowledge of God. What's the point! If all the glory is in the future after I die, then I just as well drink, cuss, smoke and be marry so I can get there quicker! If I cannot walk today in the glory of that same life that Jesus walked in, am I really born of Him? Am I not supposed to be changed from glory to glory by the image I have of Christ?[30] The image I have of Him also changes the image I have of myself, which gives me the mind of Christ and makes His life available in abundance. His life, the life of the Spirit, is that of immortality. It is the life from heaven for us now! The corruptible body is not the life, but the Spirit of Christ in the body is life. Immortality dwells in the Christ in you! The Christ manifest through Jesus is the life and power of God that healed and performed miracles. That same Christ lives in you! But My people perish for lack of knowledge.[31]

It is the natural mind that needs conforming, not our spirit. The body just naturally takes on what the spirit and soul of man supplies. If the body is supplied by the knowledge and life of immortality that dwells in it, then it is clothed with that same immortality. This is putting on the Lord Jesus Christ.[32] The body will still die because it is as clothing to cover up the weaknesses of human flesh and not a replacement of the body. It is not the complete glorified body without weaknesses, but the weaknesses are not seen because of the covering of immortality. The

---

30   2Cor. 3:18
31   Hosea 4:6
32   Eph. 4:24, Col. 3:10

Spirit of life is the down payment or guarantee of that body, but is now reigning in this life over the body it currently has.[33] By that life-giving Spirit, this body now lives in the highest order of life that is freely given to us by our Creator. A future body like His yes, but that cannot help us reign over this body we have now. The gospel is not a futuristic hope that leaves us lacking now. It is a now gospel that leaves us reigning in this life now as well as in all of our future that has no end!

Jesus only spoke by parables so that the kingdom of God would remain hidden from those who only think according to the laws of this natural earth. This was done not so they would remain blind, but so that the two could not become mixed. What does light have to do with darkness? The law was not the light. Jesus Christ is the light.[34] You cannot mix the two. So Jesus spoke in parables, and the Holy Spirit inspired others to write in types and shadows, and in parables for the same reason. So natural things in the Bible are primarily written as types and shadows, and parables of the things of Jesus the Christ and of His kingdom, which is Spirit. Therefore natural (carnal) interpretations of those same scriptures are natural (carnal) in their effect as well. Another word for natural is carnal and carnal interpretations are death. How so? It is the Spirit that brings life, not the natural. There is death in everything that is natural, just look around.

Rom. 8:5–8 — *For those who live according to the flesh set their minds on the things of the flesh, but those who live according to the Spirit, the things of the Spirit. For to be carnally minded is death, but to be spiritually minded is life and peace. Because the carnal mind is enmity against God; for it is not subject to the law of God, nor indeed can be. So then, those who are in the flesh cannot please God.*

33   2 Cor. 5:1–5, Eph. 1:14
34   Jn. 1:4

The words flesh, carnal, and carnally are the same Greek word meaning meat, flesh, natural human being or natural reasoning. It is looking at and from a natural view that comes to us by the natural world. According to this scripture, setting our minds on natural reasoning is hostility and opposition (enmity) towards God. Why? God is a Spirit! His order of thinking is much higher and He gave us His word and Spirit to bring us to His higher order of thinking. This thinking is authored by the Spirit and not the natural mind. But some of the body of Christ embraces many carnal views because it is so natural to see it from Adam's earthy worldly position because that's the world we were raised in since birth. The effects of such natural interpretations are of no help to the body of Christ. It produces after its own kind. Natural produces natural, and this scripture says natural mindedness produces death. Why, again? Natural interpretations will produce fear that brings death. Natural or physical interpretations of scriptures are not God inspired but come by natural reasoning; therefore, it cannot contain the Spirit of peace and abundant life. Don't get me wrong, we need to think and reason when we read or study the Bible. But let our thinking and reasoning be with the guidance of the Holy Spirit. The best teacher you have is Christ in you! There is absolutely nothing supernatural or life giving about natural interpretations. It only intrigues the natural carnal mind and embraces the theatrical. And the carnal mind can be as addicted to natural interpretations as the body to strong drugs. Only a strong desire for the truth that comes from the mouth of God and hearing that truth can set you free.

The Bible is, therefore, of the first and highest order a Spiritual Book to reveal to us the higher order of the kingdom of God, the life of the Spirit. Yes, the Bible is a natural history book too, but that is not its greatest intent. Yes, the Bible is also a prophetic book of coming things, but not of natural disasters. A revelation of Jesus Christ is what we need now in this life. Our living from that higher place is what the world needs most! Spiritual teachings in the scriptures only seen as natural things because of natural interpretations therefore cannot be the fullness of any of the word of God, and is not seeing Him face to face. The things we see in the natural earth were created by the things unseen, or Spirit realm by His life-giving Spirit. So, the things of the Spirit are greater than the things of the natural earth. Thus, the greatest interpretations of the Bible will no doubt be of the kingdom of God or life in the Spirit, and not a revelation of natural things.

If I can see from heaven's view point as John the revelator did, then I can see as God sees. But we don't need to be caught up in a vision or translated like John and Paul. They wrote what they saw, and we are to see the same things as they did from their writings as the Spirit reveals those things to us. The Holy Spirit will take us where He is in our understanding as we renew our minds to the Chief Cornerstone.

The Chief Cornerstone has already been laid. Anyone who believes on the Lord Jesus Christ can have a heavenly perception as that Cornerstone is made known to them. The Cornerstone is Jesus Christ, the heavenly man. He lives in us by His Spirit to reveal Himself and His kingdom to us every day, at any time, and in every situation that arises. His view of all things is always from heaven. He is not moved by our panic, fear, emotions, flesh, or wrong thinking. He is the stability or Rock of our salvation. Once we come to an understanding of the unchangeable Chief Cornerstone, we are able to see from His perspective all things. Only after we understand the foundation can we successfully proceed on to perfection (maturity). If we do not yet understand spiritual things or get off course from the word of the Spirit, then we have proceeded with the corruption of a natural mind.

Heb. 6:1–3 — *Therefore, leaving the discussion of the elementary principles of Christ, let us go on to perfection, not laying again the foundation of repentance* (a change of mind) *from dead works and of faith toward God, of the doctrine of baptisms,* *of laying on of hands, of resurrection of the dead, and of eternal judgment. And this let us do as God permits* (gives us liberty to be transformed).

Seeing from heaven can only come if we understand the foundation of these things that are all found in the death, burial, and resurrection of Jesus Christ. The study of the Chief Cornerstone is to leave a deep impression in our spirit and soul to the degree that we cannot but always look and see from that place. He then becomes the Cornerstone of our life and gives us an understanding so we can walk in His fullness.

Wouldn't it be great if we could see from God's perspective when trouble comes, or tests, and trials, and tribulation? Or, just to break the monotony of another boring day? It is God's good pleasure to not only give us the kingdom, but to show us what He sees. Jesus saw from a heavenly perspective, and lived not according to the view of the religious teachings of His day. Every believer has been given the same Holy Spirit and foundation that Jesus had when He walked on the earth. Our understanding of those things is the only difference. A different view of Christ will also leave us with a different view of ourselves. Heaven's view of both is much greater! A closer look at the Cornerstone is where we can gain more understanding and a view from heaven.

God's purpose of sending Jesus Christ into the world was to establish the kingdom of Heaven in the earth. In doing so, a whole new way of life and understanding of that life had to be introduced. The effect was the dismantling of all religious efforts on our part of trying to accomplish the same thing that Jesus could only do, and that was the fulfillment of the law and the prophets. His purpose was to lay a new foundation for this new and better way of life, and the first thing that had to be laid was the Chief Cornerstone. The laying of this precious cornerstone was the laying of Himself. Jesus Christ is the basis for all that we are to believe and have in this life of faith today.

The Chief Cornerstone is <u>not</u> certain beliefs or doctrines that we hold so dear to our hearts. The Chief Cornerstone is a person, the person of Jesus Christ! This Chief Cornerstone is the Alfa (beginning) of all the knowledge, understanding, and wisdom of truth. Not only is He the Alfa, but also the Omega (end) of all the knowledge, understanding, and wisdom of truth. He becomes the end of all knowledge when we live by His life-giving Spirit of love. That love surpasses knowledge so much so that you can't explain it, make sense out of it, or even justify it. We have no need for the knowledge of good and evil when we have the light of His life. It is not by the stored up knowledge we have in our mind that is anything, but the effect of His abiding life and love that is the beginning and the end of all that is.[35]

Anything, but anything, that does not line up with the perspective of the Chief Cornerstone is in reality not the truth concerning this new life in God's kingdom. It may contain some parts of truth in its knowledge, but a half truth is a lie and contains the power to deceive. It can cause a house to fall because it was not founded on the rock (chief cornerstone).[36] As we study the Chief Cornerstone, we'll discover some things that we have believed to indeed be the truth, and thus be even more assured of those things. We may also discover we have believed some things that after taking a closer look at the Cornerstone are found faulty. They just don't line up with who Christ is and what Jesus accomplished in His death, burial, and resurrection. This is when the mind or second heaven begins to be shaken. But that's a good thing and a God thing.

God hates anything that separates us from Him, and that includes wrong thinking. When a shaking of our thinking comes, it might shake the earth or natural things around us as well. Just as a fault line under the earth's surface can shake the things on the earth, so can a fault line in the foundation of what we have believed be shifted by a deeper truth.

---

35   1 Cor. 13:8
36   Mat. 7:24–27

That inner shifting will also shake off anything that is not founded on the Rock. The Chief Cornerstone is of the deepest part of our foundation. At the revelation of Jesus Christ, if there is anything that is faulty with what we thought was our foundation, it shall be shaken so that which is faulty might be removed. If that revelation changes what we believe, it will change our whole outlook on life and also how we see God and others. That truth will shake both, the heavens and the earth.[37] That truth will become our unmovable Chief Cornerstone and Rock of our salvation that can keep us sure, confident, and full of peace in the mist of any storm! A proper look from the Cornerstone at anything will remove the veil from our eyes and keep us seeing as God sees. Thus, His abundant life is able to flow in us and through us at all times.

After visiting many of God's churches (not to judge or find fault, but to fellowship with), I still find that we all have a mixture of grace and the law. This mixture causes lukewarmness in our relationship with our Lord. The Scribes and Pharisees thought they were hot for God based on their zeal for good works at observing their laws. Much of the Church is the same way. Observance of the law, whether established by our religious beliefs that we have been taught, or by self-imposed laws to measure ourselves, only produces the coldness of a works mentality that cannot bring about a righteous union with the Almighty. Observing the law causes our eyes to be focused on our doing good, or how charismatic we can get in church, or our doing things for the Lord, rather than on Him and His finished works. An attempt through greater commitment to do better is Adam's vain attempt to get to God based on his performance trying to make Himself equal to God. Impossible! Christ, who is our flow of life is to produce corresponding action that will manifest good works. This is Christ in us doing the works and not our flesh.

Eve was deceived in the garden thinking she lacked something from being in the very image or likeness of God that relationship and oneness couldn't produce. Just because she did not know everything in her natural

37   Heb. 12:26

mind, she wrongly judged herself as lacking knowledge. That conclusion is far from the truth! If you have Christ, you have all knowledge when you need it. You have the all-knowing God in you; therefore, you have no lack for knowledge. His knowledge is available 24/7. This was her fall and our fall that starts us on the road of trying to perform like God separate from His indwelling life. It is by these works that are separate from our relationship with God that produces the coldness, an atmosphere lacking His manifest presence. God created us for good works out of union with Him, not separate from that relationship.

God, who is all and in all, desires above all things relationship![38] It is through intimate relationship that God manifests His presence to us individually. This is that which makes us hot! Jesus was hot! He was so hot that He said He could do nothing, unless He saw His Father doing it, and He could say nothing, unless He first heard His Father speak it. That is relationship at its fullest! That is so hot that you could say that Jesus was on fire! He desires to baptize us with that same fire of His presence that purges us of anything that remains of Adam and his dead works, so that only Christ and His finished works remains. The coldness is that of Adam under the law. The hotness is that of Christ under grace making us one with God. Therefore, the lukewarmness is that of the mixture of Adam and Christ, or the mixture of the law and grace. The first is our own works for oneness with God. The second is God's works of love for oneness with Him. It is at the laying of the chief cornerstone in one's life that divides and separates the Christ from the Adam, the light from the darkness, and life from death. It is seeing and understanding the Chief Cornerstone that we are able to experience the passing away of Adam under the law and the resurrection of the Christ man that we are. Before the foundation of the world God intended us to be one with Him in all we say and do.

It is not my intent to relay the whole foundation. Once we see and understand the chief cornerstone, then we may individually examine

---

38   Eph. 4:6

the rest of our foundation and beliefs that we have allowed to be a part of this building of God that we are. God wants us open to receive a greater revelation of who He is and what He has accomplished through Jesus Christ. From the time we first believed on Jesus Christ until now, we have desired and have need of a renewed mind. But if any new revelation of Jesus Christ starts messing with some of our present set of hand-me-down beliefs, then we sometimes either stumble over that truth choosing not to believe it, or we get offended because of it.

Some might say, "That is not what my religion has taught me!" This was the typical attitude of the Scribes and Pharisee's of Jesus' day. Do not let it happen to you. It was pride in their religious beliefs that kept them in the cold rather than in the Most Holy Place experiencing God's warm embrace. They had labored all their life to try to gain knowledge and understanding in an effort to develop the greatest way of getting close to God that Adam could produce. Then this Jesus guy comes along and says, "I am the way, the truth, and the life!"[39] They probably thought within themselves: "If that's the case, then I'm wrong and do you expect me to admit that I'm wrong after all my years of studying the law! If I'm wrong, then I've got to change my whole way of thinking! So if I'm wrong, how about my parents and grandparents and all those who taught me? Were they wrong too?" You need to decide if you want truth or majority. Jesus was one standing alone on the edge of a new covenant and revelation of who the Father is and what He is like. Are you willing to stand alone and stand out from the crowd? If not then you'll always be a crowd follower and a crowd pleaser. But don't worry, there are thousands that have come out from among the crowd of the Western belief system. So, you are really never alone.

When God brings change, it is always good. Our religious pride may get hurt, and in the process our Adamic thinking may die, but without a death there can be no resurrection of newness of life. The only thing that can keep us from being one with our Lord and God is

---

39   Jn. 14:6

the hardness of our own hearts. Moses offered a certificate of divorce only because of the hardness of their hearts. Christ is our husbandman, and it is only through the hardening of our hearts that can keep Him at any distance apart from us, even though He still dwells in us. He is faithful to continue His pursuit of our soul (mind, will, emotions, and conscience) so that He may embrace our whole being until it all becomes one with Him. The Lord is good!

Christ is always pursuing the woman, the weaker vessel of our soul (mind, will, emotions, and conscience), for the purpose of making us complete in Him lacking nothing.

> **1 Thess. 5:23 — *Now may the God of peace Himself sanctify (set apart) you completely; and may your whole spirit, soul, and body be preserved blameless at the coming of our Lord Jesus Christ.***

It is necessary for our minds to be renewed or sanctified by the truth of God's word so our soul can be perfectly joined together with our spirit that is born of God. Once our spirit and soul are united together as one, the body will be kept blameless as well.

I pray that the truth of God's love will soften any hardness of heart and that we may know that the truth always produces the freedom and joy that God so desires for us. I pray we all receive the truth of a greater unveiling of Jesus Christ until we are manifest sons of God. A-men

I have learned the difference between someone that truly got born again by the revelation of Jesus Christ and someone who went through the motions of getting born again mainly because they just wanted to avoid the threatening preaching of a future hell. The one truly born of God has a driving pursuit to bring their soul into oneness with the new creation of the Christ man on the inside of them. They have a new hunger to come into the knowledge of Jesus Christ. It is not because they have been pressured by the Church to attend, but because the Christ in them is pursuing their soul so that the two might become one. Without this union the person cannot become complete spirit, soul, and body. And yet it is sad that some of the longer existing Church has hardened their hearts and cut off such a pursuit of greater revelation before the work is finished.

When is it finished? It's a continuum, which means a link between two things or a continuous series of things that blend into each other so gradually and seamlessly that it is impossible to say where one becomes the next. Jesus had this continuum of soul and spirit so that you couldn't tell the difference between the two; and we are told we have the mind of Christ. When we set our mind, heart, and affections on things above and not on things below, our mind is picking up on impression given to it that comes from the Spirit. Then the two are joined gradually and seamlessly together where there is no difference. We are now dwelling with God in perfect harmony.

> **1 Peter 2:1–8 —** *Therefore, laying aside all malice, all guile, hypocrisy, envy, and all evil speaking, as newborn babes, desire the pure milk of the word, that you may grow (up to salvation) thereby, if indeed you have tasted that the Lord is gracious. Coming to Him as to a living stone, rejected indeed by men, but chosen by God and precious, you also, as living stones, are being built up a spiritual house, a holy priesthood, to offer up spiritual sacrifices acceptable to God through Jesus Christ. Therefore it is also contained in the scripture, "Behold, I lay in Zion a chief cornerstone, elect, precious, and he who believes on Him will by no means be put to shame." Therefore, to you who believe, He is precious; but to those who disbelieve, "The stone which the builders rejected has become the chief cornerstone," and "A stone of stumbling and a rock of offense."*

We are described like Jesus as a living stone. He is not a stone of the letter of the law which is dead, but a stone of the law of the Spirit of life! In other words, Jesus is the living word that comes by the life-giving Spirit of God. Now that same word of the gospel becomes our head cornerstone from which all our believing comes from. It's important for us to understand that Jesus spoke the truth. His interpretations of the word of God were different from what Jewish believers had ever heard and understood before. It took a radical change of thinking to believe on the words of Jesus Christ. That's why John the Baptist and Jesus said to repent, change your thinking! That change was that the kingdom of heaven is **now** at hand. You don't have to work for it any longer! You don't have to qualify yourself for it! There is no need to put the blessings of the kingdom of heaven off into the future. It is here now! You don't have to suffer through your rituals, which is but a type and shadow of all that the I AM now freely gives you. Just believe His gracious words and receive it!

As believers, we have to be willing to change our thinking every day to readily receive a greater revelation of Jesus and His word. I've heard it preached before, "We need to hang onto the truth!" I still believe that, but now I wonder if they meant the truth as we have been taught it and now know it, or the truth as it comes to us by revelation of Jesus Christ? Sometimes religion teaches us things contrary to the truth but is declared as truth. These are well meaning people who love God. We are all endeavoring to share the truth as we see it or as we have been taught it. But that does not mean it is the truth. But we (I) being ignorant of the word of grace that is found in the Cornerstone sometimes have swallowed it hook, line, and sinker. Without knowing it, we then might hear the real truth or a greater understanding of scripture and find it hard to believe because of our religion. I trust we have something in common because I'm after the truth and not to become more religious and carnal minded. It is the truth that will set us free of our Adamic thinking and any deception we have.

The Scribes and Pharisees were bound to their religion and were made to stumble. They got offended at the truth. Instead of allowing God to build His Church, they became "The Builders";[40] therefore, rejecting the living stone that God offered them to build with. This stone was designed by God to build the Church. The stone lives in each and every believer, and He builds us individually as well as corporately. But, the Scribes and Pharisees saw themselves losing control over the people as God was taking the lead. They became prideful and stubborn over their religion and teachings that they held onto so dearly. So when the truth came along that was free from the law, they stumbled and became offended.

(I say this as an observation only and not to condemn.) Some Church leadership does not like to lose their control over the people. That same religious pride is seen in most churches today. Some want to control what we are to believe and not believe. In that, they are actually declaring themselves to be the Great Shepherd of the flock. We in Church leadership are not too restrict or control what others believe, but to unveil the Christ in each and every one that our Lord has entrusted us with. The flock is not ours, but His to care for, feed, build up, and protect, not to condemn or cast out. The truth will correct those who have the ear for it. If they don't have the ear for it, you can do nothing.

We have in the past created many reasons for stumbling within our church institutions because of the presence of religion and traditions taught as truth. But, the humble are made ready and hungry to receive the greater on-going revelation of the truth of Jesus Christ that will remove all cause for stumbling over such things. He becomes our living stone; the Cornerstone by which we can dwell in heavenly places in Christ Jesus and see from that place. That's the only way we can grow up to salvation.

Salvation is more than just a born again experience. That is only the beginning of a new creation life. To grow up into that salvation takes a

---

40   Mat. 21:42

renewing of the mind so our soul can come into perfect union with our spirit. The husband of the house (our spirit one with His) is pursuing the woman (our soul) to make her one with Him in perfect marriage. When the two become one is when they will rule over all the earth/flesh. Then the scripture is fulfilled that declares that we shall rule with Him in the earth. This is how God is able to make us complete spirit, soul, and body.

True revelation of Jesus Christ will never take away from the present truth we have, but it may take away the religious teachings and doctrines of men that have made us of no effect in that particular area in our believing. That's good news! None of us wants to be ineffective. The best is to have God manifest in every area of our lives. It is when we take more pride in our present understanding that we become unable to receive the greater truth that He wants to bring to us now. That is when He becomes a stumbling stone to us and a rock of offense.

> **1 Cor. 3:10, 11 — *According to the grace of God which was given me, as a wise master builder I have laid the foundation, and another builds on it. But let each one <u>take heed how he builds on it</u>. For no other foundation can anyone lay than that which is laid, which is Jesus Christ.***

The Lord is saying here that every thought, belief, and current word we are hearing to build our life on must be examined carefully to ensure that it is based on the foundation of Jesus Christ, if we are to be a wise master builder. If we don't examine it with the foundation, which is an extension of the Cornerstone, it might be sinking sand that could set us up to become offended by the true Rock. We may have used sand as a part of our foundation for believing and understanding many other things. This in turn could be why we might not have a victorious and overcoming life like the Bible says we should.[41] Neither do we have

---

41   Mat. 12:20, Jn. 16:33, 1 Jn:4:4, 5:4

the perfect and continual union that we so desire to have with Him. We thought it was the truth. We believed it with our whole heart. I mean, it has the same composition as the rock. By looking at this grain of sand up close, real close, it even looks like a rock. That's where the deception lies, in looking at the grain of sand without seeing the Rock at the same time! It is easy to see if it is the truth by putting them side by side and comparing. Sand isn't even a part of that which is already laid and finished, which is Jesus Christ. It may even sound like a rock in the way it was spoken to us, like the tale of who caught the biggest fish! Therefore, let us examine all teaching and preaching with the scriptures that produce the Rock. Examine the spirit in which it comes from, its purpose and intent. That one grain of sand can allow many more deceptions to come into our believing, which forms the basis for our drawing near to God and our walking with Him.

What does that mean? If our thinking, attitude, or view of God isn't correct according to the Cornerstone, then it will cause us to have a mixture and produce lukewarmness. One example would be having a sin conscience laced with condemnation so when we read the Bible our perception of what we have read will have a mixture of judgment, as well as forgiveness. The law breeds judgment and condemnation. The law is a reminder of our failures. It leaves us with guilt and seeing ourselves as falling short of the glory of God. This also becomes our way of how we see others because we judge them according to the same judgment that we judge ourselves. This certainly is not of the Father and is not of the new covenant. But too often we have been taught salvation by grace, but we must live by certain laws of do's and don'ts after we are saved. If we aren't taught such laws, we have a tendency to make up our own.

Example: I should read my Bible everyday. So when we don't, we condemn ourselves and see ourselves as falling short. Reading your Bible everyday may be a good idea, but that has nothing to do with your already being made righteous by faith in what Jesus has done. The same can be used as examples concerning prayer, fasting, going to church, and on and on and on we go. We may have unconsciously made laws for about everything we do. This in turn gives us a conscious awareness of if I do this then I'm a good Christian and if not then I'm not. Wrong! You're a good Christian because God made you good by the sending of His Son. Period! That is based only on the knowledge of the Cornerstone and that is how God sees you from heaven.

"Beware of the leaven of the Pharisees!"[42] Their view of God was from the perception of the law. Their own works of compliance to that law gave them the impression that God was harsh and judgmental, which is why Jesus gave the parable where one unfaithful servant declared his master to be a hard task master.[43] Under the law it (not God) demanded obedience and in some cases if you fell short of that law, then you got stoned to death! The law became their God and not the loving person that our Creator is. The law was their commander, accuser, and judge. Their view of God was not based on relationship; therefore, they saw God from a different light that was in reality darkness. Jesus said, "Walk while you have the light."[44] They have always had the law since Moses. Under the law there is no hope, and without hope there is no light at the end of the tunnel. They saw God from a different viewpoint other than the Chief Cornerstone. Their view of God was from a legal position as their chief cornerstone based on their own good works. If they obeyed, they became full of pride, and if they disobeyed they became sin conscious and full of condemnation which is why they judged others without mercy. Either way, under the law you lose!

So where we stand positionally forms our understanding of who God is and who we are in Christ by what we believe. That position or view from which we stand is supposed to be based only on Jesus Christ as our Chief Cornerstone. It just might be that we have had other viewpoints that have come from our own opinions and experiences.

---

42   Mat. 16:6, 16:11–12

43   Mat. 25:24

44   Jn. 12:35

Those opinionated viewpoints we claim as our beliefs, just might be another view point (another gospel) based on our own self interpretation of what we think the Bible is saying or what "God" is saying. It may be another view that comes from what others have said about certain scriptures. But, the reality is that any view other than that from the perspective of the Chief Cornerstone is sinking sand. Our beliefs is what forms the house that we live out of and Jesus said if we build our house (beliefs) on anything else but the Rock, we have built on sinking sand.

Unless we can clearly and sometimes quickly identify the Rock as our foundation, we can be easily deceived into thinking and believing contrary to Christ. And if it is contrary to Christ, wouldn't it then be antichrist? Most of the Church thinks of the devil when you mention antichrist. But antichrist is anything that is contrary to or against Christ. There are some beliefs within some of the Church that is against Christ and His finished work on the cross. But, there is a solution! By setting our gaze upon Jesus and His finished work, our minds can be renewed, and strongholds torn down. Then we can freely partake of His greater and more glorious life of grace more than we ever dreamed possible! Life and life more abundantly becomes a reality and keeps coming to us on an ongoing experience!

Our Cornerstone of truth is not supposed to be just any doctrine and teaching that we have formed as our belief system. That would then include what we and others have used to build our house with that sits on the foundation. Our Cornerstone is the person of Jesus Christ. So, anything that we might have added to our belief system that does not fit the description of the person of Jesus Christ and what He has finished in His death, burial and resurrection, needs to be examined to see if it lines up with the Cornerstone. If it does not, then it is heresy. I know the word 'heresy' sounds so bad that you might be thinking of someone getting kicked out of the Church. Really, heresy is what might have been keeping us in "the Church" when Jesus wants us to be "The Church". Heresy is much worse than getting kicked out of a church! Heresy means disunion.

Jesus Christ brings us into perfect union with the Father; therefore, anything that doesn't fit in the person and accomplishments of Jesus Christ actually takes away from Him and brings disunion. Those things are counted as loss and brings our life of faith to ruins.[45] So, it is not the loss of getting kicked out of a Church that's such a big deal, but to be separated from our Father is a big deal! Every deception has the intent to bring disunion. The devil (deceiver or any deception) with his lie in the garden brought disunion. It was a heresy and the devil (deception) should have been kicked out of that meeting of the minds! Well, we don't have to kick anyone out of our meetings, but we ought to at least kick out the deception. A deception has a mixture of truth and a lie. The truth baits us so we will swallow the lie with it. Otherwise, it would have no power to deceive. We just need to do as Jesus did and declare, "It is written."[46] Jesus knew the Father, the Spirit of truth, and you know Him.

By knowing Him personally as our Chief Cornerstone through the relationship of the Spirit of God, we will have access to His wisdom and knowledge to see the deception. This is wonder! The closer to perfect union with Almighty God, the more wonderful He becomes in our eyes. The Holy Spirit will declare the truth to us to keep us free. Free from what? Free from ever partaking of Adam's sin and the fall again by eating from the tree of the knowledge of good and evil; freedom from religion and traditions that has built its organizations on fear and control. Free from forming our own laws or receiving any laws from others, no matter who they are or how big a crowd of followers they have. The only law that Jesus gave His Church was the law of love, and obedience to that law cannot be produced by the works of the flesh. Love is a work of the life of Christ from within His children. Love is a fruit of the Spirit, not a letter of the law. He is able to keep you from falling[47] from grace and going back under the law by the working of the

---

45   2 Peter 2:1
46   Mat. 4
47   Jude 1:24

Spirit of love. Love is our law, but it is a spiritual law that comes from His indwelling life. His Spirit in you will quicken your mortal body so that it is made alive with love, which is the clothing of the immortal!

> **Psa. 118:22 —** *The stone which the builders rejected has become the chief cornerstone.* **Acts 4:11-12 - After the lame man was healed, Peter said.** *"This is the stone which was rejected by you builders, which has become the chief cornerstone. Nor is there salvation in any other, for there is no other name under heaven given among men by which we must be saved."*

Peter was saying it is from the Chief Cornerstone that the lame man was healed, and it is from this same Chief Cornerstone that all the fullness of salvation comes. The word chief in the Hebrew is roshe, which means to shake, head, chief, captain, highest. The Chief Cornerstone has come to shake the head as chief. His higher thoughts come to us to shake our thinking. That is how He establishes Himself as our head. Without a shaking in our thinking, we would still be thinking like Adam.

God is much better, much greater, much more loving than what we have so far believed. If we believe this, then we will not be so quick to doubt a word that puts Him in a better light than what we have at present. His works accomplished on the cross in His death, burial, and resurrection is also much greater than what we have so far understood. When more of that truth comes, it will shake the thinking of our head. Most of the church avoids those who speak different things than what they presently believe, because they don't want to get confused. The truth that Jesus spoke confused the Scribes and Pharisees. But, if more light comes, which it will, then it only showed that we were confused before that light came, not after it came. When the light comes it exposes darkness. That's good news! The darkness we have is the confusion, not the light that comes. How can iron sharpen iron if they are speaking the same thing?[48] Once both are sharpened, then they will speak the same thing, because they both are of the same mind of the Spirit. So, let us receive one another so that the fullness of Christ may bring us all to maturity.

Psa. 18:11 — *He made darkness his secret place: His canopy around Him was dark waters and thick clouds of the skies.*

God made the darkness and created the light. The darkness is how we see God hidden in the secret place not yet revealed to us. When the light comes or the understanding of the word of God comes, then that light reveals those hidden things that were in the darkness. The light (understanding) we had is joined together with the new dawning of light, and we become brighter for it. In other words, we were once in darkness and God Himself becomes our light. No matter how much knowledge or light we gain, we are still in some degree of darkness compared to what is yet to be revealed to us from the secret place. Then the place we were once in becomes a place of lesser light compared to where we are now and where we are going. We came out of Adam who was void (without the form of God) and in darkness, but God said, "Let there be light." And it was so.[49] That word is still working and coming to pass today in us. It is not a natural sunlight that gives us the true light, but the light of His Son is the true light.[50]

God has often shaken my religious thinking so that I might see Him more clearly. God wants every thought and belief that we have of Him and His kingdom to have the power to bring us into an ongoing perfect union with Him. At times, that will require that a shaking come so the

---

48   Pro. 27:17
49   Gen. 1:2,3
50   Rev. 22:5

error of some of our wrong thinking and beliefs are removed, and only that which is of Christ will remain.

> **Heb. 12:25, 26 — *See that you do not refuse Him who speaks. For if they did not escape who refused Him who spoke on earth, much more shall we not escape if we turn away from Him who speaks from heaven, whose voice then shook the earth: but now He has promised, saying, "Yet once more I will shake not only the earth, but also heaven."***

First, what is it that we want to escape? Most would say hell, but hell is not even mentioned. It is our religious thinking that causes us to think that way. If what is spoken from heaven will cause us to escape, then it must be what is spoken from below that we must escape from. There are many things that God wants us to escape from, but yet all of these things are one. The world's system and its fallen state are one with the religious system that has dragged destruction, death, judgment, hell and condemnation into the church institution. These are all one, and they come from the darkness of Adam that Christ and His marvelous light has come to deliver us out of. Jesus escaped all these things not when He went to heaven, but while on the earth. He dwelled with the Father and light be; light came to Him continually. It was this light that caused Him to escape the traps and lies of the devil which came with a purpose to cause Him to dwell in a lower state of being than what He is. This same thing happens to us! So, what are we escaping from? Anything that might cause us to think and dwell in a lower state of being than what God created us to be in Christ Jesus!

Religion always seeks a way to divide or show the difference between man and God in order to separate the two. This thinking alone causes man to see himself as a lower class of being than what God originally created him to be. He created us in His likeness. Showing us any kind of division and separation is the reason we have lived short of the glory of God. We struggle with receiving all His benefits because we think we are a sub-cultural worm of the dust. We were created in His image or likeness so we might live like Him. Jesus restored us back into this likeness of God, and any other image of ourselves causes us to fall short of what we truly are in Christ Jesus. We have a body not that identifies with the fallen earth, but as one bought by the blood to manifest heaven in the earth. As long as we live in earthen vessels, we are reminded of the fall. But, the blood of Jesus reminds us that we are new creations and that this body is the Lord's. If I believe in Christ and am established on the Chief Cornerstone, none of these things move me. Jesus came to bring us into perfect and inseparable union. Religion comes to show a separation or division that is not really there, nor is it seen from heaven's view, and it comes with a deception of false humility.

To be truly humble is to accept everything that is freely given you with thanksgiving. False humility rejects even the idea of perfect union because we see ourselves as unworthy while looking at our own flesh. The latter is false humility laced with self-centered pride. Some might think that true humility says that I am nothing without Christ. Though this statement is true, it is still deceptive if we stop there. Why? We are not without Christ. So, why even consider such a thing, and entertain the thought of being nothing. If He had promised to leave you and forsake you, then we might entertain such a thought. But He didn't and we shouldn't! That thought in itself is without faith and comes from the deceiver. If you can separate the Son from the Father, then you can separated the sons of righteousness that God also bore in this world and now come from the Father. Being born again also means I am now coming from the Father. I am in Christ and the religious efforts to try to take me out of Christ by showing me any separation is antichrist! I have a word of reconciliation (restored to oneness again) in me that bears witness to me of greater things, Oneness!

True humility takes us past all that emptiness, and declares all that Christ has done for us, until we come into the reality of the presence of Christ in us. Then it is no longer I that live, but Christ that lives in Me. The 'i' is lost in the presence of God so much so that they are One and I am. You've seen me; you've seen the Father.[51] The Son declared this kind of relationship with His Father. Why can't a son fully adopted by his Father say the same thing? Religion, that's why. This is not true because I declare such a thing, but because the blood of Jesus, the gift of the Holy Spirit, and the new creation is the reality of it. True humility freely accepts all that Christ has done for us, and no longer considers a life without Him or having any lack. This is when we are assured of His presence and are able to walk with Him by faith.

While walking on the earth, Jesus shook the earth with His presence, His word, and His works. All these things came to the people from outside their body, and were manifest to them who were on earth. Now we are of heaven, born of the Spirit of God, and our citizenship is in heaven. Our home is not a physical existence on earth, but a dwelling place in God of heaven. *We are seated with Him in heavenly places in Christ Jesus.*[52] Earth is now, for a short time, a place where we have the honor and privilege to manifest heaven. We are not at home in the body. To be at home in the body is to be absent from the Lord.[53] Heaven is my home now. It is a spiritual place that I go to not just on Sunday mornings, but a continual dwelling place. We possess and reign over the earthen body that God has given us by the life of Christ in the body. Even though I have a body, my home is in Christ while I yet have a body.

Now a promise has come to us that will not only shake the earth but also heaven. Why? Because living at home in the Spirit of oneness with the Lord will shake what the world is trying to speak into our minds

---

51   Jn. 14:9
52   Eph. 2:6
53   2 Cor. 5:6

through the five senses of our body. I don't think there is one single believer on planet earth that hasn't heard a false statement or teaching or doctrine that didn't affect their soul and beliefs, and every belief we have affects our relationship with our Father and those around us. Those false beliefs also affect our bodies in a negative way. That's when it is time for the truth to come and shake the heavens, our thinking, and our bodies.

It is not for the sake of someone being right or proving someone to be wrong. That is pride at work. But, God truly hates the false that we have believed to be true because it has the ability to keep us at a distance from being totally one with Him. He loves bringing us so close to Him that we become one with Him. This is the inspiration for this book. He hates the deception that separates our soul from being one with Him. I hate it, and I'm sure you hate it as well. In the knowledge of Christ Jesus and His finished work, there are no lies or deceptions that can exist. So, to abide in Him continually without interruption, there can be no lie or deception in what we believe, or even it will be removed by the truth of His appearing to you.

When a situation arises that tests that particular thing we thought to be the truth, but was a mixture, it will divide or distance us from the true God of our salvation. We then once again come into bondage not having His truth to keep us free. God is truth. There are times when we cannot draw as close to the true God as we would like because of the deception that is still in our thinking. *Draw near to God with a true heart.*[54] And *As a man thinks in his heart, so is he.*[55] Deception is not truth. Wrong thinking gets into our heart and affects how we approach God. Our approach would then be to a man-made idol or false image in our mind. So God brings the truth along and when it comes, it shakes heaven, the space between our ears. He shook the earth with His signs and wonders, but now He will shake heaven also.

---

54   Heb. 10:22
55   Pro. 23:7

Think about it. If you believe that God made you sick, then how would you approach Him for healing seeing how He's the one who made you sick? That false image in our thinking hinders us from receiving from the Healer. So, we don't even try to approach Him for healing, or we might plead with God for our healing thinking He made us sick. Either way, we cannot make our approach to the throne of grace with boldness (confidence, assurance, and courage) to receive mercy and find grace to help in time of need.[56] With wrong thinking and believing, we are serving a false idol because we have a false image in the heaven of our mind.

Sometimes believers have swallowed as truth such preposterous lies that even the world doesn't think of God being so wicked. Example: Some believe that God is behind every crisis that comes their way including illness, lack, pain, terrible accidents, storms, etc., in order to get them to return to the Lord or to teach them a lesson. This belief keeps them from receiving God's love, grace, wisdom, and power to deliver them during these times of tribulation. Why do they believe such an evil thing of our loving Lord who died for us and paid the price for our deliverance from such things? They were told such things and without looking at the Chief Cornerstone of their foundation, they mistakenly and ignorantly believed such a lie, trusting those things taught of men rather than the living God. In their thinking, He ought to be the deadly God to them. The world only knows that they are in a fallen cursed world because that is all they see. But they don't curse or blame God for it, unless they are taught such things by the Church.

Hos. 4:6 — *My people perish for a lack of knowledge.*

We who have done such things are not single minded. We are not embracing Jesus Christ and His finished work. This one lie hinders their perception of God, and thus hinders their intimate relationship with

---

56   Heb. 4:16

Him. Just being familiar with what Jesus did while on the earth should be enough to destroy such evil thinking. But it takes much teaching from worldly (fallen) experiences to convince people with such lies. They're reminded of the curse by their experiences, rather than believing the love that the Father has for them. If your natural father wouldn't put sickness on you to teach you something, how much more would your perfect Father in heaven not do such a thing? He teaches us by giving us freely His Spirit, who leads us and shows us the truth in His word.

> **Jn. 16:33 — *"These things I have spoken to you, that in Me you may have peace. In the world you have tribulation; but be of good cheer, I have overcome the world."***

The key to overcoming tribulation is not coming against the tribulation itself. The key is to overcome the world. There are many voices in the world and none of them are without significance.[57] These voices are the same ones that Jesus heard being tempted of the devil (deceiver). These voices come from our five physical senses and speak to our minds. If we listen to those voices then they will deceive us and steal the word of God that is sown into our hearts. But if we overcome the deception that is in the world by seeing everything from a Cornerstone perspective, then we have not given our authority to another. Now we have the power and authority to manifest the peace that we have as we abide in Him. His word spoken to us gives us peace. This is quite the opposite of what the world gives. Overcome the world and you'll also overcome the tribulation that is in the world. (More on this later.)

Under the law these tribulations might be the judgments of God against sin, but Jesus fulfilled and brought the law to an end, He took all the judgments of sin upon Himself, and He has redeemed us from the curse of that law! This is part of our Chief Cornerstone that will

---

57   1 Cor. 14:10

shake the religious heaven until truth stands alone. And once the heaven is shaken, the earth will be shaken again so all that remains is an earth that is filled with the glory of the Lord![58] The tongue of men will speak nothing but the highest truth having been purged of a sin conscience. That truth will manifest health, provision, peace, love, joy, wisdom, and the power of God! God is not glorified in such things pertaining to the curse and death. Sickness is part of the curse and a form of death on a smaller scale, and if allowed to remain, it can cause death. Poverty is also part of the curse and a form of death that can manifest starvation, dehydration, over exposure to severe weather, as well as anxiety. An unsound mind is part of the curse and a form of death, and when allowed to exist, it can lead to depression, obsession, being possessed by an evil or unclean spirit, degenerative diseases, or even suicide. God is only glorified when God is revealed in that person to the degree that they see and understand that they are redeemed from the curse, healed, and delivered!

The Chief Cornerstone (Jesus Christ) is planted in us (earth) like a hidden treasure waiting to unveil Himself to us when we search for Him as one who is born blind.[59] I was born blind and I saw Him not. But now I am beginning to see. He becomes our secret place and high tower that we run to. In the natural it is not the cornerstone of a house that people see. They see only the house that exists on the outside having been built on that foundation. How a person acts, speaks, responds to situations, their attitude, beliefs, habits and everything else that describes them, is in direct correlation with their foundation. So, if you don't like what you see on the outside, speak light into the darkness so the Christ in them will be awakened! It is only by the awakening of the Christ in them that any lasting change can come, not the pointing out of their faults.

If there are things you don't like about yourself then seek the truth so that a shaking might occur, and only the things of Christ will remain.

---

58   Isa. 6:1–7
59   Isa 59:10, Mk. 1:37

Who He is, is who you are on the inside. But until He is unveiled to our minds, we can have no victory. That unveiling will change your perception and that will change the way you think about yourself! That's good news! Don't ever be afraid of God's shaking. The removal of the things of Adam, no matter how precious we think they are, is but dung in the light of His glorious life. A shaking comes not by trials in your life. Those are tests that come to all that live on the earth. Those are opportunities to count it all joy, so that we might walk in the light of Him and overcome the world. But a shaking comes when a pure truth comes and shakes our thinking and our belief system until the only thing that remains is truth in that area of our thinking. That change in our thinking can most often cause a ripple effect or aftershock that also delivers us out of other things in our thinking.

Thomas had such a shaking that He never doubted Jesus again. Paul, who was Saul at the time of his religious life, had great knowledge of the scriptures, and yet was going completely in the opposite direction as Jesus. But when the light came, the truth shook him to the point that he unable to see anyone.[60] That is truly a wonderful thing not being able to see anyone (spiritually speaking). Saul now only saw the light of Jesus. Now the appearance of all men was hidden in the light. Saul thought he was seeing God and all men perfectly and under the law. He surmised that he was doing God a favor by imprisoning the believers with their lawless gospel (though the law of love lived in them). He thought he was seeing just fine by his religion, but when Christ revealed Himself to him, he discovered he was really blind! Has that ever happened to you? It is one thing to know you are blind, but it is a far greater witness to declare your blindness to all those around you that were blinded by you.

If only we had gotten a hold of the Cornerstone when we first believed and stayed there until it was completely laid in us, it would have saved us from so many errors. Well, it's never too late. In all the studies and years of training and teaching that created a religious mindset in Saul, only to have it all come to an abrupt end on the road to Damascus, yet he was most thankful for that change. Afterwards, his name is changed to Paul. The name Saul means to ask or question, not knowing the answer or not knowing God through the law. Paul means little and comes from a word meaning to stop and come to an end. The conversion on the road to Damascus was so life changing that it stopped Saul's wrongful journey and the once prideful Saul became Paul, little in his own eyes. A life going the wrong direction is always full of questions even though we think we have all the answers.

Paul then goes to Asia for about three years so that the Chief Cornerstone might shine more light into His understanding and be laid in him. It is at this time that his knowledge of the scriptures takes on a new form in his understanding. It takes some time for us all to get free from our habit of thinking according to the law and our religious beliefs. Later, Paul was the one that God used to point out Peter's lukewarmness, which was an error in Peter's understanding even after God had lowered a sheet down three times in a dream he had.[61] Peter still had a Jewish religious view of the Gentiles rather than a proper view from the Cornerstone. He had not fully understood that Jesus died for the sins of the whole world where all are accepted and there is no difference.

Viewpoints should most often be called opinions. One obviously believes his viewpoint is correct because of how he sees or understands something from the position in which he is looking. And from his point of view he is correct. But, what if he is positioned incorrectly? Can he see correctly? If you live in the valley, it may not be the best view of the valley. If you live in the forest, it may not be the vest view of the forest. The best view is from above, from the place at the top of the mountain overlooking the valley. The Creator of the universe has the best and most accurate view of all His creation, including us. To be established on the Rock or Chief Cornerstone would give us the same view as what

61   Gal. 2:11-13

God is seeing. So, when we are planted on the Rock we become living stones that have a heavenly view of all things. A view point from Mt. Zion! We are really seeing from Heaven!

> **1 Peter 2:4–6 — *Coming to Him as to a living stone, rejected indeed by men, but chosen by God and precious, you also, as living stones, are being built up a spiritual house, a holy priesthood, to offer up spiritual sacrifices acceptable to God through Jesus Christ. Therefore it is also contained in the Scripture, Behold, I lay in Zion a chief cornerstone, elect, precious, and he who believes on Him will by no means be put to shame.***

Why was Jesus Christ rejected by His own? He didn't fit their religious view of what God and heaven was all about. They were looking for a Messiah that would deliver them from the Roman Empire. Instead, Jesus offered them the kingdom of heaven, a spiritual kingdom. They saw natural kingdoms as being more valuable than the spiritual kingdom of heaven by which the natural was created. They saw natural things as more desirable to know than spiritual things. They didn't want to be changed; they wanted all the things around them changed by force. They wanted their outward existence changed without their inward being changed. Their attitude was, "Change them, don't change us!"

Too often we (me included) have prayed prayers for things to change and others to change, when the entire time God wanted to change our point of view so we could reign with Him in the middle of that situation. This is when He is most glorified. We've prayed witchcraft prayers in an effort to try to control or change others. His will or desire is never to control! That may come as a shock to you, but it's the truth. His way of ruling is not to control like the way of the world. His way of ruling is by being a servant to all. This Servant's will was and is to manifest the kingdom so that the goodness of God may lead all men to repentance (a change of mind). The Great Shepherd leads us. He doesn't drive us like cattle needing to be swatted on the be-hind to steer us in the right direction. "Follow Me," Jesus said. That's a love call! His great love for us calls us every day to Himself so we may walk together throughout the day. God delights in giving us His point of view.

God asked, "Jeremiah, what do you see?" Jeremiah said, "I see a branch of an almond tree." The Lord said, "You have seen well, for I am ready to perform My word." And the word of the Lord came to Jeremiah a second time, saying, "What do you see?"[62] God is very interested in what we are seeing. What we see is our point of view. If we see as God sees, then we see well and God is ready to perform that which we see. Jesus said of Himself, "I can only do what I see My Father do." There is only one right viewpoint, and it is in Christ, that we can see as God sees.

Elijah prayed that his servant's eyes would be opened so he could see the same thing that God was seeing. His servant's eyes were opened, and he saw angels all around that far exceeded the enemy![63] After that, the servant was no longer in fear. He had the faith of Elijah! You do not have to be a Prophet to have God's perspective all the time. You only need to be hidden in Christ 'till you see only Him who sits on the throne. This seeing is, of course, not with physical eyes, but spiritual eyes like Elijah's servant was given. The unseen realm is more real than the physical realm, because the physical realm was created out of the spiritual realm. So, when God becomes more real to you than the physical realm your body dwells in, then your eyes are now open like Elijah's servant, and you will have the faith to manifest that greater kingdom of heaven in the earth.

John, in the Book of Revelation, was in the Spirit on the Lord's Day, and he heard and saw glorious things that were from heaven's viewpoint. Then in chapter 4, John was told to, "Come up here!" And then he saw

---

62   Jer. 1:11–13

63   2 Ki 6:17

the throne, and One sat on the throne. That is when John was able to see from the throne's point of view. I won't get into all of it, but he saw before the throne a sea of glass, like crystal. This crystal glass was like a mirror. The sea represents the multitude of people, and they were like a mirror. So, from God's point of view, the people were an exact mirrored image or likeness of the glory of God who sits on the throne! God saw Himself in the people! He sees you the same way.

Our earthy point of view of these same people at times might be that they are a bunch of heathen sinners that's going to hell in a hand-basket! But, the Father only sees the world of people through the blood of the Lamb, who is the One who sits on the throne with Him. His offer to the world is forgiveness and all His love with full benefits! He instructed us not to look at anyone after the flesh so it must be right to assume that He must not see anyone after the flesh either.[64] Then what is left to see? Himself! Christ in you all.

He is not a fault finder. Neither does He judge with condemnation. He judges in righteousness. What righteousness you might ask? He judges according to His own righteousness that He freely gave us, which came by His own sacrifice on the cross. He remembers your sins no more! Jesus never lifted a stone to condemn anyone. With this point of view, we can understand why Jesus said that this is the acceptable year of the Lord. All are accepted! The kingdom of heaven is at hand, so receive freely the Father's blessings of that kingdom!

Jesus went around doing good and healing all who were oppressed of the devil.[65] I can only conclude that Jesus had this same perspective of all people seeing how He was the Lamb of God presently walking on the earth. This same view was given to Peter in a vision of the sheet being let down when at that time, he still saw the Gentile unbelievers as unclean sinners. Jesus is the Lamb of God and is presently walking in the earth today through His body. Jesus knew who He was from His

---

64   2 Cor. 5:16
65   Acts 10:38

Father's perspective. He had God's point of view. The Chief Cornerstone properly laid in us will give us God's viewpoint of us and others. It is a heavenly view. Hopefully, this will bring an end to the identity crises the Church and the world is having today. And we are just beginning to see from heaven.

Chapter 2

JESUS IS THE LAMB OF GOD

Jesus is the Lamb of God. This is probably the most important description of Jesus that we must be firmly planted on. He always was the Lamb of God even before the foundation of the world was laid.

> **1 Peter 1:18–21** — *...knowing that you were not redeemed with corruptible things, like silver or gold, from your aimless conduct received by tradition from your fathers, but with the precious blood of Christ, as of a lamb without blemish and without spot. He indeed was foreordained before the foundation of the world, but was manifest in these last times for you who through Him believe in God, who raised Him from the dead and gave Him glory, so that your faith and hope are in God.*

Jesus is, was, and always will be the Lamb of God in earth and in heaven. Jesus is presently the Lamb of God right now in our lives. In Revelation, Jesus is still seen as the Lamb of God in heaven. He changes not. As the Lamb of God, He took away the sins of the whole world.

1 Jn. 2:2 — *And He Himself is the propitiation (full sacrificial payment) for our sins, and not for ours only but also for the whole world.*

This is just one description of what the Lamb accomplished. Jesus didn't die just for the sins of those who believe, but for the sins of the whole world, including unbelievers, Muslims, Buddhists, Jews, atheists, black, white, brown and all the whatsoevers. *Whatsoever is born of God overcomes the world.*[66] Whatever kind of person, manner of person, sort of person, it doesn't matter; Jesus died to pay in full the enormous sins of the whole world.[67] This task seems to us impossible and insurmountable (impossible to overcome or deal with successfully). But, this was no ordinary four legged barnyard animal being sacrificed. This was God in human flesh sacrificing Himself for us; The Creator laying down His life for His creation. This was a spotless and completely innocent Lamb worth far more than all the sins of the people put together. This was the embodiment of God's love stretched out and hanging on the cross. He was declaring, "This is how much you are worth." Then He stamped the whole world as **PAID IN FULL**! So, how can our Father hold anyone's sin against him? He cannot. He will not. He does not! The Church might, but the Father doesn't.

Not all have believed and received His forgiveness is evident. But, does this mean that Jesus hasn't forgiven the unbelievers of their sin? No, it just means they cannot walk in that freedom from sin and bondage to the law and enjoy God's presence until they do believe. He has forgiven every person of their sins, and if their sins are forgiven them, then how much of the judgment of God's wrath remains toward them?

God's judgment of wrath, which is just, must be served to the full measure of the sin done by them and held against them according to the law of God and not according to man's judgment. It is not what we think

---

66   1 Jn. 5:4
67   1 Jn. 2:22

people deserve because of their sin that counts, but what the law of God judges to be sufficient. God saw it sufficient in the sending of His own Son for the full payment of the sins of the whole world. So, if the sins of the whole world are taken away by the Lamb of God, and if there remains no more sin according to that thorough work of God, then how much of God's judgment of wrath can there be left for anyone in the world? None! If God took it all away by the sacrifice of His only begotten Son, it would be a dishonor to His Son and to Himself to bring up anyone's sin as though He had done nothing. Unless we look at the world through the blood of Jesus, we cannot see the world as forgiven as God sees it.

Rom. 5:8 — *But God demonstrates His own love toward us, in that while we were still sinners, Christ died for us.*

God's love was set together in union toward us in the death of Jesus Christ while we were yet sinners. The death of Jesus for the sins of the whole world was not based on our believing for it or even our asking for it. God did it because God set His love on us. It had nothing to do with our obeying the law or not. God wanted to show the whole world His love for them, so He paid the price for our forgiveness and for the whole world's forgiveness. It is already paid. God doesn't take the payment back just because we do not believe. Christ didn't die on the cross because we believed. While I was yet in my sins as an unbeliever, Christ died for me. He chose to die and forgive. It was solely God's desire and decision based on His love for us. His death is my forgiveness, not because I believed for it, but because His blood is the redemption price paid in full for the whole world's forgiveness. If our believing or not believing can change any of that, then we can change God and what He did on the cross. But God changes not! Praise the Lord!

The old not so gospel (good news) of, "You're going to receive the wrath of God in hell if you don't repent and believe on Jesus," is a mixture. It has deception in it, and sets the stone of the law in the place of the true Cornerstone, which is Christ. It is a fear tactic that has been used by the church institution for centuries. But God has not given us the spirit of fear, but of power, love, and a sound mind. Perfect love casts out fear. Fear of hell or anything else is not God's way of saving people. It is the goodness of God that leads people to repentance.[68] (We'll talk more about God's judgment and wrath in Part 2, Chapter 3.)

The Cornerstone has nothing to do with us and our believing or not believing. The Cornerstone has nothing to do with the message of hell, or the devil, or most of our church doctrines. The Cornerstone is the person of Jesus Christ. (period) Jesus Christ came and finished it all while we were yet sinners. It is only when we get away from the Chief Cornerstone that we apply our own ifs, ands, buts, maybes, laws, observations, worldly views, religious views, and natural interpretations of scriptures. We cannot look from the view point of this world or from a religious concept and preach the true gospel of Jesus Christ. Only from the <u>Most Holy Place</u> of a finished work of rest, because of the blood of the Lamb having been sprinkled in all our thinking, can a pure gospel of nothing but good news be preached.

> **Jn. 12:31, 32 — *Now is the judgment of this world; now the ruler of this world will be cast out. And I, if I am lifted up from the earth, will draw all to Myself.***

I left out the word 'people' in the last verse because it was added by the translators' own understanding of what they thought the scripture should say. Without the word 'people' in it, we have to go back to the previous verse, verse 31, to see what the Lord was talking about. People are not even mentioned. It is clear He was talking about judgment. So I, Jesus Christ, am lifted up (on the cross) and all judgment will be

---

68   Rom. 2:4

drawn to Me. This makes perfect sense. How can the world be forgiven if there is any judgment that still remains? And how can He draw all people to Himself if He still holds the judgment of their sin against them? That would actually do the opposite and repel them away from Him. But if all judgment was drawn to Him at Calvary, then Jesus must have taken all, all, all the sins of the whole world upon Himself. This is the gospel of Jesus Christ, not of hell, or judgment, or even what most think repentance is.

This gospel will change the mind of the unbeliever (repentance) into thinking that God has already forgiven their sin and He longs to have fellowship with them right now. This speaks to the unbeliever that they can freely approach God without having condemnation and guilt. Why? Because this gospel causes him to believe in the Lord Jesus Christ and the right stone, the Chief Cornerstone that has been laid. Those still believing that there is future judgment that awaits us all or all the unbelievers are standing on the wrong stone. They are still standing on the stone of the law and not the Rock of God's love manifest through grace. One is still looking at people's performance or works; the other is looking at Jesus' performance or finished works. Most of us believers still need a change of mind because we are still looking at the wrong thing.

Repentance is not being sorry for your sins as most of the Church thinks. Repentance is a change of mind. Godly sorrow can lead you to a change of mind, but worldly sorrow can lead you into death.[69] So, it isn't having sorrow that produces anything but a change of mind. If you feel bad because you sinned, you're being sorry for it changes nothing, absolutely nothing. But, if it brings a change of mind that leads you to Christ, then that produces salvation. It is only by our being reminded of the sacrifice of the Lamb of God that can wash it all away, bad feelings and all. Those bad feelings come from our conscience. *The blood of Christ purges your conscience from dead works to serve the living God.*[70]

---

69   2 Cor. 7:10
70   Heb. 9:14

Only by seeing the blood of Jesus, and applying it to our sin, can we get past our looking at our own works and see His. That is salvation.

On the other hand, worldly sorrow produces death. This kind of sorrow does not produce a changed mind. If it doesn't produce a changed mind, then the person will harden their heart and their conscience will become seared or hardened as well. This is why we have heard the phrase, "They are hardened criminals." Nobody becomes a hardened criminal overnight. It is how we handle what this life deals out to us that will either produce a changed mind, or a harden heart and conscience. When we remind ourselves of our sins and failures, it will bring sorrow. But, it is only when we allow that sorrow to produce a change of mind that there is salvation.

If we sin, it is by looking at the tree of knowledge of good and evil, desiring its way of life, and then eating it that we sinned. We looked at our knowledge of the situation, judged between the good and evil, and then made our choice. We looked at the wrong tree, rather than at the tree of life in the midst or center of ourselves where Christ dwells, then we desired to eat of its fruit. After looking long enough, we decided to eat. Yes, it was our choice to eat of it, but if we hadn't gazed at it so long, it wouldn't have enticed us so. At this point, our desire is to live by the knowledge of those choices of good and evil. Religion tells us to choose the good and you will please God. But, that is not what the Bible tells us.

> **Deut. 30:19 — *"I call heaven and earth as witnesses today against you, I have set before you life and death, blessing and cursing; therefore choose life, that both you and your descendants may live;***

We see in this scripture that it is not the choices of good and evil that we are to choose from to obtain a greater life. That tree is what produces death. Choose life! That is eating from the life of God, and not of natural knowledge based on our five senses. Being led by our five senses is being led by this world, good and/or evil. Being led by the Spirit of God is choosing life. *Set your gaze, your eyes, your mind, and your desires on things above and not on things below, for we died, and our life is hidden with Christ in God.*[71] This is where we find life and the means to choose life.

> **Rom. 5:13 — *For until the law sin was in the world, but sin is not imputed when there is no law.* 2 Cor. 5:17 - *Therefore, if anyone is in Christ, he is a new creation, old things*** (old way of life under the law, eating of that tree) ***have passed away: behold, all things*** (all the course and way of life, now eating of the tree of life) ***have become new.***

When Jesus died on the cross, He not only took away our sins, but He also removed the law for those who believe, by giving us His life-giving Spirit. Now we live not by outward observations of the law, but by the law of the Spirit of life in Christ Jesus. Are we against the law? No, on the contrary, we go way beyond the law by living the life of love. The law is written on our hearts by His life living in us. This means it has become a living Spirit relationship that produces all our conduct rather than just the letter of the law. We no longer live by looking at religious do's and don'ts, or what we think to be right and wrong, or what we think is good and evil. It is by being brought into perfect union with the living God of the universe, we live, and move, and have our being! His life-giving Spirit in us is all we need to produce more life and have life at its fullest! It is only by seeing ourselves in Christ that the law can be taken away.

> **Heb. 8:13 — *In that He says, "A new covenant," He has made the first obsolete*** (covenant under the law). ***Now what is becoming obsolete and growing old is ready to vanish away.***

71   Col. 3:2, 3

We cannot take away the law by preaching repentance from sin. It is not repentance from sin that anyone can truly come to God, but repentance from dead works.[72] Whether we consciously knew it or not, we all had a works mentality in trying to please God. That's old covenant ways that never worked. A new covenant has to be introduced before we can change their minds. It is after seeing that Jesus took care of our sins on the cross, that we can come to God, not by our being sorry for sinning. We cannot take away sin and then take away the law. The strength of sin is the law,[73] not the other way around. You take away the law, you take away the strength of sin. It is at the preaching of Jesus Christ as the Lamb of God that changes our thinking so that the law, which looks at our own works, is removed. By no longer looking at our own works under the law, the power of sin is broken because a greater life apart from the law is established. Then are we free to go and sin no more.

It was only after Jesus declared to the woman caught in adultery that there are no more accusers and neither do I accuse you that He then was able to tell her to go and sin no more.[74] Only then is it possible to go and sin no more. Otherwise, Jesus told her something to do that was impossible. Who was the accuser? The law accuses because it creates a mindset of the knowledge of good and evil. So rather than condemning her by the law, Jesus freed her from the bondage of the law. If God doesn't accuse you of any sin, who truly can? Did God forgive her because she ask? No. He (Jesus) forgave because He is the Lamb of God who takes away the sin of the world.[75]

The law accuses; the world under the law accuses; family that is under the law accuses; and even the Church that is under the law accuses. But, one look at the Lamb of God with the marks of His

---

72   Heb. 6:1, 9:14

73   1 Cor. 15:56

74   Jn. 8:10, 11

75   Jn. 1:29

crucifixion, and hearing Him say, "Neither do I accuse you," can leave you with knowing you are free from all accusations! And if there is no one around to accuse you of your sin, not even yourself, then you are free! Why? You see no accusers because you see the law no more that accuses. Now what you do see is the righteous judgment of the Lamb of Almighty God as your final word. When the Lamb of God caused the accusers under the law to examine themselves by the law, then the accusers discovered they too needed forgiveness from their sins, and their accusing ended. The Lamb of God stops all accusations against us and our accusing others! How? We now see all things through the eyes of the Lamb of God which removes or vanquishes the law. Without the law, we cannot accuse anyone. If we truly have no more recognition of the law, by what can we accuse anyone?

The Spirit of the Lord just revealed that we will not have to wait on an occasional move of the Spirit like the occasional moving of the water to see people healed,[76] set free and strengthened. It will still be by the Spirit, but an ongoing knowledge/knowing of the Lamb of God presently indwelling us will move us with compassion to do the works of the Lord. The price has been paid in full and all the kingdom of heaven is at hand so why not expect it now? The I AM is with us and we are one with Him. These things will be done from the perspective of the Lamb of God, not by the purpose and plans of any man. The Lord says, "I don't exalt any man. I exalt Christ, and if you are hidden in Christ as His name is being exalted, then you are as one and exalted with Him."[77] To be exalted because we are hidden in Christ is a humbling experience because we can honestly say, "Why look at us as though it was by our own power or godliness we made this man walk. And His name, through faith in His name, has made this man strong...."[78] At the time that these things happen, we were hidden in Him and He is

---

76   Jn. 5:3
77   Mat. 23:12
78   Acts 3:12, 16

manifested through us, His servants. To be in Christ, one has to lose their own separate identity so as to become one with His. This is how the Father's name is written in our foreheads.[79]

I have been hearing that some are teaching that Jesus healed as one under the law because He was the fulfillment and perfection of the law. So, it therefore had nothing to do with grace, but as one being the fulfillment of the law He healed and did all His miracles. Let's take a look.

Jesus was an Israelite, Jew by natural birth, yet not born of a natural Israelite father, but born of God. The law is natural, but the Spirit is supernatural. So His birth was not by the law, but by promise. We know He never sinned and therefore He fulfilled the law and more. The more part are all the things the written law never covered and all those parts can only be fulfilled by love which is the fruit of the Spirit. We also know He was a spotless Lamb as announced by John the Baptist when he said, "Behold the Lamb of God, which takes away the sin of the world."[80] John did not declare, "Behold the Son of God that has come to fulfill the law for us all."

There were those who saw Jesus as the fulfillment of the law. They touched the hem of His garment and were healed. Some saw Him as one who walked with God because He was fulfilling the law. Touching the hem of His garment was touching the law as fulfilled which reaps the blessing of God under the laws of Moses. The promises of God through obedience to the law are powerful, and healing is one of them. Because Jesus was fulfilling the law flawlessly, He had the right to be healthy, prosperous and totally blessed.

But, that doesn't mean everybody around Him had that same right. Jesus had every right to the blessings of God because He fulfilled the law of Moses, but nobody else did. Those that touched the hem of His garment still had to approach Him by grace because they themselves had not fulfilled the law. So, they expected to be healed by unmerited

79   Rev. 14:1
80   Jn. 1:29

favor from the One who had favor with God. They were able to see the grace or favor of God all over Jesus. They found grace in the eyes of the Lord. They knew if they could only touch the hem of His garment, they too could be healed because this was the acceptable (gracious, favorable) year of the Lord. Before Jesus started His ministry, He declared that now is the acceptable year of the Lord.[81]

Only the ones that approached Jesus looking at their own works of the law didn't and couldn't be healed.[82] Why? Wrong approach! They were not looking for unearned favor from God like the paralyzed man who couldn't possibly have any good works at all, for he was paralyzed! They were set on gaining favor through the law on their own. Therefore, they were extremely limited and were not healed even though the power was present to heal them. But, others under the law approached Jesus as the One who fulfilled the law. They in turn had access to the blessings of God through Him; righteousness on His part, but grace working towards them on their part.

For Him to heal, or do anything by the works of fulfilling the law only, is to also demand judgment and condemnation to those who did not fulfill it. Why? If you judge yourself as fulfilling the written law, then you are a judge. What you judge yourself by is what you will judge others by. But Jesus didn't come to judge or condemn anyone. So there was no way that He was even looking at the law. Then what was He looking at? Jesus was looking at the love of the Father, which gave Him the Father's view from heaven. Neither did He come to commend those who thought they were fulfilling the law. He came as the Lamb of God to be judged for us all so that all judgment against us would be stopped.

Under the covenant of the law, you don't qualify if you didn't fulfill the law for yourself. My righteousness doesn't make you righteous. But, the righteousness of spotless Lamb makes all righteous, thus qualifying all! He qualified all that desired something of Him. So, all were healed.

---

81   Lk. 4:19
82   Lk. 5:17–26

Not just because He fulfilled the law, but also because He was a gracious Lamb towards all. We know that if we judge ourselves according to the law, we also judge others by the same law we judge ourselves. If Jesus would have only seen Himself as the fulfillment of the law of Moses, He would have only been a Judge sent by God to judge those under the same law. But He said, "I judge no man."[83]

The Lamb came by grace and truth, not by the works of the law. For the law was given through Moses, but grace and truth came through Jesus Christ.[84] Nowhere does it say that the fulfillment of the law came by Jesus Christ so our hope might be in His fulfilling the law for us as though we are to continue to look at the law. Jesus did fulfill the law because of the life and love of God in Him. He fulfilled the law by being led by the Spirit of God just as we are today. The purpose of fulfilling the law was to bring the law to an end, not to qualify Himself to heal others or to qualify others to be healed. Under the law the year of Jubilee was once every fifty years. But Jesus did the works of Jubilee for three and a half years. Every year is the acceptable year of the Lord because of the presence of the Lamb of God. We might have a problem in knowing and remembering who Jesus is, but He didn't.

Even though John the Baptist was an Israelite under the law, he didn't declare, "Behold the perfection of the law, by which He will heal and do mighty signs and wonders." No, it was a declaration that the Lamb of God has come, who takes away the sin of the world. That means that He removes all our failures to do the law so our approach to God can be by His grace.

The centurion and the Samaritan woman were the only ones whom Jesus declared to have great faith. Why? They were not under the laws of Moses. Their faith was based on His goodness and authority as the King of His kingdom, having grace and good will towards men.[85] And

---

83   Jn. 8:15
84   Jn. 1:17
85   Lk. 2:14

others were healed that had no idea who He was, and therefore, had no clue that He was fulfilling the law. So they didn't have any approach at all, but grace approached them! Not the fulfillment of the law only. Jesus accomplished that, but not for the healing of anyone. If it is by His stripes that we were healed,[86] then it must have been by that same Lamb that they were healed. If so, then Jesus would have had to have told them that I have fulfilled the law for you, and now you can be healed even though you have failed so many times at the law. This would have left them with self-condemnation instead of a gracious wonderful Lord who asked them nothing concerning the law, but only healed them. To whom did Jesus ask, "Do you believe that I have fulfilled the law?"

Jesus said, "I will have mercy, and not sacrifice."[87] Are not sacrifices a part of the law? But Jesus had mercy and not sacrifice in His heart and on His mind. If it were sacrifices that Jesus desired, then the law would have been His judgment and none would have been healed. How many came to Jesus based on their own good works and received healing? None.

So what can we say? He became all things to all men so that He would save all. To those under the law and knew they had failed, He fulfilled the law for them so they could make their approach to Him desiring mercy and grace on their part. "Have mercy on us!"[88] Whether they knew Him as the Lamb or only as the fulfillment of the law for them, the mercy and grace of God flowed through Jesus because **Jesus knew who He was**. He is the Lamb of God! He had favor towards them all was God's approach to man, and it had nothing to do with a law minded approach to Him. All those who approached Him wanting mercy got it because the favor of God was towards all men in the presence of the Lamb of God.

To those not under the laws of Moses, and to those who were a law unto themselves in their conscience, both had a conscience that

---

86   1 Pet. 2:24
87   Mat. 9:13
88   Mat. 9:27, 15:22, 17:15, 20:30

condemned them. But the presence of the Lamb of God, who takes away their sin, gave them the right approach by grace. They now approach Him having seen and found grace in the eyes of God through Him. Without the presence of the Lamb of God, none of those under the law of Moses, nor those not under the law of Moses could have approached Him, still having their own sins to deal with. They would have received nothing. One man fulfilling the law of Moses for them still cannot take away their sin and make their approach to God one of faith. Only seeing the grace of God working through Him gave them faith apart from the law. Look into the eyes of the Lamb of God and behold, we see the grace of God! That's what they saw. If He fulfilled the law by love, then what did they see? Did they see the fulfillment of the legalistic law or love? Both, love towards them as He was fulfilling the law by that same love.

Jesus was born under the law just like you and I were born under the law. And we found out that being under the law is a flesh life separate from the life of the Spirit. It is not inwardly that we or Jesus were born under the law, but one outwardly! Even Jesus had a flesh that was tempted like our own, but without sin.[89] How could He never sin? He lived not as one under the law, but as one born of the Spirit and only eating of that life. He was able to fulfill all the law, not because He was under the law, but because He was born of the Spirit of God. His was not a life lived under the letter of the law but as One with the Father. Being the Son, means He is of His Father. The works that Jesus did was because He knew where He came from and who He is. He is the Lamb of God that takes away the sin of the world! Therefore, the kingdom of heaven is at hand.

Jesus came to bring those under the law to an end of themselves as Adam. That is why He preached to the Scribes and Pharisees the perfection of the law. As long as they looked to the law as their righteousness, they would always fall short after hearing the perfection

---

89   Heb. 4:15

of the law preached to them by Jesus. This was done so they would discover that they needed grace to approach God. An end to the law is an end to Adam eating of the tree of the knowledge of good and evil so that they might receive the grace of God that comes through the manifested Lamb. I will go so far as saying that Jesus could have done no works at all if He had not come by grace and truth alone! Yes, He fulfilled the law. But not by looking at the law but by looking at the life of the Father in Him. He fulfilled the law by the indwelling Holy Spirit. By grace alone people were and are healed, everyone. As one under the law it is a hit-and-miss attempt because it requires us to fulfill the law flawlessly. If you are guilty of one part of the law, you are guilty of the whole law. Obedience to the law has the announcement of the blessings of God on it. But, to be guilty of one part of the law is to be guilty of the whole law and condemned by it.

There is no perfection of the law except it being done by the Spirit of life in Christ Jesus apart from observing the law! It was according to the life of God in Jesus that Jesus did everything; not because He was fulfilling the law by observing the law. He lived in the time and place where all were under the law, but He ushered in the grace of God right in the middle of that law. Over four hundred years had passed and there was no prophetic word since then. Why? No Spirit, just law.

Jesus was both man and God. He did not preach on the subject of grace because He had not yet died. He said, "There are yet many things I have to tell you, but you are not ready for them."[90] I believe that the message of grace was one of those things that was demonstrated through the life of Jesus Christ, but not yet taught or preached because they could not yet receive it as their own until after His death and resurrection finalized an end to the law. If Jesus would have taught grace, it would have been mixed with the law that all were still under. When He died, He died as one (us) under the law so that our approach to God could be one through grace having received His righteousness freely.

90   Jn. 16:12

When Paul performed many signs and miracles among the Gentiles, was it because he had a message of the perfection of the law being fulfilled by Jesus or the message of grace demonstrated through Him? Grace was demonstrated by the Lamb of God separate from the works of the law. It was the Scribes and Pharisees that could not be healed because they were set on their laws and not on Jesus' words.

Even in the Old Testament when types and shadows were done by the slaying of a lamb (forgiveness by grace), it produced miracles. Why? God saw it not as a type and shadow only, but as a reminder of the real Lamb slain before the foundation of the world. How much more when the real Lamb came into the world would it produce even greater works? But if we read the Old Testament and see such things as being a law only and not pointing us to Jesus as its fulfillment, then we begin to place ourselves back under the law.

Every belief that we presently have at this time must fit upon this cornerstone of the truth of Jesus being the Lamb of God. There are other descriptions of the Chief Cornerstone that we will look at later. But as the Lamb of God, Jesus hit a grand slam and brought us all home! Jesus Christ is the Chief Cornerstone of our foundation, and there must be only one stone who witnesses for us. The rest of the foundation is also Jesus Christ and given by inspiration of the Holy Spirit through the scriptures. The foundation is finished by an ongoing revelation and understanding of Jesus Christ from the perspective of standing on the Cornerstone already laid in us. Every doctrine, teaching, and thought we have heard and believed must come from this perspective or place of understanding, or it is heresy. It will bring disunion.

There is no other gospel message than that of the gospel of Jesus Christ. That gospel begins with Jesus Christ as the Lamb of God. If the understanding we have shines more light on the Cornerstone, which is Jesus Christ, then it is the truth. If the understanding we have shines light on anything else but the person of Jesus Christ and His finished work, such as our own works or an experience we had in this world of the dust realm, it will bring disunion. Disunion is why God hates mixture. The law shines its light on what man can and cannot produce which is really darkness. It is disunion. Grace shines light on what God has produced through Jesus Christ. This is the true light that lights every man who comes into the world. It brings perfect union.

What is darkness and what is light? We know that God is light and in Him there is no darkness. Light is a descriptive type of seeing clearly, knowing, and understanding something. God is omniscient. He knows everything! He is all knowing! Therefore there is no darkness in Him. Yet He dwells in darkness as well as light. How so? In the absence of knowledge and understanding is darkness. This may describe where we are at times, but right there within our darkness is the indwelling presence of the omniscient God, the One who knows all things. God is there in our darkness ready to unveil wisdom and revelation in the knowledge of Him.[91] It is into this place of darkness where we are at at that time that the light shines. That darkness, which we might have thought to be light, is seen in truth as darkness because the true light has dawned on us. Christ is that light, and that light is His life. Light shines into our darkness so that we might walk in the light of His life.

Why do you think there are so many various religious beliefs among the Believers today? There is a mixture of light and darkness, or grace and the law, because we have left the Chief Cornerstone of our foundation and believed the lie. What lie have we believed? Anything that we have swallowed as truth because it sounded right from a natural world viewpoint deceived us and lied to us. It may have been the outward appearance of man and their degrees or intellectual words that had us looking away from and forgetting the Cornerstone. But the good news is that natural Adamic view we have at this time is in jeopardy of being exposed by the light of His life being unveiled in us as we hear the truth.

We were at one time convinced by its wonderful presentation, and it made sense to our old Adamic (natural) thinking. But, in the midst

91   Eph. 1:17

of the darkness God said, "Let there be light," and it was so! Then a great and wonderful thing happened in that day, when the light came, it **divided** the light called Day from the darkness called Night. We are now able to see the difference between the light and the dark. Before the light came, we didn't know the difference. We are translated out of darkness and into His marvelous light![92] If we walk in the light as He is in the light, we have no need of the sun (the natural light that this world has). In other words, we won't look for the natural understanding or reasoning that Adam has, but we look at the true light of the life of Christ in us as our hope of glory.

Mt. 24:11 — *Then many false prophets will rise up and deceive many.*

One definition of a false prophet is a religious impostor. They carry about an air of religion that imitates or looks like the real thing. Jesus called the Scribes and Pharisees whitewashed tombs because of their religious outward observations of the law.[93] That whitewashed look is a self-righteous look. He spoke of them in Mt. 15:14 as the blind leading the blind, and they both fall into a ditch. They were studious at the scriptures; and therefore, they were given respect by all and believed by all. Yet, they were blind leaders. The born again believer should not be so easily deceived by giving more respect to the studious preacher than to the Christ living in them. A lesson learned by us all the hard way. You can always trust Christ in you.

Trust the Lord who dwells in you more than the words of mere men, because we all falter in our thinking at some time or other. Even the light we now have is not the whole light that is yet coming, so we sometimes error. It is easy for anointed preachers to speak the truth in one sentence and in another sentence speak an untruth. That untruth is

92   1 Pet. 2:9
93   Mat. 23:27

spoken in the same fashion as though it were anointed too. It sounded like the anointed truth on the outside, but deep within you it sounded like a stranger and felt yucky inside. You had an inward witness that was saying, "Woe, wait just a minute here." The untruth spoken gave no glory to the finished work of Christ, nor His name. It gave you an uneasy feeling in your spirit. That's God letting you know the difference! "That wasn't Me." He is still a small still voice in us leading us along.

If you will take the time right then, or later, to ask God what was wrong with that part of the message that was given, He'll show you. It might be that you just took it wrong or maybe not. Either way, we need to know the truth. Parts of it were good and right, but the parts that offered mixture He wants you to throw out. Why? Any untruth is heresy, which means it comes to bring disunion, and that my friend is what makes God angry.[94] The letter of the law is not the living truth. It is a false form of an outward appearance of a god that carves an image in our minds. It is our own opinion and mental conclusion of what we think God might be. That law can become an idol in our minds that we serve and worship. God hates anything that brings disunion, and He is out to destroy it! Not you! Not people! Not the preacher! But the lies and deception, even if they came with sincerity shall be destroyed! That's good news, unless you love the lie more than the truth. Then you will have to wait until the natural man with his carnal thinking dies before you will believe the truth.

The religious leaders of Jesus' day acted outwardly like they were so holy, but inside they were dead, without the life of God. The great deception is that those, who are as religious as they were, couldn't tell the difference between the truth and a lie because they looked at the outward appearance of that religion and called it God. Then when the Messiah, Emmanuel (God with us) came in person, they didn't recognize Him as God. Why? He didn't look like their religion. Could it be that there is more to God than what religion has taught us?

God can send a messenger our way to speak truth apart from our religion. If we trust in our religion rather than the Christ dwelling in us, we will see them and their words the same way the Scribes and Pharisees saw Jesus, as Beelzebub. Christ and His living word have to become our most focused place in our thoughts and walk, or our religion will deceive us as well.

Where do these false prophets come from? From vs. 10 in Mt. 24, believers that got offended, betrayed, and hate one another. What were they offended at? The truth, because it didn't appeal to the flesh. Being hated by all nations/people is no fun (vs.9). So, let's compromise the true gospel and start teaching as truth things that make our gospel more acceptable so that we may grow our congregations. They therefore sought the knowledge of men rather than God because they wanted followers. Their desire is that people follow them. They therefore looked for another gospel which isn't the gospel at all. They looked for a truth under the law and made it say what they wanted it to say. The judgment of God that many preach is part of that deception that declares God hates the people that sin. When in reality the true judgment of God is seen on the cross and put an end to all judgment of sin. The truth bears witness to the greatness of His love that He has always towards us that can never grow cold (vs. 12). The judgment of God according to the law is cold. These false prophets will make your love grow cold if you hear them.

Being trained by the religious traditions of men produces religious impostors. I call these religious impostors 'false reporters' because they are only reporting what they have heard from others as truth. Some of these do so with the utmost sincerity of heart trying to please God, which in itself is of the law. Some teach these things as truth because that's what they were told the truth is. Now their heart and conscience is infected with these things and error in their thoughts and understanding. The longer they continue in these things the harder their heart becomes. That is why we are told to guard our hearts with all diligence, for out of it flow the issues of life.[95]

So what happens when we don't guard our hearts and we believe false reports? Out of it will flow the issues of death or disunion from the life of God. It can keep us from entering into the promise land just like the Israelites when they believed the evil report. A mixed up heart can let good and bad flow out of it. James says this ought not to be.[96] A well-educated deceived heart will no doubt preach mixture with a greater ability to deceive others. Yet, the deceived preacher doesn't know he is deceived and preaches like it is truth. His own determination to preach another gospel having mixture is even more enthusiastic because he wants to prove that he is not ashamed of the gospel he has, even though it is not the gospel. If he will not listen to the truth when God sends him a messenger, he is just stubborn. It seems as though zeal without the knowledge of the truth produces stubbornness. Why So? The law in itself is stubborn. The law has no mercy to give, no love to give, no forgiveness, no slack, and is very ridged. So a mixture will have the same look to it underneath all of its outward appearance. Do not be deceived by outward appearance. The zeal and love some have for their religion can attract followers. But the truth is what we are out to follow, not people.

I am not ashamed of the gospel of Jesus Christ[97] is often mistaken for zeal. Not being ashamed is not a testimony of our actions to show ourselves bold and outspoken towards others about the gospel. That once again is looking at our works. <u>I am not ashamed of the gospel is a testimony of knowing the one that leaves us not ashamed.</u> It is what the pure gospel has done to us, for us, and through us. It is a testimony of the true gospel, which speaks only of Christ Jesus and His finished work that empowers believers with salvation, leaving them not ashamed

95   Pro. 4:23
96   Js. 3:10
97   Rom. 1:16

because they see sin and judgment no more. That gospel leaves people healed and whole; spirit, soul, and body. That's the gospel we are not ashamed of, because it is the power of God unto complete salvation. If our church is not preaching that kind of gospel and having us look at ourselves, our morals, and our works, then that is another gospel that leaves us ashamed. Don't be deceived! It is not about us, but it is about Christ Jesus, and then us hidden in Him.

People just like to be followers of other people. That's the way this world operates. In the natural, people have a tendency to give more respect and trust to those who have more degrees in accredited Bible Colleges than anyone who may have been taught by the Lord Himself and by great clouds of witnesses. Notice the accreditation comes from man and not necessarily from God. Bible School can be good and right, but only if one goes into it guarding their heart with all diligence by listening to the Holy Spirit who witnesses to their spirit. We are all coming out of darkness and discovering the light, and that is so exciting! But we must beware of the leaven of the Pharisees. One is not ready for Bible School until they first know the Chief Cornerstone or is taught it in the first class at that school. But even then most Bible Colleges think their religious doctrines are their cornerstone. Bible School in not necessarily a safe haven where there are no fallacies and all its teachers are speaking nothing but pure truth. They only speak what they believe at that time to be the truth, and most teach it because that's what they were taught. I know some Pastors who have told me they began pastoring because they thought it was an easy living. Such have no calling and no anointing which will produces dead men's religion.

How can we tell if it's a mixture? Look at the Cornerstone of our foundation. What lines up with it is truth, what doesn't is false. Even if it is in the Bible, that doesn't mean it's the complete truth. In the Bible there are two very different covenants, two very different men, darkness and light, life and death. One is of the truth and the other is a lie. It's how we see and understand the Bible that makes it the truth or a lie.

The Bible shows us the truth, but also shows us the lie so that we will not become deceived.

The Israelites didn't have the covenant we have today;[98] therefore, what awaited them if they disobeyed was the curse. But what awaits us is of a higher order of truth that leaves us forgiven, loved, healed, having no lack, and fully reconciled. That is what the blood of Jesus is still speaking today. Religion has trained up so many false prophets. They are confused as to what is truly the foundation for everything that should be taught from a Cornerstone perspective. Instead, they teach as foundation their doctrines and traditions (like the Scribes and Pharisees) as though it is to be heeded as their foundation. Those false teachings have produced more false beliefs that continue to increase to this day.

If this word is starting to make you lose total confidence in your pastor or teachers in your church, that's okay, if you are at the same time gaining more confidence in the knowledge of Jesus Christ and the greatest teacher, the Holy Spirit, because He will also bear witness with your pastor and teachers to the truth they do speak. That is wonderful! Our total confidence is supposed to be in God, not me, nor your pastor, nor anybody else. If what is being preached is of God, put your total confidence in that word. If it is not, you have the Spirit of truth abiding in you who will show you the truth and make all things known to you. And the Holy Spirit will not leave you judging your pastor either. If you truly have the truth then that truth will keep you from judging those who are deceived. Now you have peace towards all men. We will all eventually come into the knowledge of the truth, because a lie cannot endure without end.

How can all this deception stop? As long as we are in the world, it won't. Even Jesus was lied to by the natural mind of this world called Satan. It was in His mind that the temptations came to Him. But, He answered with the living word that abides in His spirit at the same time those lies came at Him. Not all of us do the same. An individual

---

98   Heb. 8:8

needs to pray (bear their heart) and have the desire to have the eyes of their own understanding opened. This includes being willing to go back to the foundation that was laid in you and rediscovering Jesus Christ afresh; being willing to be corrected by the Lord at the cost of having every religious belief taken away; being willing to even leave your present place of worship when this greater way of life comes; because your change of mind might not be welcomed by others. You being willing to be rejected and persecuted at the cost of learning the truth.

I am not saying you need to leave your physical place of worship, but as the truth comes, you will leave that place of worship you once had. Knowing the truth (Christ), you can't worship Him in spirit and half-truth any longer. You will not be able to worship the Lord with songs that speak of those deceptions, no matter how beautiful they sound. More truth will deliver us from the lies we have believed and from more lies that will yet come to our natural mind being in this world. Those truths will bring us into greater intimacy and greater worship. So out of truth you will correspond with greater worship.[99] You will leave your present place of worship and worship Him from a higher place of rest, the place of spirit and truth.

It is only from this hunger and desire for greater union with Him through the truth that we will even allow God and others to point us to the truth. In that process we will discover our errors of false beliefs because the light has come. But we will also discover deeper truth that will solidify what we have already known and believed as truth. It is only by first discovering the truth that one is even willing to throw off the error of their belief because the new is better. Much better! Hopefully this is what the Lord will accomplish in us all until there is a generation raised up in nothing but the foundation of the truth so as they grow old, not only will they not stray from it, but they will be manifest Sons of God.

It was the Lamb of God in human flesh that showed up when Jesus walked on the earth. Some have said that the New Covenant didn't start

---

99   Jn. 4:24

until after Jesus died on the cross. The New Covenant was completed at His crucifixion, burial, and resurrection, but the benefits of the New Covenant have been available from before the foundation of the world was even laid. *Enoch walked with God and was no more.*[100] How did Enoch walk with God? How can two walk together unless they agree?[101] No one can come to the Father but by Me, Jesus said.[102] Enoch saw it ahead of time and received it. The name Enoch means one who knows the secrets. Enoch discovered the plan of God, the sending of His Son as the Lamb of God that takes away the sin of the world. By knowing this secret Enoch was able to walk with God and lose himself in God. By observation of the law, no one can walk with God. Enoch saw the salvation of God ahead of time and walked with God and was no more.

Abraham had a covenant with God that was based on God's faithfulness and goodness, not on his own works. This is the same basis of our New Covenant cut by the faithfulness of the Son of God apart from our own works. The tabernacle of God, with all its furnishings and offerings, was a type of Christ. When the sacrifices were carried out, the blessings came because innocent blood was shed. So, when Jesus walked the earth, the Lamb of God was present to reveal the true and living God with New Covenant blessings. Because of the presence of the Lamb of God, the kingdom of heaven was at hand. The Lamb speaks of forgiveness which manifests the Kingdom with healing, soundness of mind and soul, provision, wisdom, peace, love, and many other wonderful characteristics of the God of that Kingdom. If any of our beliefs takes away from Jesus as the Lamb, it is heresy. It will bring disunion. The Lamb of God is the basis for our union with our Father God. There is no other way, no other truth, and no other life.

Before Moses could lead the children out of the bondage of Egypt, which represents the bondage we had to our sins, the blood of an

---

100   Gen. 5:24
101   Amos 3:3
102   Jn. 14:6

innocent spotless lamb had to be placed on the door frame of each house. This is the beginning of the grace of God which is now going to lead the people out of their bondage. Everything that God did from this point on was only by the grace of God, the favor of God, because of the shedding of innocent blood.

This grace was faithful in all of Israel's affairs until they came to Mt. Sinai. It is here that the people by their own choice sought a different covenant based on their own obedience to the laws that God gave them. Instead of them declaring that they honestly couldn't obey all those laws, they declared, "All that the Lord has said we will do and obey."[103] These are the same people that made a golden calf to worship! These laws that God gave them is like asking a sinner to stop sinning, a bird to stop flying, a dog to never bark again, and a person to never think an evil thought again. Impossible! It was from this place of <u>man's</u> covenant with God that Israel limited God based on their own goodness and self-righteousness.

Separate from the Lamb of God, there is no true righteousness or holiness for us. But at the cross, grace is once again faithfully at work apart from the law for as long as we choose to be free from the law. We can add to the works of Christ by adding our own personal or congregational laws. In doing so, we are attempting to establish our own righteousness and grace is eliminated. We are warned not to add or take away from anything written in the book, the book of the Revelation of Jesus Christ.[104] Why? It is adding to or taking away from the person of Jesus Christ, not just some words on a page. It is heresy. It brings disunion and sets us up for destruction and a fall, but not because God is bringing it.

When we deny the truth, we are denying God's grace and mercy that comes with that truth that was sent to set us free and keep us free from the curse. Even the world has been delivered from the curse by

103   Exo. 19:8, 24:3, 24:7
104   Rev. 22:18, 19

the works of Jesus Christ, but if we will not agree with those works, then we cannot walk in that freedom of His finished works. The same thing applies to the unbeliever. He is already free from sin by the blood of Jesus Christ. But if he doesn't agree with that work, then he cannot walk in its freedom and fullness.

There is one such teaching, and there are many others that bring this type of disunion and cause us to look at our own works to see if we are without sin. Contrary to some preaching, the Bible doesn't teach us to examine ourselves to see if we have sin in our lives, and if we do, pray at the end of the day asking God for forgiveness. There are no such scriptures in the Bible. And just in case you have sinned some hidden sin that you don't know about, you better pray and ask for forgiveness every day! Actually the Bible does tell us to examine ourselves to see if we are in the faith.[105] There's a big difference!

To examine yourself for sin is to declare that the Lamb of God has not come. To examine yourself for sin makes the Lamb without effect in your life and your sin remains in your own conscious awareness and in the mind of your imagination. To see yourself in your sin is to see yourself without the blood of Jesus. Have you believed on Jesus? Then you are without sin even when you do sin. What?! That's right! Is the word of God the same yesterday, today, and forever? Yes. Well, Jesus is the Lamb of God just as much today, right now as He was 2000 years ago, and just as much the Lamb of God that takes away the sins of your past as He is your present and future sins! Did you know that the Lamb of God never changes? The only thing that remains in question is, "Are you in the faith?" Do you right now believe Jesus is the Lamb of God that takes away the sin of the whole world? Then as far as God is concerned, you have no sin. Now, if you believe it, you have no more consciousness of your own sin, and you are free!

But, if you insist and persist on examining yourself for sin, you will develop a sin consciousness that will continue to condemn you and make

---

105   2 Cor. 13:5

you feel guilty. From then on, it's all downhill because now the mind of your imagination carries with it the curse of sin. Then to make matters worse, your body begins to develop, rather degenerate, because it is being placed under the curse that you imagine yourself to be in. The cells in your body are receiving messages of self-condemnation that is producing micro-dramas in your life. Under such pressure that is non-conducive to the environment of life that you were created to dwell in, physical sickness, disease, and poverty begin to line up with what you believe.

You can carry that line of thinking with you into a bottomless pit. But even then, God is greater than your conscience. I use the term imagination because God still sees you without sin, even though you see yourself with sin. I believe God has the right point of view. So really, the sin lies in your own conscience and imagination and does not come from God's judgment. His judgment of your sin laid upon Jesus renders you sinless. So instead of examining yourself for sin, just examine the Lamb and His blood shed for you, and that blood will speak only of your cleansing from all your sins: past, present and future. And the good news just keeps coming!

Does the Lamb of God then give me a license to sin anytime I want? No, your flesh already had that license and you can still sin all you want. In the process of partaking of that sin, you are bringing your soul into disunion, even though your born again spirit will never experience that sin. It is when your soul is not in union with your spirit, that the wrong message is sent throughout your body. You may not be sinning against anyone else, but you are sinning against the Lord, your new created spirit, and your own body which belongs to the Lord. God's forgiveness continually flows toward you while you are doing wrong, but you recognize not the presence of God in your soul and body. You in this case are not one, you are divided and a house divided against itself cannot stand.

The Bible says you cannot sin![106] This is speaking of your spirit, which is the breath of God in you. The quiet still voice of God's Spirit

---

106   1 Jn. 3:9

witnessing to your spirit will never demand its own way. That's just not the way of love; and therefore, it is not the way of God. And God will never leave your soul in hell, a place that has the absence of God. The Husbandman (Christ) will pursue you until He has captivated the woman playing the harlot (the harlot mind, soul), so He can make her His Bride, the Bride of Christ.[107] Because we came from Adam, though he has been crucified with Christ, we still have his natural mind of a fallen condition called our Adamic thinking or the unrenewed mind.

> **James 1:21 & Rom. 12:2 — *But receive the engrafted word which is able to save your soul. And be not conformed to this world, but be transformed by the renewing of your mind, that you may prove what is the good and acceptable and perfect will of God.***

It is not that God has given us a license to sin because of what the Lamb has done, but only by an ongoing relationship with the light are we able to walk in that light. It is in our natural thinking that we make natural choices, and that alone is eating of the tree of the knowledge of good and evil. We have gained a habit of eating of that tree. The world teaches us to eat of that tree. It is not learning good and evil and then choosing to do good that is right or righteous. In the world, good choices are the best you can do without Christ in you being unveiled in our knowing. Those choices are made without first yielding to the life of Christ in us so that we might freely partake of His life. That same life-giving Spirit is able to transform us by renewing our mind. We live by every word that proceeds out of His mouth, not by knowing the difference between good and evil and then making good choices.

Is it so bad for God to forgive you even while you are in the midst of your sin? Or is it better that you feel condemned, guilty, and ashamed for a season so you can experience depression and the fall of the curse

---

107   Rev. 21

and death before you receive the free gift of salvation? It seems as though it makes us feel better if we make ourselves suffer a little before we freely receive forgiveness. This too is dead works in trying to earn God's sympathy and forgiveness. It is man's effort in an attempt to reach some kind of deep repentance. I know, I've been there, and it's a lie. Deep repentance is to have a deeper revelation of Jesus Christ that changes the depth of our lowly thinking. (That might need to be repeated.) Deep repentance is to have a deeper revelation of Jesus Christ that changes the depth of our lowly thinking. Repentance is, after all, a change of thinking. It is not by our much bawling and squalling with tears that we are forgiven. Esau tried that and found no place for repentance.[108] It is by revelation of the Lamb of God that we find forgiveness and not through tearful agony over our wrong doing.

We do not learn by our suffering, but by His suffering for us. Learning by our suffering is the way of the world; and that is the knowledge that comes from Hard Knocks University. That is not the way of living by faith. We are not humbled by our suffering but by His suffering for us. All our suffering is but dung compared to the sufferings of Christ Jesus anyway. Paul prayed that He might know the fellowship of His sufferings,[109] not his own suffering in the likeness of Jesus' as some might think. To be able to fellowship with Him is so I might know and understand His sufferings that were done for me. When we know what His sufferings have already accomplished and finished as the Lamb, then we can be conformed to His death and then be partakers of His resurrection now. Did you catch it? Knowing His sufferings for us and as us will conform us to His death so we can live a resurrected life! I lose my life, seeing that I died with Him. If I now see that I died with Him, then I also find that I am risen with Him now!

The Lamb doesn't give us a license to sin. Quite the opposite is true. The Lamb gives us the death of sinful Adam and the resurrection of the

---

108   Heb. 12:16, 17
109   Php. 3:10

new man in the likeness and image of Christ so we can experience this life free from sin! When enough grace is taught and preached, we will end up with nothing but a righteous consciousness that will produce after its own kind. Preaching against sin produces a sin consciousness because it is reminding me of my sin that God has forgotten. That kind of preaching has us looking at ourselves and the works of the flesh. If I died with Him, then I have no works of my own to look at. That sure is good news. The preaching of sin or against sin only breeds more sin because it makes us more conscious of our sin that God really took away by the Lamb.

So the preaching of sin is a lying imagination conjured up by the unchanged thinking of Adam, who we are instructed to reckon as dead. If he is dead according to our thinking, then he cannot sin. The dead cannot sin, for they have no body to express that sin. Neither can they think according to the natural mind because it too is dead. So, by the grace of God, Adam died and we are free from sin. This is not a license to sin; but a liberty to live life more abundantly according to our new found life of grace that brings us into full union with the One!

Another teaching that takes away from the Lamb of God is, "We are sinners saved by grace." Impossible! For one thing, you cannot be a sinner and saved at the same time; you are either one or the other. To say that you are still a sinner is to declare that you do not believe in the Lamb of God that has already forgiven and cleansed you from your sins. That's basic Cornerstone knowledge. That's milk. Do you believe? Then you're saved! It's that simple. Declaring that you are not a sinner is not saying that you will never sin. But you are declaring that the blood of Jesus has removed all your sin; past, present and future. It is declaring that you are now a partaker of the newness of life that is found by faith in God's grace through Jesus Christ. Because of this newness of life, sin is no longer your life style. A sinner has no other alternative, but to be a good sinner. He knows no other life, and I should know; I was pretty good at it. We were all good at it because we did not recognize the life of Christ that was in us.

In the Bible and in the world only the life of Adam and the life of Christ are recognized. The life of Adam is under the law and is the partaking of sin, the curse, death, and darkness. The life of Christ given to us by His grace and is partaking of the kingdom of heaven and dwelling in perfect and complete union with the King of that kingdom. Even though the Adam of this world has already been crucified on the cross, not all recognized that truth and wrongly see themselves as Adam. Even some believers wrongly declare they are still sinners with the air of false humility. True humility is to be converted from such things and such thinking and become as a little child so you can see who we really are in the kingdom and in God's sight. If you see yourself as a sinner, you're not seeing the kingdom and you are not yet seeing from heaven.

It's becoming a child of, **of,** of God, not of Adam, that is a place of humility. Humility is not a trait of Adam. You are receiving a free gift, not something you have earned, and that takes humility. When you see the suffering and sacrifice of another, and they freely and lovingly offer the benefits of that sacrifice to you, it humbles you. The benefits of the sacrifice of the Lamb have the effect of humbling us before our great and wonderful God. We therefore, offer up to Him thanksgiving and worship. So, it is our freely receiving that is true humility, not our denying it. *We are the righteousness of God in Christ Jesus,*[110] *saved by grace*[111], thanks to the sacrifice of the Lamb of God!

Where does the Lamb of God live or dwell today? Yes, in heaven. But where exactly is heaven? Jesus said the kingdom of God is within you, and that the kingdom of heaven is at hand or in the right here and now. If the kingdom of God is within you, then heaven or the presence of God will manifest around you from within you. It is not the other way around unless another believer is manifesting His presence. When you received Christ as your Lord and Savior, He actually manifested Himself in you. A known residence of Him is in you. You are the temple of God!

110   2 Cor. 5:21
111   Eph. 2:8

The Lamb of God ascended into heaven. But, that ascension was not into some physical clouds, and then on into heaven some place five miles south of Mars. That ascension is in the cloud of the Father as in Jesus' transformation and also in the exodus out of Egypt. That same cloud has not left the earth, but lives in the many clouds of witnesses on the earth that speak of Christ and His finished works: His death, burial and resurrection. And when that witness is received, the resurrected life of Christ now manifests or makes Himself known in that one who believed the witness. In other words, Christ dwells in you as the Lamb of God. If we really believe this, then we will also believe that the kingdom of heaven is at hand wherever we go; as it was with Jesus, so it is with us. As He is, so are we in this world.[112] Jesus came as the Lamb of God and He brought heaven with Him. What makes the kingdom of heaven manifest is the presence of the Lamb of God who takes away the sin of the world!

Did Jesus believe He was the Lamb of God? Yes, even though He was sent only to the Jews, yet some Gentiles received from Him. Why were the Gentiles able to receive from the Lamb of God? Jesus is the Lamb of God that takes away all the sin of the entire world, thus leaving everyone in the position to freely receive of the kingdom of heaven. In Christ there is neither Jew nor Gentile,[113] which was known at that time to be believers and non-believers, all are equally accepted because we are all of the One that makes us one. The blood of Jesus was for the sin of the whole world and not just Jews (believers).

Jesus was sent to the Jews, not because they were something special in and of themselves, for flesh and blood does not inherit the kingdom of God.[114] He was sent because of the promise and because Israel was under the oppression of their own laws. They believed in one God and that was a plus. But their observances of their laws as a means to

---

112   1 Jn. 4:17
113   Gal. 3:28
114   1 Cor. 15:50

please God actually brought them into great bondage. It was not the oppression of Rome that had them in bondage as they supposed, but their own laws that condemned and judged one another. One is free if one is free inwardly. Only by looking at their own works of those laws, did they disqualify themselves from receiving from the kingdom of heaven that was at hand, which supersedes the oppression of the kingdom of Rome.

Another way to count yourself as unworthy to receive from God is to look at one another after the flesh. A prophet is not without honor except in His own town.[115] The words that God places in the mouths of His messengers are His words. But we might look at the flesh of that messenger and think, "I know them and they're nothing special," then we will also dishonor the words that come out of their mouths, even if it is God speaking through them. That is hearing the word of God in an unworthy manner, and the Lord can do no mighty work, even though He desires to do them. God might choose to use a donkey, if so, let us look and see by the eyes of our spirit, not with our natural carnal judgmental eyes.

The removal of sin is the removal of the fall of Adam and the removal of the curse. Knowing this, we can see people that are still in the world as forgiven and without sin. The Lamb being in us is the Cornerstone by which we can manifest the kingdom of heaven to whosoever will. We in turn can also say, "Your sins are forgiven you; arise, take up your bed and walk!"[116] Declare it like you really believe it, because you are fully convinced that it is so. Christ in you, the hope of glory, is with you and will confirm His word! The Lamb of God in you makes all power available to manifest the kingdom of heaven to all who will freely receive.

Did you notice that Jesus first said, "Your sins are forgiven you?" This was a very natural announcement coming from Jesus because He knew He was the Lamb of God. That was not a normal statement to the

---

115   Mat. 13:57

116   Mat. 9:1–6

Scribes and Pharisees, but a big-headed egotistical declaration in the ears of the religious. When you are convinced of who He is, this will also be your announcement to all because the Lamb is actively abiding in you all who believe! Then after that announcement comes the command to arise, take up your bed and walk! First the Lamb takes away their sin, and then all heaven is come with great pleasure and joy to bless. The second announcement to walk comes after his sin consciousness is removed. You cannot walk by the power of God if you are still aware of sin in your consciousness. Now that the Lamb has been manifest, the power of God is present to heal. This is a manifestation of the Lion that destroyed the works of the devil and healed the paralyzed man. The Lion and the Lamb is Christ revealed in the One, and He lives in you!

Some circles have preached that we need to get people saved and converted before they can receive healing. How many people were saved <u>before</u> Jesus went to the cross? Only a few that believed He was the Lamb of God that takes away the sin of the world. But how many were healed? All that came to Him![117] Forgiveness of sins resonated out of Jesus because He was the Lamb. The kingdom of heaven was at hand because of the Lamb being present. Most of those who were healed didn't know that He was the Lamb of God that came to die for their sins. His own disciples didn't understand that truth until after His resurrection.

The presence of the Lamb alone made healing freely available to all who came to Him. We believers like to put certain methods or qualifications on people before they can freely receive. If that's the case, then it's not free! It is you, knowing who you are, and the Lamb dwelling in you, that makes the kingdom of heaven available to all. Jesus knew who He was. Do you know who you are? Most of us, if not all, sell ourselves short of who we really are in Christ. If we are hidden in Him, then who lives now? Christ! The Lamb of God is still walking the earth in your body!

---

117   Mat. 4:24, 8:16, 12:15

Once we get a revelation that the Lamb lives in us all the time, and start manifesting His fragrance where ever we go, then we won't be able to sleep in the same bed with Adam.

> **Luke 17:34 — *"I tell you, in that night there will be two in one bed: the one will be taken and the other will be left."***

This takes place in the night, in the darkness. Where is the darkness? In the mind that is yet not renewed. Adam is of the darkness. Christ is the light. The two being in one bed together is the duality of mind. We have both the thoughts of Adam and the thoughts of Christ. The one taken away is Adam because of the revelation of Jesus Christ, and the one remaining is Christ. You are not your own; you've been bought with a price. Adam died. He was taken away in the death of Jesus Christ. The Christ is all that is left! You are God's and you are the manifestation of Christ in the earth today. The body of Christ, manifest as the Sons of God, are now ruling and reigning with Christ on the earth. This truly is making the earth His footstool.

Look what the Lord has done by sending His Son into the world as the Lamb of God! Even the angels in heaven were at awe of God's plan of salvation for mankind when they saw it unfolding. Now all of heaven sees from the everlasting effects the Lamb of God has made on the whole earth. Heaven is finished. Heaven needs nothing done to it to be perfect. The Lamb of God is seated at the right hand of God in heaven and all of heaven sees from the effect of the Lamb of God. And because our citizenship is in heaven, we too can see from the Lamb's viewpoint that comes from heaven.

Chapter 3

JESUS IS THE KING OF KINGS

Jesus is the King of kings, the Lion of the tribe of Judea. Jesus as the King is another description of who Jesus is. He reigned as the King of kings on the earth, but His kingdom was not of this world. He is the King of the Kingdom of God. It was written on His cross, 'King of the Jews', not because He was sent to the Jews only, but because of His teaching, preaching and healing, many of the common Jewish people followed Him. He was the Jew's King, but not how they wanted Him to be their King. He was their King, and they knew it not. He is the King of all the world and most of the world doesn't know it.

Jesus is the King of kings, but heaven doesn't see it in the natural form that most of us are thinking. He was not the King of natural kings, no more than He is today. If He was, then even Caesar would have come to worship Him. No, the kings that are under His kingship are all those that serve Him. Caesar, like some of our kings today, served himself and his own agendas. His disciples were kings while He walked on the earth. Did any of them lack any good thing while they walked with Him? Did any of them get sick? Were they not given authority by the King to cast out devils, raise the dead, and heal the sick? Then they were indeed kings of the King.

Yet, none of them became natural kings in this world. A true king is servant to all.

The Jews wanted a King that would lead them in a revolt against the Roman Empire. But, this King was not one that forced His rule over men like all the others. Jesus taught His disciples not to rule like other natural kings do but to rule by being a servant to bless others.[118] We are to lift up into heavenly places those who are under our leadership, not make them serve us like natural kings do. That means to serve by manifesting the kingdom of heaven by helping in natural things as well as spiritual. This will leave an impression on others so they might know who Christ is and who they are in Him. This is not for the purpose of growing the church attendance! That can be self-centered. Let God give the increase as He sees fit. As for us, let us just love one another without any ulterior motive.

If we don't see this, we will rule like the kings of the earth and think that others are to serve the church leadership. Then the Church will come to the false conclusion that God wants to rule over us the same way church leadership does. God may even what to force men's knees to bow and serve. Then God might use sickness, poverty, and all kinds of crises to force us to serve Him. Can you see how one small fallacy in our thinking can snowball? But! Jesus Christ showed us that God uses His authority and sovereignty to serve and bless, not to demand His own way. The way of this King is love.

Our God is not a hard taskmaster. Our Father is like Jesus. They are One and the same. Jesus was God and is God. God, as the manifestation of Jesus to us, died on the cross as His greatest service for us and all mankind so we could be reconciled back to God. This may not sound like any natural king that we have known in the past because love rules this Ruler. If you have ever had a boss that had laid down his life and his business for you, then you are an exception to the norm, and your boss is definitely Christ like. Most of this world, and even some church

118   Mk. 10:42–45

organizations, will use you and then lose you. If you don't dress right, smell right, and act right, then maybe you better find another church! Why do some act this way? Maybe it is because they believe all should fit their mold of what they think a Christian should be. We are instructed not to be conformed to the world,[119] so the church is trying to conform us. The work of the Church is to teach and preach the word of God so that we are transformed by the renewing of our mind, not to conform to certain looks, actions, methods, and rituals. Transformation is an inward work that will manifest on the outside. To be conformed is an outward change caused by outward pressure. That church kingdom is of this world. If you are asked to leave, it might be the best thing for you anyway. Let your peace return to you and wipe the dust (earthly, worldly impressions) off your feet and move on.

Jesus is our King forever in this life and in the life to come, and He rules with sacrificial love. He will use you only as He makes Himself known to you. Therefore, He cannot and will not ever use you and then lose you! He doesn't expect you to do anything without His leading and anointing. So if He wants to use you, He'll instruct you and empower you to do it! That's a good deal! Because then, *It's not by our might, nor by our power, but by My Spirit says the Lord.*[120]

If you have been busy doing all kinds of things for the Lord and have lost that intimacy you once had with Him, maybe it is because you are trying to do the works of God without God. He may have led you or instructed you to do certain things, but as you go about doing them, you might be approaching your work with obligation of duty rather than by resting in His anointing. You therefore, work as one under the law and not by the Spirit of life. Even if He tells you to do certain things, He fully expects you to do them with Him and as Him. It is never to be by my might nor by my power. Business is not next to Godliness. Please reconsider all of what you are doing and slow down, wait upon

119   Rom. 12:2
120   Zec. 4:6

the Lord and He will renew your strength. Then rest as you work. Rest is a state of peace spiritually and calmness mentally. God rested on the seventh day, but Jesus said that His Father is always working;[121] always working and always at rest. You are made to always be at rest. Now our work is to be done as an overflow of His life in us. Then He definitely will get all the glory!

Jesus, being the Lion or King, also means that He rules with power to destroy His enemies. Who are God's enemies? Your enemies! But this is not some people you might be thinking of as being your enemies. Our enemies are not flesh and blood, but principalities are one of the things named in Eph. 6:10. These principalities are defined as something rehearsed from the beginning until it becomes a chief corner, power, or principle in us, and in particular a principality in our thinking. Why our thinking?

> **2 Cor. 10:4–6 — *For the weapons of our warfare are not carnal (of the flesh) but mighty in God for pulling down strongholds, casting down arguments and every high thing that exalts itself against the knowledge of God, bringing every thought into captivity to the obedience of Christ, and being ready to punish all disobedience when your obedience is fulfilled.***

It is in our thoughts that we can allow strongholds to be established. These strongholds are principalities or high places in our thinking that are contrary to the thoughts of God and the truth of His word. It is here that power is given to disobey or obey. Thoughts that are against God and His ways, and are given a high place in one's thinking will empower the individual to disobey God even though they don't want to. This is the kind of ruler-ship that is of the devil. He rules by force along with a strong desire for self-centered pleasure. First tempting the

---

121   Jn. 5:17

flesh, and then gaining a stronghold in the mind. But, when the King speaks into the mind of the believer through their spirit, then faith comes, and the mind or soul of that believer is once again brought back into oneness with the Lord. Then the individual is free to obey based on a love relationship rather than by force or by observances of the law which have no power to restrain.[122]

Just knowing right from wrong doesn't give us the power to do what is right. The law was weak in that it had no power over the flesh. But, thanks to Jesus Christ! He has given us a new life empowered by His Spirit by which He also condemned sin in the flesh by hanging on the cross. We knowing these things in our hearts and minds; reckon, account, and consider ourselves to be truly as a matter of fact dead to sin but alive to God in Christ Jesus our Lord.

There are many well trained believers that have a good disciplined life. But, no matter how disciplined we become, that is not going to produce union with the Father. Discipline is not a fruit of the Spirit. It may be a noble quality, but it is nothing more than a work of the flesh. It is man's attempt to please God based on performance. The King is not ruling from within the believer who lives by self-discipline. The life of the King within us is for our ruling together over all the earth. One's own discipline is self-ruling by rules or self-made laws. As we rule together, He is the King and we are kings with Him. It is here that all things are become new and all things are of God. In other words, anything that we do on our own is of the old creation that has passed away. That way of life is not new and it is not of God. But, anything that is done in union with the Holy Spirit is of the life of the new creation.

Self-control, which sounds similar to self-discipline, is a fruit of the Spirit. Self-discipline is the works of Adam. Self-control is being led of the Holy Spirit and lets us know what course or direction we ought to be taking because love is present. It is part of the nature of God in us that compels us and restrains us by the power of His life-giving Spirit.

122   Rom. 8:3

Unlike discipline that might be a set code of ethics or a set of laws to abide by in order to achieve what we believe is Christianity, self-control looks only at Christ within. Discipline is just more works that makes us look better on the outside. It cannot offer fellowship on the level where grace is.

1 Cor. 6:12 — *All things are permissible unto me, but not all things are beneficial. All things are permissible unto me, but I will not be controlled by any.*

This is the liberty of having self-control as a fruit of the Spirit. On the other hand, discipline brings us to the place of having self-appointed laws in the attempt to control our flesh. Self-discipline is another way for us to control ourselves in an attempt to please God. But grace says we are to reckon Adam and the works of the flesh as dead. It is only through fellowship with the Lord by His Spirit and His Word freely working in us that produces corresponding action that God is looking for. A well-disciplined life means nothing. It has a great appearance before the world, but not before God. It is His abiding Spirit and word in us producing after its own kind that brings glory to God. This is how He reigns in us as our King.

He sent His word and healed us, delivered us, and saved us. How So? It is when our minds or our souls are brought into one accord with our spirit that we are able to take dominion over our body of flesh with its desires. This is why in some cases it may be needful to first hear the truth of God's word before one can be healed. Such as: your sins are forgiven you. Faith begins in the heart and brings the mind into oneness so the two reign together over all the earth (body). Not one time did Jesus force healing on anyone. It was always through their heart or spirit that He had access to before they were and could be healed.

Hearing the word of God brings one's soul into harmony with the Holy Spirit which is the dwelling place of God and His power. Now that the *two agree together on earth concerning anything they ask, it will be done for them by My Father which is in heaven.*[123] This is how earth is changed! This is how people are healed! Being born of the Spirit of God, we are His sheep and we hear His voice and the voice of a stranger we shall not follow. It is here that the King sits on the throne of your life and fills the earth (earthen vessel) with His glory.

Let's back up and identify a few of these strongholds and how they got to become strongholds. What do some of these strongholds look like? It can be a false teaching that is rehearsed enough to become a chief corner in our believing, which establishes our way of life because that is the image we have of God. It can be a circumstance that speaks to us volumes day after day until it rules our thinking and conduct. It can be words that others have spoken against us that we have allowed to affect our thinking and righteous judgment.

In all these cases, it soon develops a pattern of reasoning that exalts itself against the knowledge of God. Now we have empowered those words and thoughts to have a place of rule over our soul. We are instructed to give no place for the devil. The devil is a deceiver, and the tough part about being deceived is that we don't even know it. The truth is, the devil doesn't even exist except in the realm of lies and deception. So, if we give no place to lies and deception, then the devil has no place. This is where the war begins and ends, in our thinking! The purpose of these things coming to us is to sever our oneness with God. They come to bring disunion! The devil is a fallen or lower corrupted form of a spirit that speaks heresy. The devil knows that if the body of Christ ever comes into maturity where they know they are one with God and start acting like it, he will have no place to rule and express himself in the earth.

It was through thoughts in the mind that imagines things that Jesus was tempted as we are tempted today. Those temptations are the thoughts of darkness, deception coming into the mind of humanity.

---

123   Mat. 18:19

But, the King of kings is in the house by His Spirit to enlighten us and to bring to our remembrance all things that we have need of. *He will show us things to come and take all things that the Father has and declare them to us.*[124] Notice that what the Father has is declared. What is declared is something that comes to us and takes up residence in our thinking through words or impressions that leaves us with images first. Then those thoughts bring our soul into perfect union with the Father and empowers us to produce something in the physical realm. So, just as Jesus defeated all the temptations of the devil by the word of God so shall we. We overcome by the blood of the Lamb and the word of our testimony.[125] It is the King speaking to us that becomes the word of our testimony and the force that sends all temptations with their lies and deception fleeing. This is the authority that we as kings have been given by the King. These are the words of eternal life that cannot be taken away from us! The thief cannot steal the truth if we make that truth the word of our testimony.

> **Isa. 5:4 — *What more could have been done to My vineyard that I have not done in it? Why then, when I expected it to bring forth good* (ripe) *grapes, did it bring forth wild* (poison) *grapes?***

We are that vineyard and Christ is planted in us to produce good ripe fruit. There is nothing more that the Father can do for us that He hasn't already done through Jesus Christ! We just need to come into the knowledge of those things. Why is it that sometimes that same vineyard bears wild poisonous fruit? Because in the same vineyard was sown weeds that came from this world. The effect the world plays in the Church is most evident from individual homes where there is strife and even among church authorities that have been infected by the same.

---

124   Jn. 16:13–15
125   Rev. 12:11

(This is merely an observation and not a condemning word because I know that Christ dwells in each and every one of us.)

The completion of the ripe grapes lies within us. Christ in us the hope of glory is our ability to bear good fruit. It takes an unveiling of that Christ in us so that we may walk in Him and He in us. As we continue in His word and His word dwells in us, I am confident that He will complete or finish us. He will bring us to maturity so He Himself may eat, as well as the world, of the good ripe grapes of His vineyard. It is here that the world is being influenced by us rather than we being influenced by the world. Our kingdom is not of this world so we usher into this world a new kingdom, the kingdom of heaven; not by force, but by just bearing fruit. They will eat of you, your fruit, and taste that the Lord is good!

Another enemy that the King is to rule over is the powers that be.[126] Though a man has authority over another doesn't mean that the authority can dominate the other's conduct, or way of thinking, or atmosphere that he himself dwells in. There are all kinds of powers or authorities in the world, but none were able to dominate the Christ man. Even the crucifixion at the cross didn't produce any animosity or bitter anger from Him. He always dwelled in the Father and the Father in Him. Though people are empowered to rule over another in this world's system, none have to be ruled by them in their hearts and minds. If you are slaves, do not seek your freedom unless an opportunity arises that you may gain your freedom. But, serve the Lord Christ while you are a slave outwardly. Inwardly you are free!

They took the man, Jesus, out of the place of prayer, but they couldn't take the secret place of prayer out of the man. This is cause and effect. Because the kingdom of God couldn't be taken out of the man, the man always established the presence of the kingdom of God wherever He went. In the midst of doubting, jealousy, and hateful angry words, Jesus remained the same. He stayed in the loving place of union with the Father,

---

126   Eph. 6:12

speaking nothing but the truth by the Spirit. This is the power from on High, the power from above that empowers the soul of man to manifest the goodness and glory of God in the earth. So, outward powers that be are not to suppress the inward man of the Spirit. It is the inward man of the spirit that is to be the head or king of the whole man so that we become one in spirit, soul and body. So, let your light shine in the darkness.

Jesus demonstrated how God uses such power: He was manifest to destroy the works of the devil, the false accuser[127]. He went around doing good and healing all who were oppressed of the devil[128]. This King cast out devils. He loosed people from the bondage of sin. He showed us how we were to rule over all the earth without controlling and manipulating people, but be a servant to all. The earth was under a curse, and Jesus showed us how to rule over that curse and turn it into a blessed place. We are servants of this King, and He lives in us so we can rule and reign with Him in the earth today!

Manifest Sons of God are as one with Christ and rule out of His great love. Our King has given us the right as sons to rule with Him in the earth. We are heirs of His kingdom and have been given authority to rule in the here and now. This is greater than submission to authority as a slave or one being looked upon as lesser. This is oneness with the Authority. Jesus thought it not robbery to be equal with God. The equality part is not self being exalted by oneself but a welcomed oneness with the Father. We are more than just servants to do the will of God. We are sons that walk with the Father and are co-laborers with Christ. We were born to fulfill this role that God has called us to be. It is not just about doing, it is about being. Then as we be, then we do according to that being. The being we are is standing in Christ. Therefore, we are enabled to stand against the wiles (schemes) of the devil and overcome the world with all its tribulation. As our King so overcame the world, we who are hidden in Him shall also overcome!

---

127   1 Jn. 3:8

128   Acts 10:38

Jn. 16:33 — *"These things I have spoken to you, that in Me you may have peace. In the world you have tribulation; but be of good cheer, I have overcome the world."*

I used to read this scripture this way, "In the world you have tribulation; but be of good cheer, I have overcome the tribulation." I thought all along that it was the tribulation that we are to overcome like I thought Jesus did. But He didn't say that. He said, "I have overcome the world." That's how we overcome tribulation! If we attempt to overcome tribulation by coming from the world's point of view with its knowledge of good and evil, we will fail every time. But, if we first seek to place ourselves in heavenly places in Christ Jesus, then we will hear from heaven and have heaven's perspective. This is overcoming the world with all its voices. We'll now have the word of God concerning the tribulation. But first we must overcome the world! Hide yourself in Christ. Put on the new man of the Spirit of love. Clothe yourself with the incorruptible word of God. Let the Spirit of life quicken, make lively and empower your mortal body and thus clothe yourself with immortality. How can the natural tribulation of this world overcome the life and power of God? It can't! That means you can rule over it as you come from heaven.

Isa. 54:16 — *...And I have created the waster to destroy.*

The word waster also means the spoiler, to decay or bring to ruin, destroyer. The King is seen as having all authority and power to destroy the destroyer. The earth is laid waste, shows decay, and is coming to ruins. Is the earth the destroyer? No, it is the one being destroyed by the destroyer. The destroyer is the power of deception that has us living under a false image that we are still like the Adam of the fall in the garden. That image disarmed Adam and made him a servant to that deception. That image made the man human! Since that time the earth has been under attack because of the weakness of the human who was appointed by God to rule or have dominion over all the earth. Jesus restored all man-kind to their fullness as before in the garden.

God never used the term human. He made man in His image. The word human is made of two words, homo and sapiens. Homo means knowing. Sapiens means man or mankind. Man knowing good and evil became human. The dictionary meaning of human is having the imperfections and weaknesses of a human being. This is not how we were created! God created man, not human. Man had no imperfections or weaknesses while dwelling in the garden of God. He was complete in God, and another word for complete is perfect. We took on this fallen image of ourselves as we ate and still do eat from the tree of the knowledge of good and evil. We became good and evil in the image of ourselves as we ate. This produced humans instead of man in the image of God. It is out of this false image of being lesser than the likeness of God that the destroyer has been loosed to lay waste the earth. That destroyer is the deception, but most believers call it the devil. In that lying image those that are deceived are of their father the devil and do the works of our father. How so? As long as the body of Christ remains ignorant of the fullness of their redemption, we will serve the lie and the father of it. Instead of making the earth His footstool, we allow the destruction and decay to continue. We are to take authority over all the earth and bring it back into its original state. Jesus redeemed it. So, let's act like it is so!

Jesus, as the King, destroyed the works of the devil (deception) by manifesting His abundant life through grace. He came in the likeness of His Father, just like Adam in the beginning. Jesus was the second Adam without sin. It was by this authority of being a man (not a human) that Jesus lived as a King in the earth. Jesus mostly identified Himself as the Son of Man. What man was He talking about? It for sure wasn't Joseph, his step-father, because His real Father was God. He was talking about the first Adam without sin. This viewpoint gave Jesus the vision to destroy the destroyer. So, Jesus went around doing good and healing all who were oppressed of the devil, the destroyer. But it is important to remember that the devil is not some spirit being that goes around looking for whom he may devour. It is a spirit of deception that keeps going around seek whom he may devour and that is called the devil.

What does the deception devour? First, the deception has to try to devour the word of God that is sown in your heart and then your soul and lastly your body. That is why the earth is decaying and not just destroyed all at once by some mysterious demonic force that some imagine. I'm not saying there are no powers of darkness. But those powers only have power in their environment of darkness, which are lies, deceptions, and lying imaginations. Those powers come to bring us down into their environment of deception. As long as they can deceive then the earth will stay in ruins. They only have power to deceive. That's it! Stay out of their environment by staying in the truth and you'll stay free. Then as sons of God living in Christ we can save planet Earth. The body of Christ has been given the belt of truth to surround us and prepare us for every good work; the breast plate of righteousness as Christ dwells in that heart; our feet shod with the preparation of the gospel of peace; the shield of faith to quench all the fiery darts of the wicked one; the helmet of salvation by which no deception can penetrate; and the sword of the Spirit, which is the word of God.[129]

Sickness and disease was part of the earth coming to ruins, but Jesus destroyed those works by manifesting healing and wholeness, and there was nothing the destroyer could do about it! Why? Jesus knew who He really was. He was the Son of Man, not the son of humans. He lived as the King, not because He was God, but because He was a man with God dwelling in Him. So, He was both God and man reigning together in the earth. This is the same vision our Father in heaven has of you! Are you a man without sin? Is Christ actively dwelling in you?

129   Eph. 6:14–17

Then you must be both man and God in the flesh. As a believer you cannot deny that Christ is in you. As a believer you cannot deny that all your sins are forgiven. So that makes you a man without sin. The greatest part about you is your spirit. That's the real you. You (spirit) are of God and the Holy Spirit dwells in your spirit. He has made you both man and God. I'd make it a little 'g' but the God in you is God and not god. False idols, rulers of darkness, and graven images in the unrenewed mind are gods, but you are not one of those.

If you are born again, you have been awakened to the fact that you are not a human descendant of fallen Adam, but you are a child of God. You have been fully restored back into the royalty of the King of kings by the Lamb of God. Adam and the fall of Adam exists no more in the image of the new creation. The image of yourself is that of God and not of a human being of the fallen earth. As you keep Christ's image of yourself, you have fellowship with your Father and the Creator. If the image of yourself falls to the level of human form, you have fellowship with dead Adam and work with the destroyer.

The storm came to destroy or lay waste what is. But, Jesus stood up, rebuked it, and brought peace through the life of God reigning in Him. All the works of Jesus testify of this same type of King that He was and is today. That King came to restore the whole earth and not just mankind. Any other teaching or belief that takes away from this biblical view of Jesus Christ as our Cornerstone and how He reigns as King is heresy, and it will bring disunion.

These things we will have to ponder, meditate on, and search the scriptures to get them down into our heart if we are to come into agreement with Him and walk with Him in these things. The image you have of yourself from heaven's point of view is that of a much higher place than this world and what religion will show you. God called you a chosen generation. You are a select offspring, born of Him! You are not of human descent any longer. Your body is, but now you can clothe the mortal with immortality.

1 Jn. 4:4 — *You are of God, little children, and have overcome them, because He who is in you is greater than he who is in the world.*

Jesus said greater works than these shall you do.[130] So many believers are afraid to act like God in the earth. Some of that might be because of having a wrong concept of God as though you are to rule like the world does in a controlling bossy manner. Don't be afraid to act like the true and living God of love and in demonstrating His power to heal and deliver. What are they going to do, accuse you of thinking you're God? You could reply, "I'm not God, but I am one with God and he is my Father." You will suffer persecution from the religious bunch, but happy are you!

God has a strong desire to do more wonderful works while it is called today. Don't get the wrong idea that we are to do more and more works. The King <u>sits</u> on His throne and rules from a finished place of having all authority. The works that Jesus did was from a place of rest in the Father. Jesus didn't work real hard <u>trying</u> to do all the things that He did. He only did what He saw His Father doing, nothing more and nothing less. I might add, He sure saw the Father doing a lot of things, didn't He? So much so, that the world could not contain the things that could have been written of Him.[131]

When it comes to doing the works of the Father, it will energize and not drain one of his life. Yes, it takes energy to teach, preach and heal. But while doing those things, there is a vibrating energy that flows with the power of the greater life of God in us! Jesus was naturally tired before ministering to the woman at the well.[132] He told his disciples to go into town and buy some food. While waiting, a woman came along and Jesus began to tell her some things that only a prophet would

---

130   Jn. 14:12
131   Jn. 21:25
132   Jn. 3

know. He was ministering to her with a prophetic anointing and with compassion. After ministering to her, the disciples returned with food and Jesus said, "I have food to eat of which you do not know of." Jesus didn't have any natural food while they were gone. But He had received supernatural energy that came to Him while ministering to the woman. The Spirit quickened His mortal body with energy!

Jesus was one with the Father; and therefore, He worried and sweat about nothing, except when His hour had come and He was not fully prepared to go to the cross yet. After having been ministered to by angels (messengers) sent from the Father, He stopped His sweating drops of blood and entered into rest. Joy was the fruit of that rest. He sweat drops of blood so we wouldn't have to sweat it or worry any longer. It is no longer by the sweat of the brow of Adam that we work, but from a place of rest in the finished work of Christ Jesus. It was from this place of rest with joy that Jesus was able to do the greatest work of His entire ministry, yielding His life as a Lamb for the slaughter. So, it never becomes our work, but our working as one in Him is our joy. He is the author and finisher of our faith, and that which is not of faith is sin.[133] True faith joins us perfectly together with Christ where we see ourselves no more, but only Him who is. Now we have entered into His rest, and then we enter into His labors. God is always at rest, and yet He is always working. That is also a description of us in His image.

Have you noticed that the Lamb is first revealed before the King. He first came to us as the Lamb, and now He comes to us as the King. The Lamb came first to forgive, and it is through forgiveness that we allow a new King to come and take His place on the throne of our hearts and lives. Once the world sees Him as both the Lamb and the King, then they will come to Him and freely receive all things that they have need of. His crucifixion and ours with Him produced the death of Adam so that "human" doesn't try to rule like the kings of this world do, by force.

---

133   Rom. 14:23

We can see this sometimes among ourselves in our own homes and in the church organizations. When we try to run our house or the church organization like the world with the authorities dominating and manipulating others so that everything operates the way we think it ought to be. We wrongly demand our own way having forgotten we are born of love. Organization is needful and absolutely necessary, but it is how you go about it. God given authority is for service to lift up others, not so others will serve us under our church positional authority. We labor together and serve one another. We are not given positional authority for the purpose of demanding our own way, or using that authority to harm another. That authority needs to be held accountable.

One can rule as a dictator with the attitude that whatever he says goes. That's authority that has gone to their head. How can we be surrounded by wise counsel if we have the attitude of, "I da man!" We see that often in the world. One can rule as the owner of the organizational business end of the church and act as though he is the owner of the sheep. He sees himself as being above the sheep because he is a pastor and not a sheep. Too bad, the day that one thought he was no longer a sheep is the day he stopped seeing the Shepherd. One can rule as though he is the head, everyone's spiritual head giving no one else the opportunity to speak and minister in church meetings. That might be okay for big churches having national TV viewers, but as far as ministering to the attending congregation it will always lack meeting people's needs. In this setting the gifts that abide in the rest of the believers are suppressed. And there are people who like and want these kings ruling in their life.

Many submit to such misuse of authority without reprisal for the sake of having been taught 'submission', or they falsely think that form of submission is love. Paul did not submit to Peter's authority just because it was Apostle Peter. But Paul did submit to the higher authority, the Spirit of the Lord. When Paul corrected Peter in front of everyone,[134] it

---

134   Acts 2:11–21

brought a greater definition of true love among all the people because it brought equality among Jewish believers and Gentile believers. It also brought a pure gospel to the forefront of everyone's thinking. How could Paul correct Peter? Wasn't Peter the greatest Apostle? Yes, that is why he willingly submitted to such correction. The greatest one is servant to all. Unknowingly maybe, Peter misused his authority by implying that the Gentile believers were lesser than the Jewish believers.

As Pastors, we should be willing to receive correction from a little child when it is necessary. There is no place for pride when you have authority. Pride will cause you to misuse your authority many times repeatedly. This is when we all need to know that we do not submit to every authority, but we do submit to the higher authority. Correcting someone, even in love is not fun, but if it is received you can save both yourself and your hearer.[135] That is rewarding and that is the grace of God working together in His family. We are one and no one is above another. We have all been lifted up to the same place, the cross, and we have all been resurrected by the one Jesus Christ; and now we are all in the one Christ. But sometimes we make mental mistakes without first listening to the Holy Spirit and we need correcting. Thank you my loving brothers and sisters in Christ.

> **Rom. 13:1 — *Let every soul be subject to the governing* (higher, above) *authorities. For there is no authority except from God, and the authorities that exist are appointed by God.***

Unless you are grounded in the Chief Cornerstone and are seeing from heaven, you would think that this scripture is saying that every authority, good or bad, is from God. And that we are to submit to every authority. But that cannot be true. If Jesus was to submit to the highest authority in His church, the High Priest, He would have kept

---

135   1 Tim. 4:16

quiet and not taught, nor preached, nor healed. But did he stop. No! Why not? He obviously was not submitting to the church authority of His day. But He was submitted to the highest God appointed authority and that was Father. The word governing in the Greek means higher, above. Let every soul be submitted to the higher authorities, not the lowest authority, not every natural governing authority. If a governing authority told you to shoot your neighbor, would you do it? No! I don't care how ugly your neighbor is shooting them isn't right. So you would resist the governing authority. But yet at the same time you submitted to the higher authority of God's life of love. By doing this you submitted to the righteous ways of God, the way of love. You just fulfilled Rom. 13:1, good job!

The devil (deception) is the lowest authority there is. In fact, he has no authority unless you give it to him. A lie has absolutely no authority unless it is believed and acted upon. Is the authority of the Father gave higher than the High Priest? Yes. Then Jesus submitted very well then when He didn't submit to the High Priest's wishes and stop healing on the Sabbath. There is no authority except from God means God only recognizes God given authority above that of natural positional authority. Positions or titles that people hold in the world are not recognized by God as the higher authority in the earth if it differs from His living word. Your position in Christ is always the highest of all authorities if you are truly standing on the Chief Cornerstone and not some religious mumbo-jumbo! That is why church authorities that tried to stone Jesus were unable to do so. This is the authority that is appointed by God.

Adam lost his authority in the garden to deception and when he tries to rule from his fallen flesh, he turns out being a lying ruler and a self-centered tyrant. This authority is self-appointed. The only authorities that exist are only God appointed authorities. This authority comes not from earth; nor can a person be voted into such God appointed authority (even by a Church vote); nor can this authority be purchased.

This authority comes from heaven. In fact, unless you are in Christ, you have no God appointed authority. There is no God appointed authority outside of the life of Christ.

Mat. 28:18 — *"All authority has been given to Me in heaven and on earth. Go..."*

The one who has all authority is Jesus Christ. Do you think He is going to give any of His authority to someone who acts like Adam and is full of lust and selfishness? At least not while he is acting like that! If Jesus has all authority like this scriptures says, then who is He giving His authority to? His disciples! But that doesn't necessarily mean church going people. It means disciples and the qualification for a disciple is one who is taught, instructed, and a learner of the Lord. There is no mention of Jesus giving His authority to anyone else. But don't be deceived. Just because someone doesn't go to an organized church doesn't mean they are not being taught and instructed of the Lord. The Holy Spirit or the anointing is the greatest one on one teacher there ever was and ever is and ever will be.[136] Going to church is not a prerequisite for being a disciple of Jesus Christ.

"But what about the scripture that says not to forsake the assembling of yourselves together?"[137] It is good and necessary to gather yourselves together, but not as a commandment as though it is a law. Remember this? We are no longer under the law but under grace.[138] If this scripture is not a law, then what is it? Instruction in righteousness. It is a righteous thing to meet in order to build up and encourage one another. It is a righteous thing to meet together when you see the day approaching. The day is not the return of Jesus Christ as some preach. The day is the light of the truth being made known today. "If anyone walks in the day,

---

136   1 Jn. 2:20, 27
137   Heb. 10:25
138   Rom. 6:14

he does not stumble, because he sees the light of this world."[139] And quite frankly, some church meetings don't have enough light to walk in without stumbling. That may sound hard, but it is true. Some church meetings are so filled with other agendas that there isn't enough word of light to make it out the door without stumbling. So can we judge someone as not being a "Christian" if they don't attend a church like that? Just a little side thought, now back to the authority of the King.

> **Mk. 16:15, 17, 18 — *"Go…And these signs will follow those who believe: In My name they will cast out demons; they will speak with new tongues; they will take up serpents, and if they drink anything deadly, it will by no means hurt them; they will lay hands on the sick, and they will recover."***

Again, who is sent or who is told to go? Jesus' disciples! Now who is given authority in His name to do such wonderful things in these scriptures? Anyone who believes! A believer is one who is a learner. He has hears to hear and understand. So, again the one who has all authority is giving His authority to a believer or disciple and not to any earthly authority. All I'm saying is, your earthly position or recognized title, including church titles is secondary when it comes to God appointed authority. He gives His authority to those who live in Christ. In My name you shall… This authority comes directly from the kingdom of the King. It is the Kings authority to give to His kings, not natural kings, but kings that reign with Him in His kingdom on earth.

Verse 4 in Rom. 13 says, *For he is God's minister to you for good.* God's minister has God's authority. That's not talking about the five-fold ministry in Eph. 4:11, it includes those, but we are all ministers of reconciliation. If you are in Christ, you are a minister of righteousness. Sure, there are natural authorities that also have God appointed authority

---

139   Jn. 11:9

because they also dwell in Christ. A big praise God for that! But not all natural authorities have and use God appointed authority. In the same way not every parent uses God appointed authority over their children. God does not give parents authority to lock their child in a dark closet. When that happens, the parent has taken self-appointed authority and misused their natural position to do such a thing. God had nothing to do with it. He didn't give that parent authority to do that. But yet, if that same parent fixed a special birthday cake for their child and had a birthday party with some of their friends because love prompted them to do so, that was God appointed authority. Notice the difference in their spiritual position. The first was definitely in the flesh and demanded control. The second was walking in love and faith works by love. If your faith works by love, so will your God appointed authority. So, depending on your spiritual position and not your natural position or title, you will manifest God appointed authority or you will manifest Adam's fall.

Hitler was not a God given authority. Yet people submitted to him and millions were murdered. Why didn't the whole world submit to his authority if all natural authorities are God appointed? The authority wasn't from God. It was a self-appointed authority. Even though he was not self-appointed into that leadership position, he used that position wrongfully, thus using self-appointed authority. God didn't give him permission to murder or to start a war. He appointed himself to do such a thing and most of the whole German population followed his lead. If they had known that they were to submit to the highest God appointed authority and not just any man's authority, then they could have refused to follow him. Misusing one's authority above that which God gives you is a self-appointed authority. We don't submit to that kind of authority because God expects us to walk in faith and love.

When we submit to dominating and manipulating authority, we might think we are doing God a favor and being good servants and walking in love by submitting to such authority. After all, we don't want to stir-up any trouble. Yea, like Jesus didn't stir-up any trouble by speaking the truth. That's what got Him crucified. But by not speaking the truth, we are doing as the Israelites did when they asked for a king instead of relying on God as their King. God warned them that the king they chose would rule over them in a manner like the other kings of the world. That kind of king would dominate, suppress, and control them. But, they wanted a visible king to serve rather than God. Being unaware of such things, is this what some of the churches have gone to?

What's going on with all the misuse of authority? The Lamb is missing! The Lamb and the King are to rule together! Now the King only uses His authority to serve and lay down his life for the benefit of others, not for the benefit or profit of oneself.

Seeing the misuse of authority for the sake of submission may be where some of the church organizations are today. Some have been taught that they are there just to serve their Pastor. In this manner they feel like they're pleasing God because they're serving the "man of God". Well, that's good, but who are you and all the others in your church? Everyone is a man of God. We are to serve one another out of the life of love. We are to esteem one another above ourselves, not just the pastor as though he is any better than anyone else. Preferring someone else above yourself is scriptural, but preferring someone else above another someone else is not!

Can we stop leadership that controls and manipulates? Probably not, because most that act like that aren't hearing from God and probably won't hear from you either. I've even heard it said that sheep can't correct shepherds. But if God can use a donkey to correct a prophet, I suppose God can use a sheep to correct a pastor. But, speaking the truth in love and establishing the righteousness of Jesus Christ based on His word might give hope if there are hearing ears to hear. Even if they don't hear you, it's still right if your motive is right. Truth is always better than living a lie.

Jesus allowed no man to dominate Him, not even the High Priest. He didn't speak what the High Priest wanted Him to speak. He spoke the words of His Father, which is the higher authority. So it was by this authority that He did these things. When He was a young boy, He submitted himself to his parents as a child as long as it didn't go against His Father. In doing so, He disappointed His mom and dad by staying behind and speaking with the priests. He was about His Father's business, which at that time didn't exactly line up with the wishes of His mom and dad.

As an adult he followed and submitted to his Father as the supreme authority. Even His mother and brothers thought He was off His rocker (crazy) and wanted Him to stop. What would have happened if He would have obeyed His mother? He would have been disobeying the greatest authority in His life, His Father. He submitted Himself to all governing authorities but never allowed Himself to be dominated or manipulated by them. Thus, He was submitting Himself to the highest authority, Father God. This submission to the highest authority is how authority was given Him by which He was able to do such wonderful works. I'm not trying to bring about a rebellion in the churches or cause strife between husbands and wives. But, we need a better way of life than that of submitting to dominating authorities. We need a better way of using our positional authority than seeking our own way. You cannot serve two masters. One will put you in bondage to the world's system or way of doing things and the other will place you in the presence of the Lamb having the King's authority.

Some would say, "But I'm serving God by serving my Pastor." That might be true if they delegate authority with responsibility and your purpose for serving is right. But, if we are just trying to please our Pastor in order to please God, we have a wrong motive. Under this mentality, we are slaves to do the will of our Pastor and cannot be led by the Holy Spirit. The Pastor may like it, but our Father doesn't. We are to serve our earthly masters as serving Christ.[140] That means we are serving out of union with Christ, and it doesn't make any difference whether it's the

---

140   Eph. 6:5

Pastor or a worldly task master. Serve out of the gift that God has given you and not because you feel like you have too. It's not duty minded, but Christ minded that we serve one another by the power of His life.

Our God is our concept or understanding of who God is. Some aren't pleasing God even while serving their Pastor. How do I know? If God were to tell you in the middle of a service while the Pastor is preaching to go and minister to so and so right now, would you do it knowing the Pastor doesn't like interruptions and he might get upset? If not, you're programmed to serve and please your Pastor and not your Father. The Pastor is to orchestrate or bring order to the service as well as teach and preach, but not control it. If he is controlling the service, then where does that leave God and those who have gifts that can minister to specific needs of others? Oh, I know, put them in youth and children's ministry. No wonder those ministries are so blessed! Truly, the Holy Spirit will lead the service if we will let Him.

Granted most of the time when something like this happens, God wouldn't tell you to do it now and you could wait until after the service. But, if God wanted to change the flow of the service and manifest Himself through others, rather than just the pastor, and you just sat there because you are thinking that the Pastor isn't going to like this, then you are intimidated by the Pastor and are thus being manipulated by him in your own mind and are honoring him above Christ. You should talk to your Pastor. Faith pleases God, not whether we are serving the lower authority of a titled position or not. Myself, as a Pastor, I'd welcome such an interruption anytime as long as it is truly from the Lord. If it is of God, it will bear fruit. Even if it wasn't I would just pick it up where I left off. I know I've missed God many a time, so no condemnation to anyone. I want the Spirit of God and all His gifts flowing as the Spirit leads us along.

The whole idea about serving is how we are in action towards one another as our expression of being a king of the King. Serving is for the main purpose of blessing one another as our expression of His life in us, and is not our basis for approaching God. The Church is a living breathing God creation that is not to function like the world. Yes, there is to be order, but I wouldn't call the world a place of order. Would you? *The government shall be upon His shoulders.*[141] Christ is the ruler and leader of all He wants His Church to be and to accomplish. We don't need a Pastor run Church or a Board run Church. We need Christ leading the Pastor and the Board so the Church can run with God. We need a Christ led Church and if any of these leaders are led of Christ and not of any worldly ideas or concepts of what they think Church ought to be, then we can have Church! The atmosphere will be filled with love and power because everyone is serving in the gift God has given them and they are doing it with His God appointed authority. The body will then be tightly knit together by what every joint supplies[142] and God will show Himself strong!

Jn. 15:15 — *"No longer do I call you servants, for a servant does not know what his master is doing: but I have called you friends, for all things that I heard from My Father I have made known to you."*

We are not just God's servants, but His friends. Jesus taught His disciples to be servants to all. Now that they got that message, it was time for them to know that they are friends of God. A friend is another description of love, philos. We are still servants of God but we are also more than that, we are friends. That makes us love slaves. Because God is so good to us and we are so tight with Him, we want to be servants of Him. But, He doesn't want us just to be His servants, He wants friends! He desires for us to know Him intimately and to know His business. When we know Him, then we will know His true business. A king is a friend of the King. The King is your friend!

---

141   Isa. 9:6
142   Eph. 4:16

Once again, our King does not rule as the kings of this world. He rules over us not to control us, but to express His love by serving and blessing us; to lift us up and to unveil Himself in us, to heal us, to provide for us, to make us in every way whole, to show us His goodness, and to bring us into a continual fellowship of perfect union and oneness with our Father to be enjoyed while we are yet in the earth. Does this sound like any earthly king you know? That's because the Lamb and the King are to serve together as one. The two are laid down together in Christ and in you as well, if you can see it.

I mentioned the word control. Most of the Church thinking too is that God wants to take control or that we are to give God control of our lives. That has a tendency to give us the impression that we can give God control, and that's not totally correct. If we could give God complete control, then we wouldn't have a need for relationship. But we have a need for relationship so that there is a continual life flow and a corresponding exchange of interaction. A good father doesn't seek to control their children, but to have an ongoing relationship that will guide and influence their conduct and decisions. Any father that seeks to control their child will actually cause them to rebel. Why? They were not created to be controlled, not by their parents and not by God. But they were born for relationship and intimate fellowship as long as they both shall live. A good father actually becomes a part of them and they become a part of the father. That's how it is supposed to be. If not, then the only thing left is the laws that govern or attempt to control them, and we know that doesn't work.

One definition of control is to work or operate something such as a vehicle or machine. Is this what we seek to become to God or for God, a machine programmed to do His will? Another definition is to limit or restrict somebody or something. Is this what God wants to do to us, restrict or limit us? Yet, the most deceiving definition is this: to exercise power or authority over something such as a business or nation. Is the Father out to exercise power or authority over us? We may have been taught so, but let's look at the Chief Cornerstone to see if this is the truth.

Did Jesus exercise power and authority over people, or over the works of the devil? Did Jesus seek to gain a physical crown so He could become a physical king of the Jews? No, because control is not the power or authority He was seeking to exercise. He was seeking a love relationship that would bring them to the Father so they might both rule together as one over the earth to bless it and all who dwell in it. How can we be co-laborers if we are not equally responsible for that labor to be done? Ah, then maybe we could just put it all off on God because you know, He's in control!

Prov. 16:9 — *A man's heart plans* (plots and fabricates) *his way, but the Lord directs his steps.*

If God wanted to control us, then why did God give us individually an imagination, desires, dreams, freedom of choices, and the ability to reason and gain knowledge? It is good for man to make plans in his heart, but they will be incomplete if the Lord is not included to walk with us in those plans. I believe there are times when we need to hear from God, and we should be led by the Spirit always. But I also believe that we can live and make plans according to what we have in our heart. The main thing is that we always walk with the Lord. Our Father does not need to, nor does He want to dictate to us everything involving our lives.

If God wants to have control, then how much control does He want? The religious will respond, "Complete control!" Then God must tell you every morning what clothes to put on, what and when to eat, each step that you take when you walk, when to breath and when not to, when to go to bed and when to get up, exactly what to say and not say at all times, and you then must be without choices and never do wrong. That's complete control and that is bondage. Where do you draw the line? If you draw any line, it's not complete control. God does not want control and neither does He seek control. Relationship based on mutual love is all God pursues to have with you, and that is all He needs for us to do His will. Then it becomes, "I delight to do your will O Lord."[143] Does the Great Shepherd control the sheep or does He lead them? If they don't follow, they will get lost. Then the Shepherd goes and finds him and lifts him up and puts him carries him back to the sheep fold.[144] Is this control or is it a true love story of a real relationship that God has with us? Even if we don't follow and get lost, there is no mention of condemnation, judgment, or punishment. He only embraces us and lifts us up. Wow! That's the kind of God we serve. There is no need for control.

We were made in the image of God to have dominion over all the earth, not over one another. To exercise control over another against their will by the uses of a spell or to enchant words is called witchcraft. Is God into witchcraft? Some would like God to put some kind of spell on them so they could only do what He wanted them to do. But the "spell" or power God uses to get us to do His will is LOVE. But if you don't want to follow Him in His love you don't have to. God never created us in His image as sons to have dominion or absolute control over us, or for us to have dominion or control over one another. But, He created us to have an intimate relationship with us and to enjoy us. We can through that same purpose of relationship enjoy Him and His presence. No one is seeking to control anyone! Love is all we need. Again, love is all we need.

Jn. 14:15 — *If you love Me, you will keep My commandments.*

Love is the empowerment to walking with the Almighty God of the universe and obeying Him! Love relationship is what delights us so

---

143   Psa. 40:8

144   Lk. 15:4–6

to do His will. Love is not having control, but trusting and life-giving. If we don't trust our children, we will want to control them, and that's what rules and laws are for until they mature or grow up in the Lord. We were born filled with His love and that is all God seeks from us. *The love of God has been poured out into our heart by the Holy Ghost.*[145]

A right marriage is kept not by the husband controlling the wife or the wife controlling the husband. A marriage is not kept strong even by nobody sinning or doing wrong. A marriage is kept strong by the love they possess expressed freely to each other. Love covers a multitude of sin. So it's not the absence of sin that makes a marriage, but the presence of love. In the same way Jesus is the Husbandman and we are His wife. In that relationship are you going to tell me Jesus wants to control me? No, He doesn't need to. Jesus wants to freely express His love to me and in turn I express that same love to Him. This empowers us to obey Him because we possess that same love that joins us perfectly together as one. I obey not as a separate entity or being out of fear, but as one and the same being united together in marriage. If you are married to Christ, then you are one, not two separate beings. Because of the presence of that marriage of love, He is empowered to freely give us whatever we ask of Him. Because of the presence of that marriage of love, we are empowered to reign in this life as kings being one with the King. While in His love, you can't even ask for something outside His will.

> **Mk. 11: 24 — "*Therefore I say to you, whatever things you ask* (desire) *when you <u>pray</u>, believe that you receive them, and you will have them.*"**

Prayer is not about the purpose of asking, it is about being one with your loving Father. Prayer is an exchange of my weaknesses for His strength, my thoughts for His thoughts, my mortality for His immortality, and my corruption for His incorruption. Prayer is having

---

145   Rom. 5:5

communion, not the ritual of taking communion but having common union. In His love you can ask freely and know you have whatever you asked of Him. A loving husband thoroughly enjoys giving his wife whatever she asks of him. A loving Father thoroughly enjoys giving whatever His children asks of Him. This is not control nor is it manipulation, it is agape love. Giving at the expense of self is the definition of agape love. He doesn't have to worry about spoiling them, because a love relationship is the expression of His giving. He is not giving because they lust out of their flesh for something. In fact, Js. 4:3 says, *You ask and do not receive, because you ask amiss, that you may spend it on your pleasures.* It is when we give to our children because their flesh is demanding it that they get spoiled. Giving out of a love relationship is an exchange of life and bonds us together forever.

A child will always at one time or another try to manipulate their parents into getting their own way. This is the image of natural Adam. It is an attempt to gain control over their parents, and love has nothing to do with it. It is nothing short of self-centeredness, and if a parent gives in to this manipulative way of obtaining things, then they are training them up to learn how to manipulate and gain control over others. This is deception. God's ways are higher than those ways, and control is the lower way that God is not seeking to obtain. It is the rulers of this world that seek to control people, money and power. If this is the way of the world, can it be God's way too?

Have you ever tried to give God control and nothing changed? I'm not talking about yielding yourself to God and becoming one with Him. That's picking up your cross, and that's necessary whenever the flesh of Adam pops his head up out of the grave. The flesh needs to be crucified. But, that too is not giving God control; that's crucifying the flesh so that you might partake of His resurrection life. Living the resurrected life is not giving God control but being one with Him so there are no differences. I've tried to give God control and He wouldn't take it. He has never dictated a thing to me. Why? Because God is not a Dictator! He is never described as a Dictator that rules over us and controls us. Only those under the law can imagine God wanting to control us. Get rid of the law and what do you have? Love! And love is all you need. He is our loving Father and we are His children. That speaks of relationship not dictatorship.

The word that is most closely related to control is dominion. Does God seek to have dominion over us? No. He gave us dominion over every living thing on the earth, but never over one another. We are all equal in that place of dominion over the earth. One is not above another to dictate or control their place of dominion. God gave us dominion when He told Adam to have dominion over the earth. Unlike some that have been taught, God did not give us His dominion or control over the earth. God did not say, "I give Adam My dominion over the earth." God gave us dominion over the whole of His living creation on the earth so we could rule over them with Him as one. Our own body is one of those living things that we have been given dominion over that we may rule over it as one with Christ.

If God does have dominion over every one of us, then He's doing a poor job of running things around here. One might say, "Well He seeks to have dominion but not everyone has yielded their life to Him yet." So, what you're saying is that Almighty God can't have dominion over those who don't want Him to have dominion over them. I wouldn't describe Him as God then because you just told me He's not God because He can't. With God all things are possible.[146] If all things are possible, then why can't God at least control His own people? Maybe He's not seeking control.

What we have not fully understood is what God meant when He said, "...fill the earth and subdue it..." The word subdue it means to overcome it, conquer it, and keep it under. We also need to understand what earth is. Earth is everything that we can see with our natural eyes. What is your body made of? Earth! The hardest thing for us to conquer

---

146   Mat. 19:26

or keep under is our own body even when you are a "Christian". God gave us the authority to subdue our own body and bring it under the leadership or under the shepherding of the Lord. Then God will lead and guide us to a long and prosperous life until we are satisfied.[147] So, God gave us dominion to rule over our own flesh, yes?

This misunderstanding is why many say that when it's God's time to take you, then you're gone. They say it meaning that God is in complete control of everyone's time to die. So, if God decides it's time for a baby to go at age 2, then that innocent child will die. That is not my God! That is not the God of love! That is not within the description of the Chief Cornerstone which is Jesus Christ. So if it's God's time for you to go, then why do you want to go to the hospital to get well. Will you not find yourself fighting against the will of God? Someone saying it is God's time for them to die is judgmental on their part. It also places all the burden of caring for one another off on the Lord. "Am I my brother's keeper?"[148] Yes you are!

We shun our responsibility off onto the Lord and blame God for everyone's death or misfortunes. If you smoke cigarettes, then God decides at what age you will die of lung cancer. If you have a habit of over eating, then God will decide at what age you will die. But if you decide to stop these bad habits by conquering your flesh, you will live longer. So who's in control? You are! You are exercising your own authority over your own flesh just as God gave it to you to do. It's up to you as to how long you will live. God promises to lead, guide, and help us live a full life. If we refuse His leadership and help, we might not live as long as He desires for us to live. But that is not God taking us home early. God declared that He wants us to live a long and prosperous life and if we die early, is God in control? Only if He went against His own willful desire; then you could conclude that He lost control of Himself and went against His own will. You have been given the authority to

147   Psa. 91:16
148   Gen. 4:9

subdue your flesh and if you don't, then God cannot rule over it with you. That's how we chose to live the life God gave us. It is oneness with you that God desires, and the fruit of it will be a blessed and full life.

But here is the greater way of the finished work of the life of Christ dwelling in you: You can have a bad habit and yet have no condemnation because you believe on the Lord Jesus Christ. You are steadfastly looking at the finished work of Jesus that announces your innocence and freedom from that sin while you're still bound by it. That's the key! You cannot get free until He announces that you are free. That individual has to hear that call of freedom from the Lord Himself. It is having a revelation of Jesus Christ and not looking at your own works that is the key. Upon this rock (of revelation knowledge) I will build my Church. The grace of God will eventually fill your heart and mind until you are completely free from that sin. By that same grace that brought you into oneness with Christ, you will overcome the world and all the tribulation and temptations that comes with the world! The world point of view will point out your sin, condemn you, judge you and then sentence you. But Christ forgives even while you are doing wrong. He is as fast as light to forgive. This is grace abounding over sin![149] Now God is working with you to deliver you! You cannot conquer sin on your own.

Php. 4:13 — *I can do all things through Christ who strengthens me.*

Can you see the relationship you have with Christ as one in this scripture? By ourselves we were not created to control the earth. Isn't that obvious? Look at the mess the whole world is in because we have been trying to control the earth by ourselves! But as co-laborers in Christ Jesus we can rule the earth once again by the power of love. Because Jesus loved, the lame man walked, the blind were made to see, the dead were raised, the storms were stopped, and all catastrophes

149   Rom. 5:20

ceased. But, it was not because Jesus was seeking to control everything. It was an expression of the Father's love for us so we might be brought into that same union as the Son. Then, we too, as sons would do the same works as Jesus. Just the thought of trying to control everything would leave anyone overwhelmed and unable to be at rest.

The whole point is that the King of kings is not out to control but to rule as a Lamb that brings us into perfect union with God. Control is the devils (deceiver's) way of doing things. He seeks to gain control and manipulate people so through that control his will is done. I don't know about you, but I was even taught to pray prayers of witchcraft. Witchcraft!? I was taught it in church and I taught it too. I was taught to pray that God would save my family and friends even though I knew they didn't want to be saved. So, I would pray my will, which I thought was God's will, be done over their will. I was trying to exercise my will over another's will. Once again, God did not give Adam dominion over Eve or anyone else, just over the earth that was his. It is of course God's will to save because He has already done it, but they just didn't know it or have not yet awakened to that fact. I was forcing my will over theirs. Jesus never taught such a thing. He said to pray that labors would be sent into the harvest fields.[150] Share the gospel by the Spirit and do the works of Jesus in healing the sick, casting out devils, and raising the dead. Now they are seeing Jesus in action working through us and their choice to believe is an open door to a wedding, not a shotgun wedding by force against their will.

Control is what Hitler desired. Even "Christian" rulers in the past like Constantine desired to control the whole world to force Christianity on it. All religions have tried to do that. It will never work! We were born with a God given free will, and yet there are those who try to take that away from us through manipulation and control. Hitler was deceived into thinking we were evolving from once being apes, and that there was some that hadn't evolved as far as he had; therefore, he

---

150   Mat. 9:38

sought to make all others his slaves and control the low-life's. Is this the mentality of our God? We were made in His image and likeness, not like some lower species of apes or some other animal. The problem with most of the human race is they don't know who they are. So, some act like uncontrolled animals or as the Bible calls them, beasts. But who hasn't acted that way at times? Once you see what Jesus Christ has done, and come to have an intimate relationship with the Father, our view begins to change. Once that happens we are empowered to come out of that view of darkness and come into His marvelous light, heaven's view. We have just begun to see ourselves as our Father sees us in Christ. We do not need to be controlled by the law, but only brought into union by His great love. That union will freely yield all the fruit that He grows in us.

We were given the law by God because we sought to become like Him outside of union. It was our vain attempt to obey Him and become like Him through the law. We sought to control ourselves by the law and we couldn't even do that! Why? Because anyone trying to control others or themselves is a false king! Here we are unable to control ourselves; and yet we seek to control others? The law couldn't control our flesh and God doesn't seek to control our flesh. He sought to kill it! And He did so by the crucifixion of His Son in the flesh. His death was our death. His burial was our burial. His resurrection is our resurrection, and if we are raised with Christ, why would God seek to further control us? No need, for it's no longer I that live but Christ who lives in me. Jesus could have sinned if He had chosen to. But He didn't! Why? Was it because the Father completely controlled Him? No, because it was a Father/Son relationship that developed into an inseparable union called the love of God. That is God's way for us.

Rom. 8:35, 36 — *Who shall separate us from the love of Christ? Shall tribulation, or distress, or persecution, or famine, or nakedness, or peril, or*

sword? As it is written: "For Your sake we are killed all day long;

If nothing can separate us from the love of God, then why does God need to control us? Love is all we need.

We are one of the ONE. We are family! We can't help but express God in the earth because we are His own special people, His offspring for this particular place and time.[151] We are kings reigning in life by the One, King of kings![152] This is what God sees in us, and this is how God and all heaven sees us. This is seeing from heaven.

---

151   1 Pet. 2:9
152   Rom. 5:17, 21

Chapter 4

GOD IS LOVE

God is Love. Love has already been mentioned in part in some of the previous chapters. You just can't avoid talking about God and His love. Everything He does is an expression of His love. Everything that God is comes from His unchangeable character of love. 'God is love'[153] is taught to our children in Sunday School and Children's Church often. But, as we become adults, sometimes religion is taught in a manner that might get us confused as to what God's love really is; or is God always love; or is God always loving.

I remember as a young believer, when I started reading my Bible, I would run into things, especially in the Old Testament, that would give me an image of God doing something mean and hateful that many today call righteous judgment. I couldn't understand why God did what He did, but I knew God is love. That's the only thing I remembered as a child having gone to Sunday School a few times (very few) while I was growing up. So, I just chalked it up to not fully understanding yet, but I know God is love. I didn't understand at that time that a portion and most important part of the Chief Cornerstone was laid in my life. God is love! It helped me from becoming obsessed with the idea of God being

---

153   1 Jn. 4:8

judgmental, condemning, and out to destroy all who sin, including me. I know it seems confusing reading the Old Testament with all the judgments of God against His own people and then reading:

Jn. 3:16 — *For God so loved the world that He gave His only begotten Son, that whoever believes in Him should not perish but have everlasting life.*

It seems as though there are two different Gods, or maybe God changed somehow. But, if we can understand this one thing that in the Old Testament the God of grace was present and ready to show Himself strong to those whose hearts were upright towards Him. But, to those who chose the law to be their God, rather than the God of love and grace, then that law became the accuser, condemner, and judge of them all because we all failed when observing the law. Such as, an eye for an eye and a tooth for a tooth is the law and it's punishment.

But, Jesus comes along as truth and grace, and says, "But I tell you not to resist an evil person."[154] He teaches the way of love and grace to those who have no hope in the law. Jesus offered what the law could not. He offered an empowerment of a new life that produces love. The law had no such empowerment, and therefore always left us short of the glory of God. Then it condemned without the possibility of parole, which by the way, is where most of us had gotten our false concept of hell. The law was based on our own goodness to fulfill it. But, the grace of God is based on God's own love and goodness to forgive us and restore us in His image. By His life in us we are now able to do the commandment of love, which is not short of the glory of God, but the fullness of His glory.

Jesus is the very expression of God's love. Jesus is love. Jesus never corrected the Scribes and Pharisees with the purpose to condemn, but out of love in hope that they would see their need for a Savior. To those

---

154   Mat. 5:39

who sought to be justified by the law, Jesus gave them the perfection of the law so they might understand that it was impossible for them to obey all the law. Therefore, it was impossible to be justified by that same law. This is why Jesus taught the perfection of the law to those under the law, so that they might give up all hope in justification by their own works of the law, and turn to the grace of God that comes through Jesus Christ.

If people are stuck on the law as their means of obtaining a ticket to heaven, God is obligated to give them more law, and then more law, even the fullness of the law until they are so overwhelmed by it, that they give up and come to an end of themselves and that way of life. Now they're ready to hear the true way of salvation. Don't ever condemn anyone; just give them more law if that's where they have decided to put their trust. Give more grace, if that is where they want to go. But don't mix the two together! Never!

The world has its own idea of what love is, and because we, the Church, came out of the world (Church means called out ones) we sometimes get a mixture of ideas as to what love really is. Agape love is giving at the cost of self. The love of the world, which is really lust, is getting at the expense of others. Giving at the cost of self is a perfect description of Jesus our Lord. He came not to be served, but to serve, and to lay His life down for us. Don't forget that Jesus is the very expression of God our Father. That being the case, then that is exactly what the Father is like. If we have a different view of our Father God other than that which Jesus demonstrated, then our view is distorted. "If you've seen Me, you've seen the Father."[155]

Reading the Old Testament without this knowledge burned into our hearts and minds will no doubt leave us with an impression of God judging us and the world as He did the Israelites who were under the law and not under grace. According to their own works of obedience to the law, they were blessed, but according to their own works of

---

155   Jn. 14:5

disobedience to the law, they were judged with condemnation and justifiable penalties were given. This is a completely different system or testament of agreement that believers in Jesus Christ have today. It is not even the same God. The law was their God!

"But didn't God give Moses the law to live by?" God gave Moses the law of His love that is found in the ten commandments, but Moses only saw the backside of God and perceived it as lawful works that were to be obeyed. So Moses gave the people the law, not God.[156] Moses did not preach grace because he never found grace in the eyes of God. By that same law he judged the people. If you have a mental picture of the law as your God, you will judge others by that same law.

But our approach to God under grace is based on His own finished good works; whereas, our approach to God under the law is based on our own works, good or bad, without any consideration of God's mercy and grace. God was looking for a people who would depend on His grace and come to know His great love for them. That is why He brought the Israelites out of Egypt's bondage with blood. That is why when they began to complain and even speak against God's chosen man, Moses, God still brought them through the Red Sea on dry ground and destroyed those who once controlled, manipulated, and wrongly used them. By grace their shoes never wore out. By grace there was not one feeble one among them. By grace all their livestock survived. By grace they came out with great amounts of gold and silver.

Then something terrible happened! God confronted them with their sin at Mt. Sinai,[157] which means sin. Why did God confront them with their sin? By this time, you would have thought that they knew God was a merciful and gracious God. God had revealed His love and grace to them many times by now, and now God wanted to forgive their sins freely by that same grace that delivered them out of Egypt! Their sin was a mountain between them and God and God wanted that mountain

---

156 Jn. 1:17
157 Exo. 19

removed! Even before the ten commandments they were a law unto themselves. Now after all their complaining and mumbling against the one God used to deliver them, their conscience was filled with the awareness of their sins. God wanted to forgive their sins.

When Moses presented them with the law which they had already broken by the making of a golden calf (instead of falling to their knees and crying out for mercy), they said they were well able to obey the commandments. They delighted in their commitment to do them. Sounds like religion to me. Here you are faced with a mountain of sin, and you decide to try and do better. Because these commandments came from seeing the backside of God, they were the works of God. So, they were declaring we will do the works of God by a greater commitment. That is no more than the old Adam trying to make himself better. He is a sinner in all his thoughts and ways and yet is determined to change himself. If he got himself into this mess, how is he going to get himself out of it? Can Adam change Adam? Can sour spoiled milk become good on its own? The Israelites were doomed to fail at obeying the law. But God had a plan, plan A. "I'll provide Myself a lamb for the sacrifice, as a sin offering."[158]

Now that the law, given by Moses, became their way of approach to God, there was no more room for grace, which means there is no more room for error. You either want grace or law, God cannot give you both. Mercy finds no place in the law either. Hard times are ahead of those under the law, and that doesn't have to be prophesied. They wandered around until that generation passed away. Another generation was raised up that was able to believe the promises of God, not based on their own good works, but on His own goodness. Even Moses could not enter into the promise land based on observation of the law. He too was law minded because he only saw the backside of God, and not the face of God. Again, the backside is the works of God as seen in the ten commandments, and that became their law. The law deceived us because we did not know Him face to face.

---

158   Gen. 22:8

The only law we are supposed to live by today is the law of the Spirit of life in Christ Jesus. This law supersedes any man-made laws because it fulfills all righteousness on earth and in heaven, not just earth only. **It is based on the strength of relationship for our obedience, not the strength of our obedience for relationship.** That relationship was cut with His own blood. It is out of this relationship that we are able to do all things through Christ who strengthens us. It is not obedience and then blessings, but relationship established by the Lamb that makes the kingdom of heaven at hand and manifests blessings continually. It is because of God's love for us, that God makes Himself known to us in this relationship. According to that life, the Lamb and the King lie at rest in us, and the blessings of God overtake us.

Our works are not even considered. That's good news! Did the Lamb of God first ask anyone if they were obedient to the law before they received their healing? No. Why? The Lamb declares forgiveness thus making them innocent based on His blood. What was God's motivation for doing those things? **"I Love you!"** By way of the Lamb of God is the only approach that is acceptable to the Almighty God. It was the coming of the Lamb of God that gave us this acceptable year of the Lord. That year of Jubilee has never ended for the whosoever that will freely receive. So the blessings of the Lord will never end because His love never comes to an end.

God is love and we are begotten of Him who is love. So, I guess that makes us love too. We love because He first loved us. No person under the law can love agape style. The love of God is not found in the letter of the law no more than forgiveness is found in the letter of the law. The law produces forced labor, but love produces free volunteers that go beyond what the law requires. As long as a person is under the law, they are slaves to do the law and are not free to love by the power of the new creation. The law is the tree of the knowledge of good and evil. That is the way sinful Adam lives. The old man was under the law, but the new man of the Spirit is begotten of God and lives according to that power of a higher life. We only have the power to love ourselves and others as we freely receive of His love. God has no hate towards us or anyone. We who are born of Him have been given love, not hate. So in Him, I cannot hate, except that which separates others from His love.

As God loves us individually, then we have the ability to love others with that same love. By experiencing natural love one can love by the ability that it gives. But, that is still far short of experiencing the agape love of God and loving according to His ability. If we do not receive the love that God has for us (that includes the love He gives to us through others), then we may only have some natural love from the past to give at best. We all need to experience the genuine and sincere love of God through others, not something superficial. We need to receive from a now loving God so that His presence is felt now. The love of God abides in us constantly whether we feel it or not. We just need to know these things so we can yield to His great love in us and let it flow out of us. Knowing, which includes experiencing, His constant love for us will help us walk in love constantly. As we draw from the well of the water of His everlasting life within us, it will soon become a flowing river of His life and love. We may have to first draw it out of ourselves and others before it becomes an easy flowing river, but His love is always there without end.

Jesus was often moved with compassion[159] for the sick and hurting. Compassion is love in action. This is why Jesus said, "My Father is always working", because He is love and He is moved with compassion towards us. If He is always working, then He is always loving; and if He is always loving, then He is always moving and working. Love is always moving, always working and never comes to an end. Do you get it? Love always works!

Often the Bible refers to us as God's beloved.[160] We are the ones being loved by God. We are the apple of God's eye.[161] He has set His

---

159   Mat. 9:36, 14:14, 18:27, Mk. 1:41
160   Deut. 33:12, Psa. 127:2, SoS., Rom. 1:17, 2 Thess. 2:13
161   Deut. 32:10, Zec. 2:8

affections on us not because of anything we have or haven't done, but because He is love. What is it about us that God is so attracted to us? We all came from Him and are even now in His image and likeness. We were born into this world with a natural mind that knew nothing. Only our spirit knew of God and our perfect innocence was the glory of God. Love for His own is the motivation for everything God does. Jesus was moved with compassion and healed them all! God's love is not reserved for a select few. Just as He healed them all, all are loved. God loves even the worst of sinners. I didn't say He loves their sin, but that He loves every single person. The Lamb is everlasting proof of His love towards all. "While we were yet sinners, Christ died for us."[162] To whom much is forgiven, they love much. I don't know a better way to say, "I love you", than to die for you. That is what God was saying through His Son. He has committed His love toward us to the point of His own sacrifice of death in our place. How much more will He not give us all things that we ask of Him!

God's love never fails. I experienced how powerful agape love can be one day when a friend of mine, named Jim, and I visited my neighbor. My neighbor and I were good friends and we went to the same church. Well, one Sunday my neighbor didn't show up for church so Jim and I stopped by his house to visit. Come to find out, my neighbor's five year old son was sick and had a high fever. Jim went over to the couch where his son was laying perfectly still. Jim lay down beside him and just began to talk to him and love up on him. Jim didn't pray for him to be healed, nor quote any scriptures to him, nor preach to him. He just loved up on him awhile.

After about ten minutes, Jim got up and joined us. About two minutes later, the son jumped off the couch and ran to his bedroom to grab some toys. He brought them out to show us. Then he started playing with them and making the normal noises that a healthy five year old boy would make. The fever had broken in that short time that

---

162   Rom. 5:8

Jim had loved up on him and he was completely healed! Love, agape love never fails.

Another glorious time of God's love and power obviously working together was when I was a children's pastor. One Sunday morning I got up early and began to pray. A fifth grader by the name of Emily was on my heart. She was practically deaf. She wore hearing aids, but still had a hard time hearing. She read lips very well. As I was thinking about her, I remembered when as a first grader she started coming into our elementary age church services. I thought to myself, Emily is going to get healed before she leaves children's church and moves into youth.

Now five years have passed and her hearing hasn't changed. I lay on the floor in our basement and I started talking to the Lord about it. I confessed, "Lord, I don't know if I have enough faith to get Emily healed." The Lord said, "It only takes a little faith." My mind immediately went to the scripture that says, if you have faith the size of a mustard seed, you can say to this mountain be removed and be cast into the sea and it shall be done for you.

Then the Lord said, "But it takes pure love." "Pure love", I asked? I confessed again, "I don't know if I have pure love, Lord." The Lord answered, "I'll anoint the service (people & the atmosphere) with My love…" Then I responded just like God knew I would, "Then I'll use the little faith I have." It was settled. When God does His part, then I'll do mine with Him.

Of course our services had to last as long as the adult services which was anywhere from two to two and a half hours. I don't even remember what subject we ministered on that day. But after some fun ice breaker games, then praise and worship, then teaching, puppets, more teaching, a drama skit, more teaching with object lessons, then lastly we did a worship song. The love of God filled the whole room. It was not church as usual!

Then I knew it was my turn to respond with His love that was so present among us. I turned to Emily, who was seated with her sister on the front row, and said to Emily, "Emily would you come up here please. God wants to heal your ears." As she was standing up, I said, "Take your hearing aids out." She took them out and handed them to her sister. As she stood in front of me, I had her turn around and face the class. Then I said into my lapel microphone, "Emily can you hear me?" No response. So I said loudly into the mic, "Emily can you hear me?!!" Again, there was no response. She was just looking around the room at the other kids. Even her sister felt so bad for Emily that she covered her face with her hands. "How would you feel if you couldn't hear?" I said.

We had about 80 - 90 children in the room and some on the back row were our ornery, but good and fun boys who rarely ever got serious. Even they were giving their 100% attention and were being moved with compassion! "Well, we're going to believe God for Emily's ears to open up. Do you want to pray with us?" I asked. The kids started getting a little bit fired up and excited. I had Emily turn and face me. Then I placed an index finger into each ear and said, "In the name of Jesus Christ, ears, I command you to open up and hear." I removed my fingers and had Emily face the children again. Then I said into the mic, "Emily can you hear me?" No response. So I said a little louder, "Emily can you hear me?!!" Emily then said, "I can hear you."

Well, the kids started going nuts! I said, "Wait, wait, wait, that's not good enough. Don't you want Emily to hear better than that?" The whole class said, "Yes!" So we prayed again just like the first time. After I removed my fingers out of her ears, I asked again in a normal volume using the mic, "Emily can you hear me?" She said, "I can hear you." Now the kids really started voicing their excitement. So this time I whispered into the mic, "Emily can you hear me?" No response. I then said, "One more time!" All the kids stretched their hands forward and we prayed. Again I said in a normal volume, "Emily can you hear me?" And again Emily said, "Yes, I hear you." So, I whispered into the mic, "Emily can you hear me?" This time she responded and the kids started going ballistic!

After calming everyone down, I then turned my mic off and whispered, "Emily can you hear me?" "Yea, I hear you," she said. Well, it was a good thing all the church services had ended about that time, because the kids were about to tear the doors down running out of there to tell everyone what had just happened! And it all began with the pure, perfect, and complete love that God has for us all and then a little bit of faith. It was also the love of God manifest that brought all the children and adult children's ministers together in perfect unity. Wow! Love, God's love is so good and so powerful!

God's love is also unconditional. We cannot merit it, or earn it, or do anything to deserve it. Neither can we disqualify ourselves from it by what we have or haven't done or are presently doing. It was God's idea alone to set His love upon you, not yours. You can't run fast enough to get away from God's love; you can't hide from it; you can't even sin enough to escape it. It's too late; Jesus has already shed His blood for the forgiveness of our sins because He has already set His love on us.[163]

Jesus was the expression of the Father's love to the whole world. If God healed or blessed based on our good works, then He would have healed by merit and not with compassion. Then the blessings of God would have been: some deserve it and some don't. But, Jesus did away with that approach to you and with such thinking and healed them all based on the Father having already set His love on us all by the sending of the Lamb. Because of the presence of the Lamb, which is the measure of God's love, (if it really can be measured) grace and mercy abound towards us so that all the kingdom of Heaven is made ready to meet our need. *It is the Father's good pleasure to give you the kingdom.*[164]

We cannot change God's love for us. God changes not, and His love endures forever. His love for you will endure through any sin, calamity,

---

163   Psa. 91:14

164   Lk. 12:32

the darkest thoughts, and all past problems. We cannot control God and His love for us. Aren't you glad about that?! He is love and greatly desires to express His love to us always.

> **Mt. 23:37 — *O Jerusalem, Jerusalem, the one who kills the prophets and stones those who are sent to her! How often I wanted to gather your children together, as a hen gathers her chicks under her wings, but you were not willing!***

You may have read this scripture before and thought that Jesus was really letting the Jews have it. He was fed up with their religion and rejection of His word, and He nailed them. But, try reading it with God's caring love and compassion for His fellow Israelites that He has loved for so long and still loves. The word 'wanted' means more than He only would have liked to. God's love is stronger, much stronger than that! It means how much and how many times I desired to, delighted to, determined to, loved to, and have rather gathered your children together, as a hen gathers her chicks under her wings. God longs to gather all mankind together and love, comfort, provide for, and protect us all like a mother hen caring for her young. God's love for His creation, which we are, has never changed since time began in the garden. And to think, there have been times that we turned away from Him because we were not willing to let Him be to us all that which He so strongly desired to be.

On the surface from Adam's point of view, we may read judgment, but there is hidden treasure within the same scriptures that reveals the heart of God where His steadfast love longs to gather us to Himself. It is our old Adamic thinking that sometimes gets in our way. From an earthly view point, we cannot see the heart of God and see nothing more than an exterior of the law that demands judgment against us.

If mercy triumphs over judgment,[165] then we ought to read it and look for that mercy until we find it. The mercy part is an expression of God's love for us. The judgment part is the response of the law without God's greater love being fulfilled toward us. Love covers a multitude of sin, not to hide it or cover it up, but to destroy its hold on us and to show us His mercy rather than judgment. Judgment is not God's expression but the law's expression. So the wrath of God that we see in the Old Testament is the judgment of the law and that law was their God, not the living God of grace. Grace was present all along but never by looking at the law. God had it all along to forgive, love, and heal them, but by them only seeing the law He could not fully express the fullness of His love for them. The law hinder them from entering into the kingdom that was already prepared for them. If I had preached a message on the law to those same children on that same morning, it would have prevented the love of God from coming into that room and healing Emily. All you need is love (and a little bit of faith).

The tree of the knowledge of good and evil became our God. If I do good and not evil, then I'm okay. That produced in our minds the observances of the law as our source of approaching the true God and receiving His blessings. This was a foreign approach and view of God that was not there in the beginning. God is love, and the letter of the law knows no such thing but only duty. When we get to the place where we can stop saying, "It was my duty to do such and such," and start saying, "It was the love of God in me that prompted me to do such and such," then we are free from the law and are living by the power of His life-giving Spirit. God is love and that is His greatest expression to us all.

God is love to the degree that it has no end and cannot be contained. Creation began and continues to this day as an expression of God's love. Exactly how far or how big is God's love? Can you measure all of that which He has created, and is now creating, and yet shall create? Immeasurable! We can't but just begin to see it all and understand it

---

165   Js. 2:13

all even less. God is so big that He is everywhere present at all times. Knowing this, then where is God's love? Where He is, everywhere! But if you're under the law or caught up in this world, you don't even notice Him. Boy have I missed a lot!

You can't separate love from God or God from love. There is no such thing. If we think there is, then we have created or molded a foreign imaginary God in our minds. Sometimes by what we might hear or think at times, we're not really sure if God really loves 'me'! That assessment comes from looking through the eyes of the flesh according to how the world is treating you. There is no such view from heaven in the presence of God. God is not of this world. He is in the world and the world knows Him not.[166]

The law will declare to us that God loves me if I do the law and if I don't then God doesn't love me. The law will declare that if everything goes well today, then God loves me today. If things go wrong, then God doesn't love me as much as He did yesterday. So the law actually becomes our guide and God barometer, and is based on knowing the good and evil that is in this world rather than the person of Christ that is constant love. The whole world is under that sway of the law, and we are not to be moved by it. We live, and move, and have our being in Christ.[167] We are to be moved by the life of Christ in us, and what His finished work brings to us, and that is a stable place in His great love that remains the same always. God's love towards us is a constant state of love no matter what this temporal world is declaring.

The world in its chaotic condition may sometimes try to overwhelm us where we cannot see the love of God anywhere. But that's why there is a finished work that we can look at. The Chief Cornerstone of Jesus' death, burial, and resurrection was all for us; and you have been given a witness on the inside of you that bears that truth of God's love for you. When we listen for that witness, He will cause us to rise up to the place where He

166   Jn. 1:10
167   Acts 17:28

is.[168] Where is He? He is from above. His dwelling place is Mt. Zion, the high places of God. There is a heavenly view from where He is.

The Holy Spirit that He has given you is thrilled to reveal the Christ in you at any time day or night and in any situation or circumstance. So, we ought not to be fooled by what we see or hear, for we do not walk by sight but by faith in Jesus Christ. We have a more sure word of prophecy than someone telling us all the good, the bad, and the ugly things going on in this world. It is the written word of God and the Teacher, well, He is the Spirit of love.

> **1 Jn. 4:16 – *And we have known and believed the love that God has for us. God is love, and he who abides in love abides in God, and God in him.***

God's love for us has been written and established in heaven and earth. Even though we know that, it still must be believed before it has the power to bring us salvation. Placing your hope and trust in God loving you is your great faith of believing. I then come to rest in His love and now faith is like a flowing river out of me, for faith works by love. Everything and all things that ever I do now are by faith that works through His love. This is how in vs. 17 that love is perfected or made complete in us; not that we loved God perfectly, but that we know and believe His love is perfect or complete towards us; not based on anything I've done or not done, but on who He is and what He has done. This is what gives us boldness or assurance on the day of judgment.

When is the day of judgment? Most everyday we are either judging ourselves or someone else is judging us. But, this is not the same judgment that stands for us now and for eternity in Christ and His finished work. That's why Paul said that He doesn't receive the critical condemning judgment of others, nor does he judge himself by himself.[169] The only

---

168   Exo. 12:31, 1 Thess. 4:16, 17
169   1 Cor. 4:3

judgment that really remains for us is that which comes after the cross. The judgment that was against the whole world was placed on Jesus at the cross, and Jesus nailed all that judgment that was against the whole world to the cross. All judgment against us is finished. It is done!

It is by allowing our own judgment against ourselves and the judgment of others (which is contrary to the judgment God has for us) to have a place in us that we don't feel or recognize the love that God has for us. This is making a place for the devil who is the accuser of the brethren. God's work done through Jesus Christ made sure that His love is perfected, completed, and is without interruption moving towards us. Knowing and receiving this perfect love casts out all fear.

We are not to be fooled by the accuser of the brethren. Jesus was not fooled by the knowledge and wisdom of the Scribes and Pharisees who preached the law. Jesus knew His Father and worshipped Him by the Spirit and the word of truth, not by the letter of the law. He also knew He was begotten of Him, so He was like Him. Once we get a handle on the Chief Cornerstone and all that He is and all that He has done gets a hold of us, we will be able to drink any deadly thing and it shall not harm us. What do I mean by that? We'll be able to hear all sorts of religious babble and accusations against us because of the mixture of the law, and not take it to heart by believing it. Those poisonous lies will have no effect on us, because the Branch has been thrown into those bitter poisonous waters, and the knowledge and understanding of the Cornerstone is unaffected by such nonsense. These lies are poisonous waters. But, the Branch in us keeps pure the water of His present life. Jesus had sweet waters and the religious Scribes and Pharisees had bitter waters poisoned by the condemnation that the law brings. Instead of helping people enter into the kingdom of God, they hindered them.

When we do not know Him and His finished work as our Chief Cornerstone, we are vulnerable to the leaven of the Scribes and Pharisees of our day. They are gifted in their knowledge of the Bible and have great titles and degrees that come with their names, but if they are not grounded by the Chief Cornerstone, all without exception, will error in rightly dividing the word of truth. Who are the Scribes and Pharisees today? Those that preach the law, or even worse a mixture of it. They are deceived and they are deceiving those who had such liberty of no condemnation in their walk with God, at least until they heard a mixture preached. The law makes it impossible to enter into the kingdom and a mixture causes confusion so we don't know whether we're in or out; but if we do this we're in, and if we do that we're out. Some would have you to think that we came in by grace, but to stay saved we have to obey the commandments. Myself, I believe what got me in will keep me in.

If we started by grace, we will be finished by grace. Grace, the favor of God working towards us is solely based on His love for us. God has been continually showing us His love since the creation of the world. But, because of Adam's fall, which we all partook of, all were blinded to His love for everyone. This is why Jesus came to open the eyes of the blind. Grace, not the law, is where we can see God's love on a continual basis. God is love through and through. A-men!

The knowledge that God is love is the Cornerstone of our foundation. If what we believe doesn't fit the Agape love of God, it is not the whole truth and can cause some separation or disunion. Beware of the leaven of religion that condemns you. It's just not the truth of our living God. If the law produces sin and death like the Bible says it does, then how can it be of the righteous God who came to give life more abundantly? The law came through Moses, but truth and grace came through Jesus Christ as an expression of God's great love for us. The law is not the truth because it brings death. But grace is the truth and brings eternal life, completely absent of death. The law is good in that it convinced us that we were sinners and needed a Savior. It also kept us as slaves and tutored us until we became mature sons and heirs.[170] Let only the truth of God's grace abide in you and God's love will abound with faith unhindered. God is love! A viewpoint from within agape love is seeing from heaven.

---

170   Gal. 4:1–7

Chapter 5

GOD IS GOOD!

God is good all the time and all the time God is good!

> **Js. 1:17 — *Every good gift and every perfect gift is from above, and comes down from the Father of lights, with whom there is no variation or shadow of turning.***

This scripture helps me to understand that any part of my thinking that believes God is the author of any calamity is absolutely untrue, it's a lie.

> **Jn. 16:33 — *"In the world you have tribulation. But be of good cheer, I have overcome the world."***

The problem is we are still in the world. But just as Jesus overcame the world with all its upheavals, the world is still under the influence of those who rule over it. Who is it that rules over the earth? Man, mostly humans. Though he was made to rule over the whole earth in the image of God who created him, he fell and now rules from the flesh until the image of himself is changed. The fallen image is Adam. Every person on earth is a ruler over earth. The earth will be restored when man walks in the image he was created to be, the image of God, and God is good.

Jesus' death was the death of Adam in his fallen condition. The burial of Jesus was the place of darkness where the knowledge of that life of Adam is buried. But, God spoke into that darkness and light came. That light is the life of Christ being unveiled in that man. After the light came, then the resurrection life of the new man is brought forth! This is not Adam being changed or being made a better person, but a whole new species of being! You are that new creature that God created in the beginning! The old man of sin, Adam, doesn't even exist anymore except in our unchanged mind that still has images of him. The completion of the work of our being buried with Him, is a totally renewed mind that no longer identifies itself with Adam, but with Christ, who is good.

Adam, a sinful and sin conscious human in a fallen condition, was not good. Not because he was not made in the image of God, because he was. But he was not good in his own image of himself because of the view he had of himself after eating of the tree of the knowledge of good and evil. While in our sins, we saw ourselves as not good because we are still eating of the tree of the knowledge of good and evil. There are two ways of seeing good. One is through the eyes of Adam, who became a judge according to his knowledge dividing good and evil. God is not seen in this state, nor can He be. The other way of seeing good is by seeing according to the life of God all things and in all circumstances, good or bad. Even in the bad or evil, we can see through the eyes of God how He perceives it and be assured of overcoming the world. So, good is not merely an observation and judgment based on knowledge like Adam has, but the partaking of and the intervention of His greater life manifest in spirit, soul, and body.

Adam could only see the dust or corruption of the earth, its fallen condition. Why? The devil (deception) is a fallen angel (message). Angel literally means messenger. We need to get beyond our mentality of thinking that he is a spiritual-being with wings. Another term for spirit is unseen breath. So, the devil or Satan operates in the unseen realm. God has the breath of life. The devil has the breath of death. The highest unseen realm is the Spirit realm of God. The next lower unseen realm is that of the mind; mental, psyche, thought realm called our intellect. It too is unseen. That is the realm that the devil operates in. He does not dwell in the highest realm of the Spirit. There is not a war going on in the highest realm of heaven. The devil cannot go there because that is where God is, and where God is, there is no corruption. The war is in the second heaven, the mental or physic realm. It is here that the battle begins and ends.

The devil was cast down from that place where God is, into a lower dwelling place. The devil or Satan, being a fallen messenger, has a lower or corrupted deceptive message than that of God. We could more easily and accurately identify the devil as any corrupt message that is lower than that of God. His message bears witness with Adam of the lower or fallen state in the unrenewed mind. God's message bears witness to the spirit of the man created in His image and then to the mind. That lower corrupted message has death in it.

> **Jn. 10:1–5 — "Most assuredly, I say to you, he who does not enter the sheepfold by the door, but climbs up some another way, the same is a thief and a robber. "But he who enters by the door is the shepherd of the sheep. "To him the doorkeeper opens, and the sheep hear his voice; and he calls his own sheep by name and leads them out. "And when he brings out his own sheep, he goes before them; and the sheep follow him, for they know his voice. "Yet they will by no means follow a stranger, but will flee from him, for they do not know the voice of strangers."**

The devil or deception comes to us by another way. Our Lord comes to us from our born again spirit and speaks to our mind. The false message (devil) is a thief that comes to steal our birthright to the kingdom of God. He comes to steal the word of God sown in our hearts so we won't know the truth and thus lose identity with His voice. That deception comes up, meaning that it is from below, the lowest realm or dust realm. It is the voice of a stranger that does not belong to or come from our Father. It is the voice of corruption and death. This voice always comes from the dust realm or natural fallen physical realm and then into our minds. Even if an evil thought comes and nothing around us prompted it, the seed of it came from the dust.

Jesus Christ is the shepherd. The door is the incorruptible word that comes from heaven. It is the door by which the voice of all truth comes. Nothing enters or comes out of heaven that is corrupt. Only good enters and comes out of this door. The Shepherd uses this door and speaks heaven's truth. This door is of the highest realm, the realm of the Spirit of Almighty God. Deception, darkness, evil, lies, destruction, and death does not come by this realm and it comes to steal that which has been given to us from the highest realm, which is God.

Jesus Christ is the doorkeeper. "No one can come to the Father but by Me."[171] He is the doorkeeper of heavenly things. Having the Chief Cornerstone is having the doorkeeper. The Spirit of truth and the word of God is the door and Jesus Christ is the keeper of it.[172] Looking at Jesus Christ and only seeing Him seals our foreheads and makes us wise so that we follow not the voice of strangers. Anyone who receives the word of truth like a little child enters the kingdom of heaven.[173] That one hears His voice and knows His voice and follows Him to where He is and that is in heavenly places.

---

171   Jn. 14:6
172   Mk. 16:20
173   Mat. 18:4

Yet the sheep are earth dwellers that eat of heaven and not of the dust. They live in heavenly places in Christ Jesus while physically dwelling on the earth. The sheep know the Shepherd is always good to them and they can trust Him. That is why they willingly follow Him and not the voice of strangers. There are many voices of strangers in the world. But none of them have the same sound as the good Shepherd. His voice always rings with the sound of heaven. It is a spiritual sound and not a physical sound that comes from a well painted tomb. It has the Spirit of life and truth in it even if the sheep hear it first with their natural ears from earth. God dwelling in all three realms manifests Himself to and from those three realms. Yet it always has the same sound of the voice of the Shepherd. It is the sound of heaven. Though we may first hear it from earth, it rings true that it originated from heaven. Though we may first have heard it in our minds, if we'll check, we know it came from heaven and then into our minds.

The devil was cursed by God, so lies and deception carry a curse with it. The devil (deception) would eat of the dust all the days of his life. That life can be short lived if we'll hear the voice of the Shepherd and only eat His body as our food and only drink His blood as our drink. To understand what it means to eat, we know that if we eat good food, our body will respond with good health. If we eat bad or corrupted food, our body will respond with sickness. It is the same way in the physic or mental realm. If we eat the good word of God, we will grow strong in the Lord and in wisdom and in health. The devil eats of the corrupt dust realm only. That leaves him or the message corrupt only. If we eat of that message, our soul will be corrupted and our health will be destroyed.

Jesus instructed us to eat of His flesh and drink of His blood. Some thought He was speaking of naturally eating His flesh and drinking His blood, which grossed them out. So, they left Him. But, Jesus is the word of God made flesh. Eating His flesh is eating the living word of God. *The word became flesh.*[174] How do you eat the word of God? It is

---

174   Jn. 1:14

a spiritual enlightenment into our mind or mental realm that we chew and chew on until we have gotten all the entire flavor out of it that we can. That's called mussing. So the intellect of man is eating eternal spiritual food for everlasting life in that realm of the second heaven. It is for the renewing of the mind that Jesus instructed us to eat of His flesh. The drinking of His blood is the absorbing or filling up with His life. *The life is in the blood.*[175] Drinking His blood or life will actually bring His life into our flesh. God is good! There is everlasting life in the blood of the Lamb. That drink will sustain us with a sound mind that is clothed with the incorruptible word; and it will clothe our mortal bodies with immortality.

When we think of the devil, we ought to be thinking of a message that is out to bring us lower than what our birthright declares. We are of God little children! A deceptive message is corrupted and carries death with it. That lower message separates us from God in those realms, and God doesn't like it! He hates lies and deception for that reason. He is a jealous God and a consuming fire. Remember, God is good and never changes. So His fire must be good as well. He will send the fire of His presence and pure holy word to consume those lies so that we will no longer are separated from Him in any realm: spirit, soul, and body.[176] Seeing how God dwells in all three realms, He desires us to be with Him in all three realms. Oh, how he loves you and me!

1 Cor. 14:10 — *There are many voices in the world and none of them are without significance.*

There are many voices in the world that are of this world and the reasoning of this world. If believed or meditated on long enough, they carry the power to kill and destroy. If we meditate on thoughts that are corrupted or lower than the thoughts of God, then our mind will

175   Lev. 17:11
176   Deut. 4:24

become sick. It will take on a lower state of thinking that leads to death. That thinking affects the physical realm that we live in as well. The lower corrupted thinking brings worry, stress, fear, and anxiety that affect even the cells in our body. That process is called degeneration that produces degenerated cells. They become abnormal in their structure of DNA.

On the other hand, there is only one voice in the world that is of God. It comes to us from the highest place, the dwelling place of God, the third heaven. Even when someone speaks to us a word from the Lord, we hear it with our ears naturally, but that word has to first be heard in our spirit before we can believe it and understand it with our mind. So ultimately, God always speaks to our spirit first and then our mind can understand it in the Spirit that it was spoken to us.

Rom. 8:16 — *The Spirit Himself bears witness with our spirit that we are children of God.*

God always speaks by His Spirit even when spoken through another person. His life-giving Spirit bears witness with our spirit and it always, always, always witnesses to us that oneness of relationship as we hear the word of His voice. His message never tries to divide or bring up differences that ultimately bring us lower than He is. His message will always leave us seated in heavenly places in Christ Jesus. Why? Because God is good! And He didn't make no junk!

The false message is to make us human (an imperfect and weak form of man) in our knowledge, understanding and body. But the angels (messengers) of God declare we are made in the image of God as a man. Human or humanity is a lower corrupted form of man. Jesus redeemed us all from that lower corrupted form and restored us unto our original form as the man in the garden of God in the beginning.

At the time of Noah, the human race was seeing and eating only from the dust because of the lower corrupt message gained by eating of the tree of the knowledge of good and evil. Therefore, man's heart was evil continually. God, being good, saw the corruption and repented that He had made man from the face of the earth or dust.[177] In His repentance, He flooded the earth so that man could only see the waters that reflected the heavens. Man has this knack of becoming like whatever is put before his face. If we will but put the Chief Cornerstone always before our eyes, we will always see heaven and thus see from His perspective.

And no man (Adam) shall live and see God. The first time we see God in flesh is in Jesus Christ. This picture of God then kills Adam on the cross. Adam saw God and died! That's good news! Now we can see Him face to face and live, really live! Now we are born of God and belong in His presence! Being born of God as dear children, we can freely look upon our Father and be partakers of that same life that we see in Him. Now as dear children we see that God is good through and through and has no evil in Him. It is only through the darkened and blinded eyes of Adam that we falsely thought of God doing something evil because we probably deserved it.

God is not the law, and the law is not our God. It was given so that we might see what God is like. He is the fulfillment of the law and the prophets. He knew we could not do the law because we were blinded by the fall and stooped over by the weight of the law on our backs. We no longer saw ourselves in His likeness. So, the law is good in that it reveals to us what God is like. It shows us our fallen condition and need for God's mercy and grace.

Sometimes religion confuses us into calling good evil and evil good. Like when I heard some youth say, "We bad!" But really meaning "we good", or awesome, or cool. This is the same confusion that is in most of the churches today. Example: An earthquake happens and false prophets proclaim as loud as they can that it was the judgment of God. Is the earthquake good? No. But religion says that something good can come out of it so it was God. People will get born again out of it so

---

177   Gen. 6:5-7

the earthquake was good. Tell that lie to all those who died and their suffering families! It will torment them, not save them! And if that is true, then why did Jesus still the storm that was about to sink the boat and kill the disciples if something good could have come out of it? If it were true, then Jesus would have sounded like some and said, "This came to teach you a lesson, and there is nothing you or I can do about it." In the end, 'you dead', and didn't we learn a valuable lesson? How confusing! Is destruction good or evil? If destruction is good, then the thief is good because the thief comes to steal, kill, and destroy. But some say God does these same things. To destroy evil is good. But to destroy good is evil. How much more is it evil when God called what was very good (you) is being destroyed?

This same confusion is what Jesus was taking about when He declared to the Scribes and the Pharisees that they were close to blasphemy of the Holy Spirit, which can never be forgiven them. Why were they approaching something that could not be forgiven them? Now this was the Lamb of God talking. They were calling the good things that Jesus had done and saying they were done basically by the power of the devil, which is evil. When this type of confusion comes, then it is impossible for God to save that person from being Adam because God is good and they interpret it as evil. It is the goodness or kindness of God that leads men to repentance, not the evil. God never ever uses something evil to make Himself known. He never uses bad things as a wakeup call. God will never use evil to glorify Himself. It is always the good being done in the midst of the evil that glorifies God.

God causing an earthquake to happen so some good can come out of it would be like someone burning their neighbor's house down so he could in the midst of that fire and pull out a burning child and then be called a hero. In the ignorance of men he's a hero. But what if another started the fire and the neighbor pulled out a burning child? He is a hero. The other is the one who seeks to steal, kill, and destroy, that is the devil, the deceptions; man still thinking he is the image of Adam instead of the image of God. That's right, the devil in flesh is Adam filled with deception, lies, and a fallen perception of himself. He lacks the image of God within himself and is powerless to still the storms of this world. But a man hidden in Christ is God in flesh and lacks no good thing!

What is bad? Anything harmful or hurtful to anyone's spirit, soul, or body is not of the life of God and is therefore bad or evil. God completes and keeps (protects, preserves) us: spirit, soul, and body. So, if someone got in an accident or became sick, was God the author of it? No, He can do no evil. Did God allow it to happen? No, we did. "But if something good came out of it, like they got saved, then God allowed it to happen, right?" No, we allowed it to happen.

> **2 Pet. 1:3 — *...as His divine power has given to us all things that pertain to life and godliness through the knowledge of Him who called us by glory and virtue*** (the Christ man).

God is the giver of life, not death, nor any form of death. Who's the giver of death and any form of it? Most would say the devil or Satan. But more accurately, it is the tree of the knowledge of good and evil. God said, "The day you eat of it, you shall surely (die) die."[178] It is by eating of that tree that death and any form of death comes. So the root of all death is the eating of the tree of the knowledge of good and evil.

I'm sure you've heard the expression, "Well, God called them home," meaning that they died. There is absolutely no scriptural basis for such a terrible witness about the God who suffered and died for us. Who wants to get saved! Get saved and God just might kill you and call you home! No! No! No! God is good and He calls us to glory and virtue. Maybe some are confused as to what glory is and they mistakenly think it's heaven after you die. Glory is everything that God is, has, and does.

---

178   Gen. 2:17

Heaven is glorious, but you don't have to die to go there. *The glory of the Lord is risen upon you.*[179] Here the glory of God is seen upon men who are alive. This is a description of the man of God that is filled with the glory of God and manifests that glory on the earth.

He calls us by glory and virtue, not by accidents or by sickness. To call us to Himself by glory is to reveal His love to us, His goodness to us, and His life-giving power to us. Again, His glory includes all that He is, all that He has, and all that He does. Looking a Jesus Christ as our Cornerstone, accidents and sickness doesn't fit in any of His descriptions. It is to the glory of God to heal, not make sick. It is to the glory of God to prevent accidents, not cause them or even allow them. He calls us to Himself by showing us His glory and virtue.

The word virtue comes from the Greek meaning a male man, not a male human, but a male man, the Christ man. God calls us to Himself by revealing the Christ man to us and in us. The Christ in us calls us to His image and He keeps calling us until we come to that place of oneness with Him. God is good!

One day I was driving a large truck heading east out of Topeka on a road that was filled with hills and curves. I was doing about 60 m.p.h., just driving along worshipping the Lord in my heart, minding my own business when I detected in my spirit a nudge to slow down. Without resistance I began to slow down, wondering why? When my speed dropped to 50 m.p.h., I then got an 'Okay' in my spirit. I drove for less than a minute that way and then I got an 'Okay' to speed back up. Now, that seemed really strange to me. I was asking myself, why? About that time, I came around a blind curve and coming at me was a semi-tractor-trailer that was trying to pass a car. There is no place for passing on that road and it has no shoulders and deep ditches on both sides of the road. But, there he was! Because I had heard the witness of the Spirit on the inside of me, that's all I had to do was let off the foot-speed a little and that gave him just enough time to complete his pass.

---

179   Isa. 60:1

Now I knew what the slowing down was all about! The Lord led me to slow down and that saved my life and possibly the lives of others. But it was still my choice to slow down. If I had been at that time (at times I have been) stubborn enough not to slow down because I reasoned within my mind that I had to get where I was going, then disaster would have struck. Did God allow it? No, I did.

He is faithful to show us things to come.[180] He preserves us by leading us by His Spirit. He will never be a controlling God. And He is not a God that allows us to learn the hard way. He always leads us and directs us on the path of life where there is peace, joy, love, health, safety, and provision. There is no shadow of turning with Him being good. But it is up to us to hear and not harden our heart by eating of the tree of the knowledge of good and evil. If we persist on living by our natural mind eating of that tree, then death and any form of it will be reaped. But rest assured, God doesn't allow us to eat of it; we allow our<u>selves</u> to eat of it. Do you not have authority to eat or not to eat? Didn't God give you authority to eat of any tree in the garden, but of the tree of the knowledge of good and evil, you shall <u>not</u> eat? See, God actually told us not to eat of it. His word didn't allow us to eat of it. His desire was for us not to eat of it. So He didn't allow us to eat of that tree, we misused our God given authority and self-appointed ourselves to eat of it.

While we were still living in the small town of Scranton, KS. and attending church in Topeka, I was driving home one night after a Wednesday night service. I thought I would pop in a tape of Pastor's message for that evening. I had ministered to the children that night, and it was my habit to listen to the Word while driving home. But this time, I got a check in my spirit to pray instead. It was nothing startling or urgent in my spirit, but just pray. I didn't have a clue why or what to pray about. So, I just hooked up with the Holy Spirit and began enjoying the fellowship of prayer.

---

180   Jn. 16:13

Just before coming into my home town, there is a country road that crosses the highway. It was dark and I could see that a car was approaching the intersection on my left. They had a stop sign, and I thought nothing of it. They stopped and I kept going. Just before I arrived at the cross road, the other vehicle started quickly across the highway. The timing of the whole thing did not allow me to do anything but very slightly jerk the steering wheel right and then back left. I had no time to even apply my brakes. There was no natural way possible to avoid an accident!

But, it was as though the other vehicle had passed through my pickup just behind the driver's seat in the back fender area. The other car showed no brake lights from the side coming on before or after the incident. It was as though the car had passed right through my truck. I know, you think I'm exaggerating, or I didn't see what really happened. But after we passed through one another, I immediately looked in my mirror, and they were across the intersection. There was still no indication of the car applying their brakes or even slowing down. I was dumbfounded, at awe and amazed at what had just occurred. Of course I was thankfully praising God later, after I changed my pants.

What if I had not obeyed the Spirit of life and went ahead and listened to the tape? Maybe the accident would still have been avoided, maybe not. If not, I would have allowed the accident to happen. Either way, God wanted to prevent it and protect me. He is good to all. "Well Randy, you must be special to God." You're right. I can't argue with that, but so is every one of you! All are special in the eyes of God because you all came from Him. There is not one of us who is more special or more highly favored than another. We are one! And God will show Himself strong to those whose hearts are upright towards Him. Why? They're listening. That's it. That's all there is to it. Eating of the tree of the knowledge of good and evil is not having a heart or mind or an ear that is towards Him. If you are eating of the wrong tree you will go deaf! And God doesn't allow that eating of the wrong tree either, we do!

By now, some are asking, "What about the scripture where it says all these things work for the good?"

> **Rom. 8:26–28 —** *Likewise the Spirit also helps in our weaknesses. For we do not know what we should pray for as we ought, but the Spirit Himself makes intercession for us with groanings which cannot be uttered. Now He who searches the hearts knows what the mind of the Spirit is, because He makes intercession for the saints according to the will of God. And we know that* <u>all things work together for good</u> *to those who love God, to those who are the called according to His purpose.*

If we just read 'all things work together for good', then we would assume (which is the lowest form of knowledge) all things is anything and everything. That would imply that everything is going to produce good. If someone dies in an accident, then that is good because good will be produced. The family is in a state of shock, but that must be good too. There is great sorrow and mourning, but that's good. There is the loss of a witness of God in the earth, but that's good. So, let's praise God that a loved one died or is suffering great pain from an accident because God is going to make good come out of it. Why cry with those who cry because good is going to come out of it? How cold hearted can we get! Religious thinking produces a cold heart and deaf ears. But, maybe that's good too!?

Even if someone gets born again through it all, it was not because of an accident and loss of another's life. It was because God called him by glory and virtue. The accident is not good and produces no good thing. The premature death is not good and produces no good thing. If a seed must, according to God, produce after its own kind, how does an evil accident produce good? Can good seed produce evil? Can a poisonous well bring forth good water? Does God use evil to produce good? Is not God good enough to use good to produce good? Maybe God is running short of good and has to use evil to produce good?

This is the kind of thinking that comes from eating of the wrong tree. Life produces life, and death produces death. But religion tries to complicate things and mixes the two together. We must not read part of the word and quote it out of context. To have fellowship with God, we need to read it as God said it in context. I used two examples of how the Holy Spirit helped me stay alive. It wasn't God alone that saved me. It was God working together with me that saved me. He works together with us.[181] If God wanted to be the Lone Ranger (I'm giving my age away), he wouldn't have made you and me.

So, when we need help and don't know what or how to pray, like I was when I was driving home, then the Spirit helps us in our natural human weaknesses. It was good that I didn't know. I couldn't eat of the wrong tree. He intercedes for us <u>as we</u> pray. We're still working together. The Spirit is interceding and God is hearing the mind of the Spirit. We're still praying together with the Spirit, and now the will of God is being made known in the unseen realm. That's where the power of God originated from to create all things. And now, all <u>these</u> things <u>work together</u>. What things? The Spirit of God, us, and the mind of the spirit are making intercession together as one. In fact, the word 'helps' means to join together in partnership against. They are all working together according to God. We are praying with our heart and spirit, and the Holy Spirit hooks up together with our spirit. Now God is working from the unseen realm of the Spirit towards us. All these things are working <u>together</u> for good to those who love God.

These things work together. Together means they interact with one another, a joint effort, and in company with. Does light keep company with and interact with darkness? Does God keep company with and join Himself together with Satan? Does the truth of God's word keep

---

181   Mk. 16:15-20

company with and interact with lies? Then how can evil work together with God or with good and produce good? I believe God to be holy, and that He doesn't touch the unclean things that we have called 'all these things.'

Who loves God? This scripture only says that it works for those who love God. So, it doesn't work for the unbeliever that supposedly gets saved out of it. It only works for those who love God! Why? Once again it is the Spirit of God working together with us to make intercession. This scripture is about union with God, those who are born of His love. Those who call upon Him love Him. Those who pray or have fellowship with Him are as one working together. These things only work for those who love God. This is not about God loving everyone. He does! But not everyone is willing to work with God or even seek Him. This is about the Spirit working together with us and as a result, the good will of God comes out of that working of togetherness. Those who don't love God won't work together with God and no good can be done. But those who love God enjoy working together with Him.

Jesus could do no mighty work in His home town because they would not work together with Him. They looked down on Him because they saw only His natural flesh. Therefore, they would not join themselves together with Him. Faith in God causes us to work together with God, not by ourselves. So, together with God, nothing is impossible.

Amos 3:7 — *It is as though God will do nothing unless He reveals His secret to His prophets.*

A prophet speaks what God says to him. That's what a true prophet does. When the believer asks the Spirit to help him pray, the Spirit isn't praying on His own. He joins Himself together with the believer and the believer prays what the Spirit is speaking. In that way, the Spirit makes intercession and that makes ready or brings to pass the things prayed according to God. Unless His word is voiced into the earth, it's as though God will do nothing. That's also what a believer does. He speaks the revealed will of God into the earth.

> **2 Cor. 4:13 — *But since we have the same spirit of faith, according to what is written, "I believed and therefore spoke," we also believe and therefore speak...***

That is how Adam had fellowship with God in the garden, together. God works together with us, confirming His word with signs following. Without His life-giving word, we are in darkness. But together with His Spirit and His word, we are as God in this world! We are in His very likeness as we are hidden in Christ.

In the midst of darkness, God can be manifest, not as darkness, but as a light in the darkness. Are we looking for the light? Are we drawn to the light? If we are in some darkness, and that is where we feel most comfortable, it may not be so easy to let go of the darkness and cleave to the light. I'm talking about a change of thinking and eating of the tree of life. It was our habit to eat of the other tree that produced darkness. Breaking that habit is sometimes not so easy or comfortable, or else it wouldn't be a habit. But now, we are born of the life and light of God. We are a new creature born in the Day.

God is not the darkness, as is the knowledge of the other tree, but the light. Did the darkness manifest the light? Impossible! When we now see that there is darkness all around, we search for the light and that light comes because God loves us and knows where we are at. He is moved with compassion and reveals Himself to those who are searching for the light. God, who is good, doesn't need evil to testify for Him. He doesn't use the evil no more than He uses the devil. James says that God tempts no man with evil. Why? God has no evil to tempt anyone with. If God doesn't have any evil, then He doesn't and couldn't use it for His glory even if He would, and He wouldn't. But, in the midst of that evil God will manifest Himself in that person to deliver him from that evil, if he is willing and able to hear, believe, and receive.

God is light and there is no darkness in Him. So, how can darkness (evil) come out of Him? All evil is done in darkness, because they hate the light less their deeds be exposed. If God did evil for the sake of good coming out of it, then His evil would be exposed, and He would be an evil God. It just doesn't make any sense to think that God does evil or uses evil for good.

But, those who do the truth, do it in the light so that their deeds may be clearly seen; that they have been done in God.[182] God does good in the midst of the evil. The truth of His goodness, in the midst of that evil darkness, manifests the light of His life. The darkness was not God. The evil was not God. The darkness and evil came from the god of this world. But, that is not the God that created you, died as you, and arose as you.

"Well, didn't God destroy the earth by the flood?" Yes, it was god. The law is not God. We must understand that even the Hebrews that were inspired of God to write the scriptures understood God to be the law, which produces sin and death.[183] If their law was God, then God was producing sin and death. The law was their god. Just look around you. The law is the way of this world and the god of this world. People are taught from childhood to live by the law. It is worshipped as God, but in truth it is god, a lower form of God. The world does not live by the Spirit of God, but by the law. The flood came from the god of the law, but God was able to save those who listened to Him.

If you believe that the same God that destroyed the whole earth with a flood is also the same God that saved some from it, then you have just described a house divided against itself. The earth was under the curse because of the fall of Adam, and that fall was from being under the law that the tree of the knowledge of good and evil produced. The earth was

---

182   Jn. 3:19-20

183   Jn. 8:2

not under the cruse because the God who created it cursed it. No, He blessed it and called it good. God did not reverse the blessing, but He did reverse the curse through His death, burial, and resurrection. After Adam ate of the tree of the knowledge of good and evil, he gained a sin conscience. With sin consciousness it is impossible to see God for who He really is, because guilt, judgment, and condemnation is the image of ourselves. This only gives us a view from that lowly fallen place of sinful Adam. Once the law is removed, then the veil that covers our eyes from seeing Him clearly is removed. Only grace can remove the veil; and if it is grace that we now see, then we are looking at Jesus Christ the Chief Cornerstone who is in heaven.

The law that still remains in us to this day covers the light of the glory of Christ in us. It is after the law is removed from us that the veil is removed and we see Christ clearly. Moses had a veil over his face, that veil was the law. The law and its judgments are set into motion by the continual eating of the tree of the knowledge of good and evil. It was and is the eating of the wrong tree that brings the curse of that god, not the one God! Jesus didn't say that He will confirm the laws of Moses with plagues and destruction. Really Jesus and Moses didn't have much in common. Abraham, the father of faith, yes, and David, yes, but not Moses. That is why the Scribes and Pharisees thought Jesus was against their laws, because He was the true God and not their god of the law. Jesus fulfilled the law and the prophets by the life of love, and yet He broke their laws. Once again, the law is a picture of who God is, His character; it is an image of Him. But it is only a shadow of Him and not the life of Him.

Noah found grace in the eyes of the Lord. Noah saw the true God apart from the law. There is no grace in the law. None of the ten commandments included grace. None of the other laws that were added to that ten included grace. But Noah found grace in God eyes. He saw the true God of grace and not a shadow. The law is a shadow cast by the tree of the knowledge of good and evil.

But even these things such as the flood were written for our learning. We even see death differently than God does. The death of the bodies during the flood was not the end of them forever. It was actually the end of their flesh and a new beginning for them all. No longer having the face of the earth to look at, they could actually see God face to face. The flood destroyed the corruption that was in the world. Do you want God to destroy the corruption of your world of sickness, poverty, lower state of thinking, depression, and anything else that is not of Him? I say, "Bring it on God!" God repented of making man from the face of the lower corrupt state of the earth. I thought God made man in His image. But here it says that God made man from the face of the dust or earth. God did give man an earthen body, but he didn't make man face to face with that dust. The tree of the knowledge of good and evil did that. It projected a false image of man being like the fallen cursed earth. Men had the wrong image of themselves because they were still eating from the wrong tree.

If there were no truth being spoken today, everyone would be eating of the wrong tree today. The knowledge of good and evil is the god that places people who eat of it face to face with the fallen curse of the earth. I might be so bold as to say that Adam made it flood. Remember, God gave Adam authority to rule or have dominion over all the earth. Did God lie or take back what He had given to Adam? No, the flood of death was the works of Adam.

Why did Adam and Eve eat of that tree? It was so they could become like God. They were already in the image and likeness of God, right? The real eating of the tree of the knowledge of good and evil was when Eve became deceived by the deception in her mind and she agreed with it. At the moment she agreed with the deception that was her eating of it. After that she became god just like the devil (deception) said she would. She was now a separate god from the living God that gave her life. This separation from her original life as one with God cut off her life source which is God. Death began the day she ate of it. She now began to rule as god over the earth that was given her. Her rule was from the dust realm of the fallen sinful condition of the earth.

If we can see this, then who brought the flood? She did! If she hadn't have eaten from the wrong tree, then she would still have been seeing nothing but God. Of course I'm not talking about the individual person 'Eve', but that same person that is produced by all that eat of the tree of the knowledge of good and evil. Instead of placing the blame on God for the destruction that comes upon the earth, this puts it all back on those who still eat of that tree.

> **Gen. 6:13 — And God said to Noah, "The end of all flesh has come before Me, for the earth is filled with violence _through them_; and behold, I will destroy them with the earth.**

Remember, this is the god of the law doing this and not the God of grace. This was a people that did not seek God and therefore found not His grace. It was through them (Adam) that the earth was filled with violence. The end of all flesh is death. They came before God with nothing but flesh, and no flesh can stand in the presence of God. God saw that the end of their flesh was coming to pass. They were bringing swift destruction upon themselves. They were a people that were a law unto themselves and the works of their flesh demanded death. Complete flesh = complete death. By their own authority, they demanded death. How so? Whatever a man sows that shall he reap. That is a principle of the law and not of grace. If you sow to the flesh, of the flesh you will reap destruction.[184] If you sow to the spirit, you will of the Spirit reap eternal life. The flesh was sown and death was its reaping. Sowing and reaping of the flesh is under the law of sin and death.

I have shared these things with you so we might understand that there is truly one God and that is the God of grace. In this understanding we

---

184   Gal. 6:8

can now see the possibility of the real God being good only. It is only by our eating of the tree of the knowledge of good and evil that we sow to our own destruction and God is not responsible for that destruction. In fact, He will speak truth to you and send you messengers in order to deliver you from all destruction. God is good! God is good only! But don't get condemned thinking every tribulation that comes along means you've been eating from the wrong tree. Just being in the world you will have tribulation. And when it does come, eat of the tree of life which is the overcoming of the world and then you can conquer the tribulation.

Now for our spiritual learning: God flooded the earth so Adam would be buried under the waters (baptism) and the Christ man is raised in the image of the waters. The waters reflect heaven for it is a type of the Spirit. It is the Christ man raised in us that enables us to see that our dwelling place is in heaven now and not just after we die. No one can do the will of God on their own authority or power. Adam represents all humanity trying to make things happen on their own power of the flesh. It is the new man from heaven that can do all things. Once again, man saw himself as the dust of the earth that was corrupt and under the curse, and thus he became like his surroundings.

So God repented or changed his mind and desired to flood their souls with the goodness of seeing themselves for the first time as made in the image of God. So, God sent Noah to them to preach the grace of God that he had found in the eyes of the Lord. If received, this message would change their whole view of who they really are, made in the image of God! Then there would have been no flood.

In our small thinking, we see this life on earth in our time frame only. That time frame is the eternity in our natural thinking. But, God sees all things from the place of His life of eternity and looks back. If the world in the days of Noah would have continued, the future of it would not have had a place in it for you and me and the other 6.9 billion people. The flood didn't just save Noah and his family. It saved the whole world as we know it today. God is good!

Yes, the law brought the destruction, but God raised up a new earth out of it. It was sown in corruption and was raised up a new.

Noah means rest, resting from his own works. By hearing the message of Noah, the people could have entered into the same rest that he had in the grace of God. As long as you're looking at the law, you cannot enter into His rest. God wanted a new man formed in our heart and in the image of our thinking, not from the dust, but from the water that is a reflection of heaven, God's dwelling place. God longs for us to abide in His presence so that we might have fellowship with one another.

God didn't just decide one day that because the world was so evil that He was going to destroy it and most of the population of the world with a flood. Adam (humanity) was under the law and the law has no flexibility in it to receive the grace of God, which is salvation. So as long as Adam stays under the law, then the law which is already set into motion and cannot be nullified or stopped without grace will condemn, and Adam will reap what He sows. An eye for an eye and a tooth for a tooth is the law, and the law works that way. That image of the fallen condition of the earth controlled Adam's image of himself, and because of that image, he was facing a death sentence. The law has the ministry of condemnation, not God.[185] If the flood was an act of condemning the world, then it came by the ministry of the law.

Noah found grace in the eyes of God. That means Noah saw that God is gracious. His message for the people was that of the grace of God. His message included that of a great flood. Just like most of the people that did not understand the parables that Jesus taught, they didn't understand what Noah was preaching to them.

How do we know that Noah preached to the people? Noah found grace in the eyes of God and he walk with God. Jesus said out of the abundance of the heart the mouth speaks. Unless Noah was unable to speak, he but naturally shared about the God who he walked with.

---

185   2 Cor. 3:6–9

He built a houseboat. Noah had a vision of saving the world by that houseboat being built. How could you stay quiet?

The flood is a parable of water baptism. It teaches us of the washing away of our sins and the death of that man of sin. Adam is buried completely, but out of that water another man is resurrected. That man is a new creation. Old things have passed away and all things are become new. Now the risen man out of the waters would have the image of himself as being in the likeness of God.

If anyone had listened with their heart, they would have understood Noah's message. But, the people rejected Noah and his message. In reality, they rejected the salvation of God. Therefore, God could not stop that death sentence, it was the law of eating of the tree of the knowledge of good and evil. The day you eat of it you shall surely die. God delights in the death of no man. But, the law declares what is good and what is evil, and a reward for each. The letter of the law is the ministry of death.

God had set out to destroy the dust face image that Adam had through the preaching of Noah, so that a new man might arise in the image of God. The boat that Noah built was not designed to save the whole world. The message of Noah was. Now the flood had to come.

The law and the judgment that comes with the law are ended when grace appears. Noah found grace in the eyes of the Lord, not because of what he had done, but because he saw the true God of the universe without the influence or image of the law. Noah was not blinded by the law because Noah saw who God truly is. He is a God of grace, not one of lawful condemnation. Noah and his household would be saved, though they too were in the world that was about to be judged by the law. God saves in the physical realm and mental realm as well if we are willing to hear what He is saying in the Spirit. That is God's desire for every single person because God is good.

Seeing all things from the perspective of the Chief Cornerstone truly enables us to live by the power of His life-giving spirit. From the cornerstone we can see ourselves as being complete in Him, just how God sees us. The god of the law saw man as corrupt. But the living God of mercy and grace sees every man as being in His image lacking no good thing. The cornerstone is laid and God cannot see anything that is made except through that finished work of His death, burial, and resurrection. Now we are a divine expression of Christ in the earth. For as He is, so are we. That's the only way God can see us.

God cannot stop the law from ministering condemnation and death. So, He showed us His grace that came through Jesus Christ that He might save us from the judgment of the law.

> **2 Cor. 3:5–9 —** *...but our sufficiency is from God, who also made us sufficient as ministers of the new covenant, not of the letter* **(of the law)** *but of the Spirit: for the letter kills, but the Spirit gives life. But if the* <u>*ministry of death,*</u> *written and engraved on stones, was glorious, so that the children of Israel could not look steadily at the face of Moses because of the glory of his countenance, which glory was passing away, how will the ministry of the Spirit not be more glorious? For if the* <u>*ministry of condemnation*</u> *had glory, the ministry of righteousness exceeds much more in glory.*

What was written in the letter that kills is what was written and engraved on the tablets of stone that Moses carried down the mountain. The letter of the law or the Ten Commandments on stone are observations of the backside of God, or the works of God. And if we try to do the works of God by only looking at the law, it becomes an impossibility because the law is weak through the flesh not having the expression of the life of God. The letter of the law is the ministry of death and condemnation.

"But Moses' face shined with the glory of God, didn't it?" Yes, because he saw the back side of God. Seeing the works of God is glorious. The letters on stone were written as a revelation of the works or goodness of God. Moses saw the goodness of God and had letters to prove it. But the people saw the letter of the law as a way to please God and earn His benefits. They didn't see those letters as a description of the goodness of God. Because the letter was received as a means to approach God and not as a revelation of God, the law pointed out their faults, thus condemning them to death. It was their pride that led them to declare, "We are well able to perform all that is written on those stones!" Our response to the law ought to be, "Wow, isn't God good! Only He is well able to do all these things!" And then realize the new creation we are and that He has done all these things in us, and He will do them through us!"

As long as man looks to the law for his justification, then he will find his flaws by that same law. The harder we try to please God by the works of the law, the more we see the perfection or fullness of the law and still fall short. It's an unobtainable and delusional battle to try to please God by the law. The only thing that pleases God is faith in who He is and what He has done. And that is what our Chief Cornerstone is all about.

The Scribes and Pharisees thought they were doing great at observing all of God's laws and even their own additional laws until Jesus preached to them the perfection of the law. Why did Jesus preach to them the perfection of the law? So they might see it was impossible for unchanged men in the image of Adam to do all the works of the law. Then in turn, they will see the need for a Savior that only comes by the grace of God, the unearned favor of God. But, to those who knew they were unable to do the law and were looking for the grace of God, He gave them no such laws. He taught and preached the way of love and that the kingdom of heaven is at hand. Then He healed them all, manifesting that kingdom in the earth.

The goodness of God is manifest in His grace and not under the law. Jesus remarked only twice about great faith.[186] And the only thing these two separate people and events had in common was they were not Jews under the law. Jesus declared He had not seen such great faith, not in all Israel. They were looking for the grace of God and His goodness outside the law and they found it! So don't be fooled by the law believing that destruction, sickness and disease, disasters, and tribulation of all kinds are good and come from God. They are nothing more and nothing less than the ministry of the law that brings with it condemnation and death. Hidden in Christ we are just as free from these things as Jesus was when He walked the earth. Knowing who He was in the Father and one with the Father, He was well able to overcome all that was in the world. We are in Christ and our fellowship is with the Father and with His Son, Jesus Christ. We are one in the family and one in the Lord by the grace of God.

God is so good in that the shedding of His own blood redeemed and restored all that Adam had lost in the garden. He is the good seed sown into the ground of all humanity so that all might believe and experience that redemption and restoration now. That's why this is called the gospel or good news. Telling people that they are sinners and going to hell is not good news. And neither is it **the truth**! I know what some might be thinking right now. So, let's look briefly for a moment at what the Spirit and the word of God says is the truth.

Jn. 1:17 — ...*but grace and truth came through Jesus Christ.*

Here we understand that nothing can be truth unless it comes through Jesus Christ, and grace comes with the truth. The word 'and' is a conjunction that brings two words together so that they are one and the same; they work together. It is not the truth unless it contains grace,

---

186   Mat. 8:10, 15:28

the unmerited favor of God. The law has the power of condemnation unto death in it. The gospel of grace brings the power of God unto the salvation of everlasting life. If hell is the truth, then it came through Jesus Christ. If hell is the truth, then it would have to have grace in it because truth and grace work together as one. Really, the preaching of hell (not as a topic, but as a place reserved having an eternal future for sinners) is the preaching of Adam from his viewpoint, not of the viewpoint of Jesus Christ from the throne of Heaven.

Why is it the preaching of Adam? Adam is the human that lived before Jesus was crucified. When Jesus was crucified, He took the sins of Adam which were the sins of the whole world. In the taking of Adam's sin, Jesus became the man of sin for us. Jesus became Adam. That is the identity we had of ourselves before we believed on Jesus Christ. But now, we know that Adam was crucified on the cross and lives no more. He was buried. Only the Christ man arose from that death, not Adam. If Adam is still in that grave, then why do we preach hell as though Adam has not been crucified? Adam is the man of sin that was destined for hell. If you preach hell to the world, you're preaching Adam to a people that already have the image of Adam. Big help we are.

How can the preaching of Adam save Adam? Can Adam save himself? We need to preach the death, burial, and resurrection of Jesus Christ. This will give them the true image of who they really are. They have all their life lived under the false image that they are Adam and are suffering like Adam under the curse. And if a mixture of hell and heaven is preached, isn't that mixing truth and grace with lies from the law that contains condemnation? If one believes in such a mixture, will they not still have a conscious awareness of their own sin and condemnation even though they believe they are saved? "I'm a sinner saved by grace." How confusing! If you preach hell as your approach to sinners, what more are you giving them that they don't already have? No, we preach Christ unto them. He was crucified, buried, and raised for them and as them so they might believe the truth and receive the grace that comes with that truth. That is why we are not to look at ourselves after the flesh as though looking into a natural mirror, but we are to look into the mirror of God's word so that we might see the Christ in us, the person we really are now and forever.

Well, then let's just preach a moral gospel. If you do good, then you'll go to heaven; or if you do good you'll please God. This is the preaching of moral laws. It is still the preaching of the law. The law is good, not in that it contains the means of salvation, but that it reveals the character and likeness of God to us. It also makes us aware of our need for a Savior. So, if the people in your church do not know they need a Savior, then preach the law hard to them until they do.

"If I can just do more good things like God, then I will be good and pleasing in the sight of God." Not! It is not by our outward appearance or works that makes the inward man better, but a new man of the heart that produces the good works. How can a bad tree of Adam bear good fruit? How can a contaminated well spring forth good water? The law without the life of God, is therefore, not a means to an end in that it is unable to change the heart or condition of the man. But thanks be to God and our Lord Jesus Christ that through His sacrifice, He has saved us.

Js. 1:17 — *Every good gift and every perfect gift is from above, and comes down from the Father of lights, with whom there is no variation or shadow of turning.*

God is good and there is no shadow of turning with Him. It's interesting that the word shadow is used here, because the Old Testament is full of types and shadows where Christ is hidden from them. Under the shadow of the law they were seeing a god full of variations and the real God was yet a mystery. That mystery is Christ in you, the hope of glory. Where Christ is hidden in shadows of the Old Testament, He is clearly seen in the light of the New Testament. The word shadow comes from two Greek words meaning off or departure from and shade of darkness. <u>There are no gray areas or no departures from God being good!</u> He has no hidden agendas or motives. God is love, and God is good. That's why He only does what is good.

I will always remember an event years ago, when I was a young pup of a Christian. My sister-in-law had asked us and our church to pray for her and her baby she was carrying. The baby, after six months in the womb, had formed a large bulge on one side of its head. A scan revealed that the bulged side of the brain had nothing but water in it, and the other side had some water on it too. The Doctor said if the baby would live it would be a vegetable. We prayed and believed God.

She was reaching out to God the only way she knew how. She didn't go to church, but there was no one on earth who could help her. She did what the doctors advised her to do, and they took the baby by C-section six weeks later. To the doctors amazement the baby's head was normal size with just a little water on the one side that had no brain earlier. This was a miracle! We were all praising God. We still believe if they had not taken the baby six weeks early, the miracle would have been completed.

I was pondering those things in my mind one day when I was working. I thought to myself, "I know why God did that miracle. He did it so my brother and sister-in-law would get saved." Immediately after I had that thought within myself, I heard what sounded like a loud strong voice that declared with authority, "I did it because that's who I am!" It was so loud that it startled me. I looked around the room to see who said it. I knew it was God, but I had never heard His voice with such volume and authority. It sounded like the blast of a trumpet.

That straightened out my thinking right away that God has no ulterior motives to doing anything. He does everything just because of who He is; He is love, and He is good! That's right; God doesn't do anything to get people saved. If they get saved, the angels in Heaven will even throw a party. God is gloriously pleased. But, that is not why He does anything. He does what He does because He can't help it; He is love, and He can only do good. It is our own reaction to His goodness that ends in salvation. His motive is just to reveal Himself to you personally (period). He loves <u>you</u>! Even if no one was to ever get saved by believing on the Lord, He would still love us all and do good because He cannot deny Himself.

God is so good, that He sees things differently than we do sometimes. He already sees us as one with Him. **He looks at us and sees Himself.** Remember in God's word (1 Pet. 2: 4-5) that He says, He is a living stone? Then He proclaims that we are living stones. We are one of the same as though God really meant it when He said, "Let us make man in our own image."

Too often we read the Bible as though it is only a history book that kept track of all the evils that mankind had done. But, the whole purpose of its writings was for our learning, that God loves us all, and that He is good to all. Now that same book is being written on earth and in heaven of our righteous works as a result of us seeing His righteousness in us. As our Father looks at us, He sees Himself! And as the Chief Cornerstone is unveiled to us, we can see that God has already done everything that needed to be done to make us His finished work so that we are now in the image of our wonderful and great Creator. That is the glorious work of Christ hidden in you.

It is the truth throughout all ages. God has already made you and me in His image today. It is in our mind that God is still doing the work of forming the image of the Christ man in us. The Lord speaking His word to us today is what forms the true image of who we really are today. It is in our minds understanding that we had fallen short of the glory of God because we had a sin conscience. But, Jesus has cleansed us from a sin consciousness, and now the knowledge of Him bears witness with our conscience that we are the righteousness of God in Christ Jesus. The Holy Spirit also convicts or reminds us of having His righteousness. He is still molding and fashioning us in our thinking as the Potter does the clay from what already is in the inner man. That inner man now lights up our mind's understanding so that we might know that we have been made one complete new creation in the image of God.

Pro. 20:27 — *"The spirit of man is the candle of the Lord, searching all the inward parts of the belly."*

Why is our inward man (spirit) searching all the inward parts of the belly? Jesus declared that the belly was where the presence of an overflowing river of God comes from. What He has placed in us is Himself, so that we might bear His image on the outside as well. He has never spoken a condemning word to us, the law does that. When we hear His voice, He is only speaking works of encouragement and revelation of who His is so as to reveal the Christ in us. In this we are able to see who we really are, children and sons of God. It is not in Him, His character or His ability to speak a negative word against us. God is so good! He is so good that He is only good.

As He continues to show us His Son in us, we will continue to see from His perspective what we really look like. This is heaven's viewpoint and this is who we really are. For too long the fallen condition of the earth has convinced us that we are a hopeless case bent on selfishness, greed, and destruction. But Jesus Christ crucified that man named Adam, and He has given us a new name that fits us according to that new creation made in His image. It is the image of the Christ man and you are a man of God! (No gender reference)

It is only through our Adamic thinking or lack of understanding that we think we see some variation in God being good and for that matter you being good. This opinion might come from some experience we have had or from how we had viewed certain scriptures. Experiences can be poor teachers of the greatness and goodness of our God because that teacher is of this world. In the world you will have tribulation, so if we base our view of God from times of tribulation, God is in no way perfectly good. In fact, He's down right mean and cruel at times, and we had better catch Him on a good day!

Here's a good rule of thumb to see by; I believe God is always greater and better (gooder) than I now know Him to be currently. So, if I hear or experience something that is trying to tell me something different than that, I set my mind on things above, and then He clearly shows where I am missing it. Often, it is a greater revelation of Jesus Christ that I had not understood up to this point in my life. Never, never, never has it been the other way around where God turns out being worse than what I thought Him to be. Others have shared their opinions that tried to convince me He is worse, but too late, I know Him better than that. This perspective opens me up to hearing something better than what I've heard and understood in the past. But, I still check it out by the word and the Spirit for more witnesses before it can be established in my life of faith. *Let everything be established by the witness of two or three.*[187]

1 Jn. 2:1, 2 — *My little children, these things I write to you, that you may not sin. And if anyone sins, we have an Advocate with the Father, Jesus Christ the righteous. And He Himself is the propitiation for our sins, and not for ours only but also for the whole world.*

A word that we have often misread is the word 'with'. Most of my life as a believer, I thought Jesus was my Advocate or Intercessor between me and the Father. But with the Father means with and not trying to convince the Father. 'With' means by the side of, near to, among, because of, together. So if Jesus Christ is my lawyer (intercessor) and the Father is by His side together with Him, than who is the judge that they are approaching to get me acquitted? The law was my accuser.

187   Mat. 18:16

It is any accuser of ours, including our own consciousness of sin while in our fallen state of mind. If we condemn ourselves when we sin, Jesus and our Father will defend us all the while that we are accusing ourselves. God only sees a finished work and Jesus Christ is that finished work. They are declaring that the new man they see didn't do it because everything is under the blood and forgiven. It was no longer I (the new creation) that did it, but my consciousness of sin and that image in my mind of the old Adam of flesh that did it. Jesus Christ and the Father now come before our conscious thinking, and declares to us that we have already been forgiven, and He made us innocent. He then reminds us that we are a new creature and a righteous man! He convicts us of our righteousness!

It is we that need convincing, not God. It is we who sometimes walk in the darkness of Adam having his image and not God's image of us. This scripture is God working to convince us that we are acquitted and free from all our sins, not only us, but the whole world! This is why we have been given the ministry of reconciliation. In the same way when we are accusing ourselves and He finally convinces us that we are reconciled to Him through Jesus Christ, we minister that same word to others. God and us work together to convince the world they too are acquitted because of the goodness of God that produced the finished works of Jesus Christ. His death is the forgiveness God has towards the whole world. Jesus Christ is declaring it! The Father is declaring it! The Holy Spirit is declaring it! And now the Church is declaring it!

As we grow more mature and see more clearly by the knowledge of God and His grace, we will always look for God's view of every understanding we get from every scripture in the Bible. There are only three views of the Bible. One is from the perspective of Adam as being under the law and having nothing more than his human fallen mentality to paint him a picture. The second is that of Christ, the Cornerstone of the new man as being under grace, and we are already made complete in Him. That has God as the artist that paints the picture of Himself in our minds. The third view is a religious mixture of the first two. That is what makes God vomit them out of His mouth. In grace, we are one with God's word being spoken out His mouth. He speaks, we speak. We are one as His mouth. Under the cold law we labor endlessly trying to please God by our works. He has a word for them and it is 'rest'. "Come to Me, all you who labor and are heavy laden, and I will give youi rest."[188] It is the mixture of the two that makes us double minded. One moment we sound like God and the next we sound like Adam under the law. God cannot use such people to speak His word unless they have a change of mind, so He spews them out of His mouth.

When I read the Bible, I often read it with tones in the words as though I am hearing them spoken. Well, as a result, when I was a part of that mixture, I read some with harsh tones of condemnation, especially when it came to words with hell, torment, darkness, gnashing of teeth, and anything else that had some dramatic images to it. I'm sure that comes naturally, because I am in the world, and we all like drama. But now, I read the word with Christ centered in my thinking as absolute love and good having no condemnation. It's a joy to study His word.

Most of the preaching of the 'end times', as an event yet to be fulfilled, comes from over dramatized minds of Adam that only interpret the scriptures by the natural carnal mind. They cannot yet see Jesus Christ and His finished work because they still speak of God's judgment against sin. Anyone not born of God can do that because of their sin conscience. And when comparing natural current events with natural interpretations of events in scripture, it is obvious that those interpretations are only natural minded and not spiritually inspired or discerned. It doesn't matter how they are presented or who is presenting them. It's a waste of our natural time and resources when we ought to be preaching the good news of the kingdom of God, which by the way is a spiritual <u>super</u>natural place. God dwells in a place that is above and superior to the natural. Yet, He manifests His goodness in the natural realm from being positioned in the highest realm.

---

188   Mat. 11:28

Somehow, we got confused along the way. If we see natural events in the Bible and compare them to natural events in the news, we believe that Almighty God who dwells in the highest realm of a Spiritual heaven has to do or is going to do all those events because we were smart enough to figure Him out. Somehow, the natural mind has evolved to the degree that we know what God is going to do because we studied the scriptures frontwards and backwards. Back in the old days, the Spirit of the Lord came upon His prophets, and they spoke by inspiration things that were going to happen in the future. But we must not need the Holy Spirit today because we have it all figured out.

True prophecies still come by the Spirit of God. But now they seem to come from natural interpretations of scripture and comparing it to CNN news or some other daily news events. Both are natural and no more inspired of God than Adam was when he ate of the wrong tree; and when the false prophets of old prophesied from the same tree only having the knowledge of good and evil. 88 Reasons Why Jesus Is Coming Back In 88 was man's attempt at naturally interpreting events in the scriptures and putting a time frame on it. He was a false prophet. But now, he's a rich false prophet. Why? Most of the Church loves those things and willingly threw their money in a ditch to have a blind guide. The Church has need of knowing the living God, who is a life-giving Spirit that reveals the Chief Cornerstone so that we are no longer deceived. Unveiling the Christ in you will cause you to look to Him and trust Him to be your guide instead of looking for the spectacular.

Even the false prophets of old knew the scriptures forward and backwards. But that didn't make them true prophets, just good fakes. It generated their popularity and their profits which is what also appeals to our own flesh. People get the wrong impression thinking that just because someone is on TV that must make them approved of God. Well, I've seen the devil (deceiver) on TV and I know he's not approved of God.

The truth is found in Christ revealing the kingdom of God. It is not about a natural farmer sowing seed in a field. It is all about God being the sewer, and the seed is the word of God, and we are that field. It is about spiritual things being revealed using natural parallels, not spiritual parallels revealing natural things. Those parallels are call parables, types and shadows, or the word signified. A prophetic word of wisdom can reveal something in the future, but it is most generally used to minister to individuals and it is always used to build up and not to destroy. There are greater things to be discovered hidden in those prophecies of old that can bring us to a greater revelation of Jesus Christ. That in turn brings us to a greater understanding of who we are so that we might walk in oneness with our Creator.

Tell me, how are natural interpretations of natural events going to do that? All I'm saying is be wise; get God's perspective of all things by standing on the Rock called the Chief Cornerstone and don't be tossed to and fro and carried about with every wind of doctrine by the trickery of men, in cunning craftiness by which they lie in wait to deceive.[189]

Mat. 6:10 — *Your kingdom come, Your will be done on earth as in the same manner that it is in Heaven.* (paraphrased)

Calling those things that be not as though they were according to the will of God can only be done as we have seen it or heard it in heaven.[190] Having God's perspective is having God's faith. An earthly perspective makes it impossible with men to foretell the things that are of God, because an earthly perspective is natural or carnal. But with an earthly perspective you can foretell the natural things of this world. Weather people do it all the time and hit it about as much as our natural prophets. But that has nothing to do with God!

As a new creature hidden in Christ, he sees as Christ sees and then all things are possible with him because God and him are one. That man

189   Eph. 4:14
190   Rom. 4:17

can do nothing of his own authority, but only what he sees the Father do, he does. And that goes outside the limits of this natural earth and its weaknesses and an earthy mentality.

God is good and we should know better than to allow thoughts or words to deceive us into thinking God is otherwise. God is not the author of destruction. Man without God and under the law does a good enough job of that all by himself. God is good and doesn't need to destroy that which He has already fixed! Fixed? The death, burial, and resurrection of Jesus was God's plan from the foundation of the world to solve every problem on earth. And destruction wasn't part of His plan, but the Deceiver's! God is good and He is not out to destroy the very ones He died for. That doesn't make any sense, unless you are religiously deceived. I know, I've been there and I used to teach and preach the same thing. But now you have the opportunity to have a change of mind and to gain a heavenly view.

And we will all have a problem of understanding the judgment of God if it is not viewed from the Cornerstone. But I've got good news for you. God is good! Later in the book we will address this subject of judgment even further. But yet a fuller description of the Chief Cornerstone must be revealed so we can properly understand the judgment of God from a Cornerstone perspective. Never forget, God is always good and that will never change. This is being seated with Christ and seeing from heaven.

Chapter 6

WHO IS GOD

There might be some confusion about the God of the Old Testament because there was little mercy and grace revealed and so much judgment. Most believers in the U.S. think it was the same God that introduced the law back then that we serve today, sometimes grace and sometimes judgment, but mostly judgment. The God of the Old Testament seems so contrary to the God of the New Testament. It is the same God of both, but in the Old, the law judged the people and God was hidden in a cloud so you couldn't see Him clearly.

> **2 Tim. 1:10 — *but has now been revealed by the appearing of our Savior Jesus Christ, who has abolished death and brought life and immortality to light through the gospel.***

It is in the New Testament that Christ as God is clearly seen and now grace is our judge. The New is much better! Both are seen today. There are those who serve the god of the law, and there are those who serve the God of grace. More would serve the God of grace if more of the Church would preach words filled with grace. Any message having grace in it reveals the kindness and goodness of God that leads all people to a change of mind (repentance) of who the real God is. He is their help in the time of trouble;[191] He is not their trouble.

In the Old Testament we see glimpses of God's mercy and grace showing us that from before the foundation of the world, God had already counted His Son as slain for our sins. God at various times showed His people, as well as strangers, that He is a merciful and gracious God. All of the miracles of bringing the Israelites out of the bondage of Egypt were by grace. The I AM is full of grace because He sees the Lamb slain now and not just in the future or the past. The blood on the door posts was the shadow of the real Lamb to come. But being in the shadow of the law, they did not understand. So the I AM was with them and delivered them by grace. Though they doubted God and Moses in times when they felt trapped, God still delivered them. That's the same God of the New! Did they have faith? No. But God had a vessel named Moses that spoke God's desire to bless and deliver them and it was so.

If the people would have said, "No, we know we cannot obey these commandments that God has given us; we want forgiveness, mercy, and grace; for we know our weaknesses," then God could have lived among them as the Lamb and the Lion. Instead they wandered around in the wilderness for forty years when they could have entered right into the promise land. Why? Because then they would have only been looking at the goodness of God and His ability that comes through grace rather than at their own goodness to obey the law by their own natural ability. The law causes us to look at our own ability and then we wonder why we don't have faith?

But they said, "We are well able to obey all that is commanded of us!" With those words, God had no choice but to give them back to the law because they chose a natural king to rule over them, the law. The law is natural and a tutor like Moses when he judged the people, but

---

191   Psa. 27:5, 37:39, 41:1

it was not God. It was only a description of Him and was not the real person and life that He is. It was a backside view of the works of God and not a face to face view that reveals His love and grace. That's why they couldn't do the law. The flesh is powerless to produce the works of God. The commandments were a description of a holy God. The law in turn brought them into judgment and condemnation. Moses led them by the spoken word of God and then the law led them into the wilderness to die. God gave Moses the law because the people constantly doubted God's word spoken by Moses. By their own choice their God was therefore not the God of the Spirit or of Heaven speaking directly to them, but the god of the letter of the law which is of this world.

When Adam ate of the tree of the knowledge of good and evil, it became a law unto him. After that point, he tried to live by it. The Israelites ate of the same tree, and they desired to eat of it and ate. The tree was in the natural garden all along and it is call natural knowledge. It was a lower form of life and God told them not to eat of. It was a life of the curse because God was not the author of those thoughts. The law as a word of the letter is inspired by the natural; whereas, the word of God is inspired by the Holy Spirit. It was a life style of trying to live by the knowledge of knowing the difference between good and evil. It is in knowing these things that we have a tendency to identify ourselves with these things. One day I'm pretty good, the next I'm not so good. But God only knows the life that produces abundant life. Jesus ate not from the tree that was also in the midst of his garden. He chose only to live by the life of the Father in Him.

The difference between the tree of the knowledge of good and the tree of life that produces good is the first tree comes from the natural which is temporal and subject to change. It also has a goal of pleasing the flesh. The second tree mentioned comes from the highest form of life, eternal life that is ultimately and unchangeably good. It ultimately fulfills and makes whole the total being of man. Mentally knowing good doesn't make the motive or purpose good; neither does it carry with it the power of changing a person's life. It is a good thought that might come from duty rather than from a life of abundant joy. Good done by the Spirit always leaves a lasting impression in the spirit upon others. A good deed done because they mentally determined to do so only leaves a mental impression. It has no life in it, only the letter of the law. Spiritual begets the eternal. Natural begets the temporal.

Example: When Jesus healed the man born blind, it left such an impression on the man's spirit that he taught the Pharisees when they asked how he got healed on the Sabbath. His answers confounded the studious Old Testament Bible scholars. Jesus never taught the blind man such things. Who did? The Spirit of God that touched the man when He was healed. When Jesus ministered healing to him, it left an eternal impression of that same Spirit, which is why Jesus said, "But that the works of God may be revealed **in** him."[192] Wow!

Jesus was given a name above all names. Jesus only bore the fruit of grace and not that of the law. His name has life in it and is therefore above or greater than the law. The law is powerless, even if your name is Jesus, to make men complete and one with God. It was weak through the flesh of man, and Jesus was a man having flesh. Yet He relied not on the flesh to accomplish anything. The living word became flesh and dwelt among us. This is a living word and not a dead letter of the law of commandments. If being born under the law, He fulfilled the law by the power of the law, then let us look to the law. But He fulfilled the law by the life of the Father in Him that expressed agape love. This life brought the grace and truth of God into the whole world!

Even in the Old Testament, God is worthy to be honored and exalted in those times of His mercy and grace when the people allowed Him to be to them all that He really is. So we will take a look at a few of His names that are all found in that one name that we recognize today, Jesus who was called the Christ.

---

192   Jn. 9:3

We really don't have to know all the names of Jehovah in order to receive all the benefits of being in the kingdom of God. But it might help us to know that God wants to be to us all these things that His names describe Him to be. Today, names are usually given because that's the one we liked the most for some reason or another, or we remember someone we respected or loved with that name. But in the beginning and throughout the Bible, names were descriptive of that person, and when God calls you by name, it empowers you to be all you are to be.

We have a daughter we adopted at the age of two months by the name of Roslind. She was named by her birth mother. That name didn't really strike a bell with us, and we were considering renaming her. But when we looked up the meaning of her name and found out what that name meant, we couldn't change it. It fit her perfectly. Her name means 'giver of love'. She was a gift from God to us after we had been married for 25 years and hadn't been able to have any of our own. We ministered to, loved, and cared for other parents' children, but we knew we were really missing something special, especially during the holidays. It's a long and wonderful story that my wife has shared many times that often gives all the hearers goose-bumps. It would take another book to put it all down on paper the way she explains it. So I won't attempt it. God did some awesome things to get her into our hands in a very short time and love is what it was all about. So we kept the name Roslind.

All the names of Jehovah are a description of who Jesus is as our Cornerstone. These names are once again proof of God's love for us and that He is good. We will list His seven redemptive names:

1. **Jehovah-Tsidkenu — 'The Lord our righteousness.'**
2. **Jehovah-Shammah — 'The Lord is there' or 'The Lord is present.'**
3. **Jehovah-Ra-ah — 'The Lord is my Shepherd.'**
4. **Jehovah-Shalom — 'The Lord our peace.'**

5. **Jehovah-Nissi** — 'The Lord is our banner' or 'Victor' or 'Captain.'
6. **Jehovah-Jireh** — 'The Lord will provide' an offering.
7. **Jehovah-Rapha** — 'The Lord our physician' or 'The Lord that heals you.'

If what we believe takes away from any of these descriptive names of Jesus, it is a lie and a heresy. There are yet many more descriptive names of Jehovah, but these are the redemptive ones' of most importance. By studying these names, we can better approach our God with boldness or full assurance to receive grace in the time of need. We can also praise and worship Him more fully as He deserves. Even if we are familiar with all these names, it would be productive to meditate some more on them. It is not enough to know about Jesus so that we might grab a hold on Him. That is only a mental approach to God. It is enough when we get to know Him so that He has grabbed a hold on us to the degree where we lose our own identity in His. It is His name that He writes on our forehead so that we might not only know the truth but live the truth as one in Him.

Why do we use the Old Testament name Jehovah as though it is the same as Jesus. Only when the true God of grace is pictured in the Old Testament is He also the same person of Jesus Christ. There is only one God with three different names to fully describe all His manifestations of who He is: Father, Son and Holy Spirit. The god of the law of the letter of commandments written on stone in the Old Testament is not God at all and that letter produced death. That god is therefore not a true description of the true one God. So whether we use the name of God as Father or Jesus or Holy Spirit, it makes no difference for they are one just as your spirit, soul and body are the fullness of your make-up.

Like most of us, I have been taught many doctrines and some traditional beliefs that confused and hindered my loving relationship with my Lord and God, but I didn't know it at the time. For years I believed some things that I thought were the gospel truth. Of course, I even taught those same things. Along our journey while going to church we learned many things that set us free. And then we also learned some things that put us in bondage that we didn't have even when we were sin conscious sinners. But after God had separated us out of the organized church for a short season, He began to take us back to our foundation and clean it up. I didn't even know it was dirty! I didn't know I had become so religious. I thought I had the truth and nothing but the truth so help me God!

For three and a half years in our little house church, God began the work of refining us. That doesn't mean everything I had learned before then was wrong by no means. But I had gotten as far as I could go based on my present foundation and what I was being taught. I wanted more! As we study briefly each one of these names, I will give you some brief examples of some confusing beliefs we had ourselves, as well as some we had heard preached that we didn't believe but others do. But it is not my intent to condemn or sound like I know it all. I don't! I only aim to know Him and His life more abundantly that flows in me at His unveiling. I hate disunion even if I am unaware of it. I want to be fully joined together with Him without any separation that comes as a result of my wrong believing and understanding.

Examples of wrong believing: One might declare, "I'm saved and born again, but I'm still a sinner," or "I'm a sinner saved by grace." Then you have just denied Jesus as your righteousness (Jehovah-Tsidkenu). It is impossible to be saved and still be a sinner. We are saved from our own works and have believed in His works on the cross as our righteousness. So our righteousness never looks at our own works, good or bad it makes no difference. We aren't even told to examine ourselves to see whether we are in sin or not. But we are told in the Bible to examine ourselves if we be in the faith which is the grace of God that comes through Jesus Christ.[193] There's a big difference. One looks for our own faults.

---

193   2 Cor. 13:5

The other looks at the works of Jesus Christ only. Big difference! So we ought to be saying, "I'm saved by grace, and I am the righteousness of God in Christ Jesus."[194] This by no means brings glory to me, but to the name of Jesus because He accomplished this work in me, and when I recognize it and proclaim it, it magnifies Him.

Now I am not declaring I never sin or will never sin. That has nothing to do with it. Once again, that is looking at myself and my own works. My righteousness is of Him, not me. If I do sin I have an advocate, Jesus Christ; who stands in the heavens and declares me forgiven and without sin by the price He paid with His own blood. Jehovah-Tsidkenu is all about the righteousness He freely gives us period, end of story, and don't look any farther. He is our righteousness and let any other thought or preaching of any other gospel be accursed and fall to the ground as dead, having no effect on you.[195] Jehovah-Tsidkenu is a part of that name that is written on our forehead which is Christ.

Another example: Some people always pray, "May the Lord be with us." To pray such a prayer is to deny His name that He is already with us always and will never leave us nor forsake us (Jehovah-Shammah).[196] We think if we pray and ask for such a thing, it just might happen. But if something bad happens to us, then I guess He wasn't with us. Why is there a need to pray such a thing when He indwells us always? He said He will never leave us nor forsake us! I'm sure God meant it when He said that so we should mean it in our believing. We cannot let the tribulation in the world convince us that He is not with us. Just because we don't feel Him with our feelings doesn't mean He is not present with us. God is never described as a feeling, but He is Spirit. We only need to believe what He said about that and enter into rest.

Jesus even explained that, "I go to prepare a place for you, so that where I am, there you may be also." Some put this off into the future

---

194   Php. 3:9, 2 Cor. 5:21
195   Gal. 1:8, 9
196   Heb. 13:5, Deut. 4:31

after they die. And maybe this is the only place that they know of where He will be there with them, some place in the future when they can only see into the unseen realm of the spirit. What they are saying is, "Seeing is believing." But blessed are those who have not seen and yet believe.

Jesus said, where **I am**, there you may be also, not where I am going after I die. Jesus never left heaven to become a baby. He left His place of reigning in the realm of the Spirit only to becoming a physical earth man of the Spirit so God with man might reign also on earth. Thy will be done on earth as it is in heaven."[197] He was born of the Spirit of heaven and therefore never left heaven to become a man. He even said, "The kingdom of heaven is at hand." He brought heaven with Him when He came and manifested that kingdom in the earth. Every time He spoke, He was coming from heaven and its point of view. So not only is the Lord always with us but His kingdom is always at hand and He shows us His view from heaven. Just believe and receive of that kingdom through His name given to you. You are sealed by His name written on your forehead. Sealed means a sure deal as far as God is concerned! And being sealed on your forehead means it is also a done deal in your thinking as well. You are now in agreement with God and are now walking with Him. He sealed you, you didn't seal yourself. You're a done deal, made complete in Him lacking no good thing! And He is ever present and ever ready to show Himself strong to you!

Another example: "Its flu season and I'll probably get the flu." Or "So and so got sick, so I guess it's my turn." We have just denied one of His names again. He is the Lord our healer and the Lord our banner or victory (Jehovah-Rapha & Jehovah-Nissi). A thousand may fall at my side and ten thousand at my right hand, but it shall not come near me would be a statement of faith in that name of Jesus.[198] When it comes to sickness and disease, the Chief Cornerstone of Jesus being your healer had better be in you. The world is full of the bad news of sickness and

197   Mat. 6:10
198   Psa. 91

disease, but Jesus took full payment for our healing. He is the Lord that heals you! Any other news contrary to this description of the Chief Cornerstone is an attempt to bring disunion so that this great seed of blessing is stolen from you. Chief means of greatest authority, power and importance. Let His word be established in you so that Jehovah-Rapha is Chief.

Another example: "God made me sick to teach me a lesson." This statement denies Jesus as the Healer and our Good Shepherd (Jehovah-Rapha & Jehovah-Ra-ah). It's statements like these that really shows one's unbelief of the very person in whom they have trusted for their eternal salvation. Somehow we have come to believe that God is able to save us for eternity, but He can't save us for a little while on the earth. He'll be good to me in heaven, but He's not so good to me on earth. But it's not just their fault. They were probably taught such things from pastors or teachers who were taught it at Cemetery (I mean Seminary) School. I'm not belittling Seminary. But if Seminary is teaching such things, then it has death in it. These false teachings are then spread by all who have believed their evil report which may have included us all at one time or other. So there is no condemnation but restoration by the truth.

How do people come up with such false teachings? By their experiences in the world they conclude their beliefs about God. This is trying to see into heaven from a fallen position in earth. This is the mentality of the woman who was bent over for eighteen years and could only see earth in its cursed condition.[199] She may have assumed that God must have done this to me because it happened to me and I'm not healed. But when she saw Jesus, when she looked at Jesus, when she gazed at Jesus, when she focused on Jesus, her thinking got changed from doubt and unbelief to that of faith and she was healed. Seeing Jesus is seeing from heaven's viewpoint.

The Good Shepherd will lead us into the truth. The truth is the written word of God and nowhere does it say that God puts sickness on us to teach

199   Lk. 13:11

us a lesson. You may have learned more about Jesus while going through those things, but Jesus is always willing to show those things regardless of whether you're going through anything or not. Jesus didn't say I will teach you by the hard knocks method. The teacher lives in us at all times. Jesus healed them all. You and I are in that **all** somewhere! The world will try to teach me something by sickness and disease, but God gave me His Holy Spirit to lead me into all truth as my personal Teacher.

> **1 Jn. 2:20 — *But you have an anointing from the Holy One, and you know all things.* Vs. 27 - *But the anointing which you have received from Him abides in you, and you do not need that anyone*** (by the name of Sickness) ***teach you; but as the same anointing teaches you concerning all things, and is true, and is not a lie, and just as it has taught you, you abide in Him.***

Does the anointing teach us by sickness? I've never known sickness to be anointed by God and I'm sure you haven't either. We've experienced the real anointing and it doesn't produce sickness but quite the opposite.

> **Acts 10:38 — *how God anointed Jesus of Nazareth with the Holy Spirit and with power, who went about doing good and healing all who were oppressed by the devil, for God was with Him.***

God's anointing healed all. That should settle it, for it is written. Only religious people under the law of this lower natural earth realm would disagree with God himself. But the unchangeable word has been there all along, but some just prefer to be taught by their worldly experiences rather than from the life of the word of God.

When bad news comes, most of us have a tendency to lose our peace. But really, we haven't lost it. We just haven't yielded to it because we're looking at the evil report right now. Just as God is love so is He our peace. I've even heard preaching and teaching that has tried to rob me of my peace. As a matter of fact, I used to hear it on a weekly basis. But yet at the same time while that's going on, I have a witness of greater things on the inside of me. If this witness in me isn't enough, I can take the time to analyze what was said to what is written with the help of the Holy Spirit, and I'll discover the deception every time. Why? God doesn't want anyone of us deceived. Jesus said, "My peace I give to you, My peace I <u>leave</u> with you."[200] He left us His peace so that we could be led with peace and go forth with joy. Our next step to be taken is always that of peace. Don't take it if you have no peace.

Paul had peace about going to Jerusalem even though it was prophesied that he would be bound and thrown into prison.[201] We cannot be led by prophecies. That particular prophesy had a warning with it, but you still have to follow peace and that is what Paul did. Paul went <u>not</u> being disobedient to the Holy Spirit of peace. The saying is true, "Follow your heart." He could have taken the warning and went the other way. But the trouble that lay ahead seemed like nothing compared to the peace he had about going. He was kept by that same peace and witnessed to some high ranking authorities that he would not have been able to if he had not gone. God is able to keep our soul in peace as we look to His leading and listen to His voice. His voice always speaks and will settle our minds in peace. Even in the valley of the shadow of death,[202] He is Jehovah-Shalom!

Death of the body of the believer is not a fearful thing that all must suffer. Though the body dies, we experience only life as the body is passing away. With each moment that our body draws closer to death,

---

200   Jn. 14:27
201   Acts 20 & 21
202   Psa. 23:4

our spiritual eyes are being opened wider and wider. How exciting! This is why the scripture says, "O death where is your sting."[203] The transition from the natural death of the body to the fullness of dwelling only in the higher realm of the Spirit is smooth and glorious! Only the ones left behind might grieve over such a glorious and wonderful transition of a greater experience of everlasting life because of their loss. It is to our gain that we depart and be with the Lord.[204] But our leaving is a loss to the world. That is why every life is so precious and valuable to us here. We all come from God with a calling and a purpose, and we all go back to God. That is why it is such an atrocity and an attempt to cut off God's plan for us all because of abortion. But have some peace in this: that baby just came from God and was in peace while being aborted. He never left the presence of God and His goodness. Like the Lamb of God, the baby gave himself for us. It was our loss, not his. That baby even forgave as God forgave us all. The baby knows not the torment that we have known from its death.

Jer. 1:5 — *Before I formed you in the womb I knew you; Before you were born I set you apart and appointed you...*

I'm grieved just thinking about that precious gift from God being rejected by us. And if you went through such a thing, you too are grieved even more by the loss. But know this; God has no condemnation or ill thoughts toward you. He and your baby forgives you and loves you, and they both desire that you fulfill your calling and be a gift to the world. And God would say to you, "Live! Live to the fullest the life that I have given to you through the knowledge of Jesus Christ!"

The Lord is our banner, flag, captain and victory. "Well, I guess it'll all be better in the sweet by and by," some have said. This statement is

203   1 Cor. 15:55
204   Php. 1:21

a depressing place of hopelessness for the now present time because it only places one's hope in the future. It denies Him of the victory in our lives that now dwells in our spirit. A depressing hopeless attitude is not of Christ and if it is not of Christ, then it is of Adam. Jesus the Christ earned the right through His death, burial, and resurrection to carry the name of Jehovah-Nissi. In fact, such a statement is a dishonor to His name and that's the last thing we want to do. And because we want to honor His name that is above every name like a banner or flag, we therefore must choose to believe and yield to our Captain and Victor.

It's okay to give up and throw in the towel at times. With only an earthy view, we have no other choice. Such action describes the end or death of Adam, but the resurrection of Christ awaits you! You have come to the place where you now say, "Okay God I'm done. I fully depend on you. Speak Lord." Now He will direct you and show you the way of abundant life so that you might see as He sees. Though the report says disaster, or cancer, or lack, or sickness or depression, and the doctors add to the evil report that your body has been telling you all along. But God created the earth body and earth realm, and He is Lord over all His creation if we will just agree with Him. How can two walk together unless they agree? So our Lord says to wave as a wave offering high above the head (our natural lowly thinking) the name of the Lord as our Captain and Victor!

This is not something we do out of our own strong self-will as though we are trying to obey some lawful process to make it happen. But out of a revelation of Jesus Christ being all those things to me personally, I am moved by His Spirit to do those things. Corresponding action of what you now see in Christ is faith in action. I'm not telling you to do anything. But if your response to what you have just heard makes you want to do something, **RESPOND! Do it!**

Now I do it more as a thank offering based on relationship rather than following a three step or ten step sermon on how to get the victory. The first one is based on relationship and corresponding action where the Lord is the author. The second is based on a law that if I do this, then He'll do that. If He instructs you to do this, then He will to that. But the Spirit authored it and not our own reasoning. Corresponding action to that relationship of faith is a liberal reaction and expression of one's own faith that Christ authored and not any man. When it comes from God, it's eternal and nothing can move you off that stand. It was authored by Christ, and it came from heaven. Jehovah-Nissi, the Lord our banner, flag, Captain, and Victor. Expect to hear from your Captain and respond without hesitation for He sent His word and healed them.

Many believe and say, "If I pay my tithe, God will bless me!" I've seen the prosperity message come and go into all kinds of ditches. But that doesn't mean that Jehovah-Jireh, the Lord our provider, has changed His name. Did you notice that this name literally means the Lord will provide an offering. We think religiously that if we bring our tithes and our biggest offering to church, then surely God will be pleased with my offering and bless me. It just ain't going to happen Cain. Cain brought earthy substance of value to offer to God as his first fruits, which is the tithe. It was the very best that he saw or understood that he had. Cain brought it as the first fruit of all his increase and God rejected it! God rejected Cain's tithe.

But God accepted Abel's offering of a blood sacrifice and blessed him. In fact, Abel only brought a blood sacrifice and no other offering. The Cain family didn't realize that all our efforts to please God are in vain if there is no blood sacrifice first. Jesus is the first fruits and the first fruit is the tithe. Jesus fulfilled the law of tithing and now all other offerings are acceptable to God because blood was offered first. The blood sacrifice established the greatest covenant for mankind. It was not and cannot be made by man in any way. That has to be the first offering before anything we give can be accepted. God made the new covenant between Himself and Christ Jesus; then He offered that covenant to all mankind. We entered that covenant and are blessed by it only because of our believing and our freely receiving of that finished work of that covenant cut by Jesus Christ. We are the recipients of that covenant and not the one by which it was made. God made the covenant between God and Himself. He is therefore faithful to fulfill all the promises contained in that agreement of covenant. The covenant was cut with us in mind so it therefore contains everything that we have need of within that covenant. If God had made the covenant between Himself and us, then it is exactly like the covenant of the law where if we keep the law then God will keep His promises. Aren't you glad He made a new covenant based only on His own goodness and faithfulness and not ours so that we can receive of that covenant all His promises at any time?

We seek God to bless us and I want His blessing too. But the only offering that is acceptable and worthy of blessing is the One He provided, Jesus Christ! Like Abraham said. "My son, God will provide for Himself the lamb for a burnt offering."[205] God has provided Himself an offering for us, the offering of Himself. If you can give something of greater value than that in approaching God, then bring it on, tither. It will be rejected as a tithe. But bring all you want to or as little as you have after first recognizing the one and only acceptable tithe as your first fruits, the Lamb of God! The tithe has been paid in full by Jesus Christ. Now we can all give with peace and great joy in knowing God provided an offering for us every time we consider giving so we might have faith in His works and not ours. Now that's faith and not works! Come to God with that offering and it works far better than our tithes and offerings of material things. It's a sure and unchangeable covenant sealed by His own blood designed for your being blessed!

2 Cor. 8:9 — *He was rich, yet for your sakes He became poor, that you through His poverty can become rich.*

---

205   Gen. 22:8

God so much desires to prosper us and bless us in every way, but not by our own works and our own sacrifices. That just wouldn't be consistent enough or reliable enough for God. That is why He made the covenant with Himself. It is far more reliable than anything we could come up with! Our tithing cannot make us rich. Jesus took poverty upon Himself on the cross so we can become rich.[206] Why would we ever want to get back into our own works and declare that God will bless it? Only faith in what God gave us, in His offering He provided, can we have an abundant supply.

Men and church organizations have been made rich at our expense preaching another gospel. Jesus being our first fruits or tithe is part of the Chief Cornerstone because He is the Lamb of God. He is the sacrifice offering that God supplied for us. Now, let your giving be done out of love knowing that the first fruits (the tithe) of the blood sacrifice has already been given and you'll fulfill all that God desires to do through you and you'll have no lack. He's got you covered because He is Jehovah-Jireh!

Many more things could be said about each one of His names, but what is most important is that we know His names are true and unchangeable because He is the same yesterday, today and forever. We cannot change God. We can only change our mind about who God is. Let these names forever settle our minds about who God is and not be fooled by any man's wisdom. The world will declare bad news because they still only see the earth from the viewpoint of the earth under the curse. That view is from below and is under the sway of the world. But we see from heaven the earth as redeemed and speak much better things than those. We cannot control the world that is given to another, but we can have dominion over the world that belongs to us. Let us allow the Chief Cornerstone to reign in us and through us so our earth is restored as in the beginning. Looking at Christ will cause us to rise up with wings of eagles high above the lowly viewpoint of the natural fallen

---

206   2 Cor. 8:9

condition of Adam. God also gave the eagle eyes so they can see earth clearly from heaven's view. We are those eagles.

These names of Jehovah were made known in the shadow of His future coming. He has now come, and His name is being manifest in the light of all that He is. As we see Him within these names, but not limited by these, we are seeing from heaven.

We have looked at who Jesus Christ is as our Chief Cornerstone and there is no book written that can contain all that He is and all He has done and is doing and yet will do. But I hope this part of the Cornerstone of Him who is laid in you is better understood so that you may abide in Him and He in you with greater oneness. We will now take a look at what Jesus finished or accomplished while on the earth that was established from heaven and is also now being established on earth through His body.

PART 2

THE FINISHED WORK

Chapter 1

AN END TO THE LAW

We have briefly discussed the person of Jesus as our Cornerstone. The Finished Work is what Jesus accomplished by His death, burial, and resurrection.

> **Jn. 19:30 — *So when Jesus had received the sour wine, He said, "It is finished!" And bowing His head, He gave up His spirit.***

What did Jesus mean, "It is finished?" There are many things this statement means and still speaks today. But the most accurate meaning is found in the very context of this verse. Jesus had just received sour wine. This represents the law. How do we know this? Jesus taught that there is old wine and new wine, and the new is better. Would you call sour wine new wine or old wine? The old wine of the law is bitter, sour, and hard to swallow or hard to bear. It leaves a sour taste in our mouth knowing that we always fail because it represents our own works by the law which always falls short of the glory of God. The glory of God is all that He is, has, and does. Our own works can never measure up to His by looking at the law because there is no life-giving impression left by our good works. Jesus said the law is finished right here and now because He received the sour wine and nailed the law to the cross.

The law was our tutor until we came to Christ. Now we have received the inheritance as sons, and with our Father/Son relationship based on the blood of Jesus, we have no need for the letter of the law with outward observances. In Hebrews, it says the law is passing away.[207] As we mature in Christ, He gets a hold of us until there is no more need for the law. It is no longer by our observation of the law that we are blessed and our relationship continues, but by the blood of Jesus. This letting go of the law is not an easy or immediate experience, but a passing away. The more we recognize His death as our death places us in the position of it's no longer I that lives but Christ that lives in me. When we experience these times in our life, we can also say, "It is finished!"

The 'it' that was finished is the law that held us under its power to condemn and punish us. When 'it' is finished for us individually, we only see ourselves under grace. Then we have also come to the understanding that we are His finished work. How so? Christ in us, the hope of glory, is what manifests and that causes the law to come to an end. With Christ manifesting Himself to us, we have no need for any laws. The age of the law is finished, done, and has ended concerning us who have believed.

The last Adam of sin was crucified on the cross and we would have not known sin if it were not for the law. It was the law with all its condemnation and judgment that nailed Jesus to the cross, not because He had sinned, but he was our substitute. So the law with its condemnation was nailed to the cross with Jesus who represented us as fallen Adam. The law came to an end when Jesus died on the cross

---

207   Heb. 8:13

so that the accuser would lose his case every time. If Adam was raised from the dead, then the law is still alive. Though Jesus died representing Adam, it was Christ who was raised, not Adam. And if Adam was not raised, neither was the law. The law therefore is finished.

This is what happened in the garden when Eve ate of the tree of the knowledge of good and evil. Eve represents the weaker vessels that we were once, before we were awakened and born again. Adam was not deceived like Eve, but He ate anyway.[208] Adam represents Jesus Christ, a man without sin, who was not deceived but ate of that same fruit for us and died on the cross with us (Eve). When did Jesus eat of this fruit of the tree of the knowledge of good and evil you might ask? When He declared, "My God, My God, why have you forsaken Me?"[209] God never forsook His Son even after He took our sins upon Himself. He was the Lamb of God that represented God and His covenant that was being cut with blood. Why would God forsake Himself? He didn't. If God the Father forsook Jesus at the cross, then God was not present to ratify or establish the covenant that was cut with blood at the cross. This covenant was established between God the Father and His Son. If God forsook Jesus, then He turned His back on Himself and His own covenant in the making. The first Adam ate of the tree freely as a proclamation of the last Adam that would also eat of it so He could save the bride He loves so much. The bride was Eve that represented you and I! We have all been deceived and were therefore like Eve.

Corruption was sown in the ground, but God raised up the incorruptible! When Jesus accepted the sins of the whole world upon Himself, He became the last Adam. He took on our corruption even though He had never sinned. That corrupted man died. But Christ Jesus was raised up and given an incorruptible body because there was no corruption in Him to corrupt the raised body. He didn't take the corruption in Himself, but upon Himself. Thus Adam died when Jesus

208   1 Tim 2:14
209   Mat. 27:46

died, but only Christ arose. That means Adam was finished, done, all gone, and exists no more. The last Adam was buried and left there in the tomb of our Lord and Savior.

Some believe they have found the remains of Jesus' grave clothes or covering. But those belonged to Adam, the real Christ is risen! You can't find Him in the tomb, and touching or wearing His grave clothes isn't going to do anything for you but increase your imagination. The remains of Jesus' death are that of Adam and not of Christ. Christ is risen and you can't find anything good in His tomb! It is an empty tomb that is declared as good news because now He is risen and is free to dwell in us all! See yourself as Adam no more, for he died and now only the risen Christ in you lives! If Adam is dead, then so is the law as far as you are concerned.

Rom. 8:1 — *Therefore there is now no condemnation to those who are in Christ Jesus.*

How so? An end to the law is the end of all condemnation. Only when we bring up the dead works of the law can any condemnation come to us. Adam was never meant to be raised up from the dead. Only Christ is raised. Condemnation happens because we do not see the truth that we died with Him and are now always under grace. Therefore, we are not to judge ourselves according to our works as though we are still under the law. We are **not** instructed to judge ourselves to see if we are doing good or bad.

2 Cor. 13:5 — *Examine yourselves as to whether you are in the faith.*

The eating of or believing on the tree of the knowledge of good and evil is what got us all into this mess. But Jesus Christ got us out, and only that truth can keep us free from eating again and again of that other tree. Every time we look at our do's and don'ts to examine ourselves to see if we are good Christians, we have just eaten from the tree of the knowledge of good and evil. Grace never looks at the law or at the one's own works. Grace only looks at Christ's death, burial, and resurrected life. The resurrection part is the life of Christ in you that produces the fruit.

Eph. 2:8, 9 — *For by grace you have been saved through faith, and that not of yourselves; it is the gift of God, not of works, lest anyone should boast.*

We either live completely by grace, or we just as well live completely under the law. You have to decide. Grace always, with 100% consistency, saves us. The word 'saved' is the Greek word sozo. It means to deliver, protect, preserve, heal, do well, and make whole. In other words, by the grace of God we are always blessed! But under the law, we might qualify for a blessing and then again maybe not.

So, let's examine ourselves to see if we qualify. Well, I didn't react to that situation quite right. And then when that happened, I was madder than a hornet! After that examination, I hope God will heal me. Can you see how clumsy living under the law can be? Whereas under grace we can always come before the throne of grace, that we may obtain mercy and find grace to help in time of need.[210] But whatever you do, don't mix the two together!

In fact, Adam and Eve were kept from eating of the tree of life because the two don't mix.[211] You're either under the law because you eat of the tree of the knowledge of good and evil, or you're under grace because you eat of the tree of life. How we eat of the tree of life is found in eating the flesh of Jesus and drinking His blood. In other words, as the word became flesh in Jesus, we now eat of that living word and

210 Heb. 4:16
211 Gen. 3:22–24

then become the body or flesh of Christ now in the earth. As we drink of His blood, we become partakers of the covenant that flows with the life of God. That life that now dwells in us. Jesus Christ is the tree of life that we can eat of freely.

But of the tree of the knowledge of good and evil we can still eat of it too; God tells us not to, but we can if we choose to. Why do you think there is such a mixture of law and grace preached and taught today? One is eating of the tree of the knowledge of good and evil by the law being preached and we therefore examine our own works. Then in another sentence we are fed from the tree of life. Is there any wonder there is so much confusion in the church. The mixture is confusion and brings lukewarmness, and maybe that is why the world is also confused. Because of so much confusion in the Church today, there seems to be no stability anywhere.

Jesus was the Rock that walked the earth, and He said He would build His Church upon this Rock. That Rock was the revelation of Jesus Christ and nothing else. We cannot continue to try to build the Church on the law or even on moral laws. It can never be the preaching of good morals that causes the Church to be founded on the Rock. Jesus was not good morals. He was and is the life of the Father. The Rock that the true Church is built on is the Chief Cornerstone already laid in us, and from that heavenly view we can offer the Church and the world stability. Not just advice, but the way, the truth, and the life; the source by which all the earth shall become new. Christ in you and in them is all of our hope of glory! It contains the truth and power to save the whole world!

Doomsday prophets today still exist because they can find an ear that will listen and an open billfold in the Church. Christ speaks much better things than those. Only a flesh (natural) minded preacher under the law would read their Bible and try to interpret it in the natural. The Bible is first a Spiritual book to be understood as a revelation of Jesus Christ and the kingdom of God. All the destruction we read in the

Bible is nothing more and nothing less than the destruction of Adam and the deceived mind of Eve. Period. And that's all there is to it. It's simple. The gospel never changes, just different parables that say the same thing. Even the adulterous in revelation is the Adamic (mankind born after Eve) mind that is eventually captured by the Husband, who continually pursues her until He has made her His bride. And the beast is the untamed tongue of Adam as found in James 3:8.

We don't need another gospel. The whole gospel is Christ crucified, buried, and raised up as one with God. The Church doesn't need all this hoopla of destruction being just around the corner. There is a much greater witness of much greater things, everlasting things, that the Spirit of God is speaking that has not yet been revealed to the Church yet, and the world is waiting for it! The course of the world can be changed by the truth of the gospel just like you were and are being changed by it. The law with all its fantasies of destruction coming from God has been a great hindrance to the Church. It brings disunion from the true God who laid the Chief Cornerstone. But it is Finished! Can you see it?

Do you still believe on Jesus Christ? If we have allowed the old habits of the flesh to dominate us, then let us once again gaze upon Christ so that we can see Him as He is. In doing so, we realize we still believe and are in Him. This eliminates making room for the devil, the deceiver, who always questions us about our new identity. "If you are the Son of God..."[212] Seeing only Jesus and seeing only Jesus in you also eliminates all condemnation that comes with the works of the flesh. God does not want us to know anymore condemnation, only the fullness of His grace that puts an end to the law that condemns.

Set our gaze upon Him and "It is finished!" This is not about some fictitious make-believe license to sin and get away with it. No one can get away with sin because all sin is nailed to the cross! Every time we sin because we have a lying view of ourselves being in the image of Adam, we get nailed with Him to the cross. This is all about restoration, not

---

212 Mat. 4

condemnation! The death of Adam brings an end to all condemnation. Being reminded of the new creation we really are brings us into perfect and complete union with the Father who is able to keep us from falling through that ongoing relationship.[213] It is by the power of His life in us that enables us to do all things because it is no longer we that are doing them, but Christ in us!

An end to the law is only part of what Jesus came to do. Another part is a fulfillment of the prophets that spoke concerning Him.

> **Luke 24:44 — *Then He said to them, "These are the words which I spoke to you while I was still with you, that all things must be fulfilled which were written in the Law of Moses and the Prophets and the Psalms concerning Me."***

Concerning the things written of Christ by the Prophets, Jesus fulfilled them all. That is part of what He came to do, and He did not fail! If Jesus did accomplish all that was written of Him, then there is nothing left undone for Jesus Christ to fulfill. Then why have we been taught that there are yet some things that Jesus will come back to accomplish? This leaves us with a sweet by and by mentality. No, the kingdom of heaven is in you now! There are too many things concerning the kingdom of heaven that our Father has already given us, and He wants us to experience those things now. But if we put them off into the future as though Jesus left some things unaccomplished in His first coming, then we will lose out. God always shows Himself as the 'I am' and not as the 'I will be someday, someway, somehow' God. No, 'I am' is with you! I'll speak more on this subject of Jesus being the I AM in the last chapter.

A fulfillment of all that the Prophets wrote about the Christ brought to us a new age or a new beginning. It was an end to fallen Adam and the beginning of the rising of the Christ man in the earth. It was

---

213　Jude 1:24

an end to a law-based attempt to curb sin and get to God. It was the beginning of a God given full acceptance based on the sacrifice of His Son. It marked an end of an age of Adam for us who now believe and the beginning of the rise of Christ in our flesh.

It was prophesied that the government would be placed upon His shoulders. The Jews were looking for Him to do this physically and force the end of the Roman Empire over them. But a wrong natural interpretation of the prophecy got them looking for the wrong thing, a natural event! They therefore missed His coming and denied Him as their Messiah. The government that He came to establish in the earth is to rule the very life of each and every individual person from within the earth that you are, not to rule as the world rules from the outside with laws and judgment. That kind of rule doesn't work even if it was done by God Himself, which He wouldn't and doesn't. Why wouldn't it work? Moses tried it and it failed because it lacked the power to change the heart of man. Hitler tried it and it failed. Any and all governing authority that rule by force will fail eventually. God's government rules from the heart of man as one with man.

To rule through a loving relationship that continues to speak volumes of His life in us is the way of true communion (common union). To rule as the Good Shepherd by first feeding us, caring for us and then leading us is the way of the life of our Lord. We then become free-will sheep of His pasture and not oppressed slaves. If all were to allow Christ to be their life, then there would be no need for any of the laws and governments we have today. Wouldn't that be heaven itself! Love would be the way of every man. Well, that's how God has chosen to do it, and the more we put such things off into the future as though it is not already accomplished in us, the more the world is going to continue on the path of destruction. We have the message that can save the world from destruction!

I still believe in the physical return of Jesus, but not as most of us have been taught. Jesus is not physically coming back to establish a physical kingdom. Wait all you want and you'll miss His true coming as the religious Jews did. It is through His body that Jesus comes to rule your world now. He has come in us and does so everyday! Again, I'm not saying Jesus will never come back physically. I believe He will once we establish His kingdom and the enemies of our Lord are made His footstool.[214] But that cannot be done by force. Love is the principle way and only way of establishing the kingdom of God in the earth and in all of the whosoever wills. The seed has already been planted in them; we just need to awaken the Christ in them by speaking to the One that is in them.

To some degree most of us have been taught physical events of prophecy. But Father chose to speak of physical things so we might see and understand the things of the Spirit or the kingdom of God. Even when Jesus prophesied of the destruction of the temple, He wasn't speaking of just a physical temple made of stone. The temple represented humanity, just like we are the temple of God now. The stones that built that temple represented the stone tablets of the law that condemns. It was a temple or people filled with laws. Not one stone of the law would be left to add to another, upon another, and another. All of the law was weak through its inability to change the heart of man, and those laws were coming down. That would put an end to that whole way of life. Not a physical end to the world but to that way of life. It was a prophecy concerning you and every believer in the Lord who would find grace in the eyes of the Lord; of how the law would come down and a life of grace would take its place.

So, it is not about a physical temple being torn down unless you are more concerned with natural things than spiritual things. A physical temporary temple being destroyed is not a big deal with God, with the religious Jews, yes, but not with God. The Bible says that God cares for you. It never says that God cares for your religious temple made of gold. Those are just temporal things, but you are the apple of God's eye

---

214   Mat. 22:44

and the love of His life. He has no need of gold, but He wants your fellowship because you came from Him and are His offspring.

Eph. 3:20, 21 — *Now to Him who is able to do exceedingly abundantly above all that we ask or think, according to the power that works in us, to Him be glory in the church by Christ Jesus throughout all ages, <u>world without end</u>.*

Many have tried to prophecy an end to this physical world. No matter how many ages go by or how many ages we go through, the world will never end.[215] The present state of this world will change with each age that the Church goes through, until it grows up and gets past all this religious stuff that holds us back. We are to mature and become the sons of God. Each individual believer goes through, or rather is supposed to go through, different stages in their life that brings about a new age or growth of life than previously known to them by the further unveiling of Christ in them. This is our being changed from glory to glory. And when this happens, we don't want to go back to the old understanding to live according to that lesser glory. We will gladly refuse to go backwards and live according to that way of life that had less light and life.

The light of His unveiling is the life that we are to live now. So we walk in the light we have. But when greater light reveals the Son in us, we don't continue to walk in the same light that we had before, but we live in the greater light. And there are times when this light brings such a change that it is as though we have been born anew all over again, and we are amazed by Him like we were the first time we saw Him. We have just pasted into a new age and the prior age of life is not as good as this one. We are brought into a greater awareness of Him through the knowledge of Him. He becomes greater in our own image of Him, and we become absorbed into Him.

---

215   Eph. 3:21

Now back to the physical temple of Israel. There was so much pride in the construction of those stones, which represents the law, that it grieved Jesus to think that His own disciples had missed the purpose of His coming. God allowed the building of that temple and against His own will (His word) He allows the Church to build more and more laws into their way of thinking and living. He will send messengers, but if they are not received, then they missed His appearing again and will wonder around in the wilderness that the law gives them. The death, burial, and resurrection of Jesus Christ is also the death and burial of that old lawful temple built on man's efforts. Then by grace a new temple is built not with man's hand, but its builder and maker is God.

Abraham knew these cities that were built by man through laws. So, He began looking for a city whose builder and maker is God.[216] Now we are the temple of God where no stone has been left upon another. No stone of witness against us can remain! Christ will see to it that every stone of accusation against us is torn down! No stone of the law that condemns can be thrown at us! That's why they could not stone Jesus. He represented the end, fulfillment, and finishing of the law. It was physically impossible for Him to be stoned or condemned because that was the way of the world; and He lived by the life of the Spirit of God which is much higher and greater. To stone Jesus is to stone the Father. Impossible! Can that which has been created, say to the Creator, "I find fault with you, and therefore, I accuse you." How can he who was created judge the One who created him? A lawful mentality sets us all up to critically judge ourselves, one another, and the Lord.

When they stoned Stephen, he laughed with joy because he saw Jesus, the Lamb of God standing at the right hand of God.[217] If there was any guilt of condemnation in Stephen, he would not have seen the glory of God, nor Jesus standing at the right hand of God. The stones they threw only killed the body, but lacked the power to change the

---

216   Heb. 11:10
217   Acts 6:15, 7:55

countenance on his face because of the revelation of the Lord Jesus Christ. People can hurl stones at you all they want, but the joy of the Lord is your strength knowing that there is no condemnation left for you because you are no longer under the law but under grace! Even if your Pastor or an elder in the Church hurls condemnation or accusations at you, none of those stones can stand upon another against you to keep you separated from your Lord. He Himself will tear each and every one of them down! If you ever feel condemned, the Lord will come to you again and again until all those stones are torn down so that you may be freed to come into oneness with Him. There is no condemnation to those who are in Christ.

Now, we are not of this world built with stones, not natural stones, but a life under set laws engraved in stone. So we too have come to such a great time of salvation, to walk in the Spirit, not fulfilling the lusts of the flesh. Now are we being sanctified, set apart, and separated from being dominated by this world's system. The authority of all the kingdom of God and heaven operates from within us because we have not been built with hands of the laws of men, but by the hand of God through His Spirit. We are His temple! We are the building of God that Abraham had longed to see and searched for diligently! Together we are the city of God! We are the finished work of Christ Jesus and the unlimitless kingdom of God dwells in us.

But if we, the Church, keep putting off what is a revelation of Jesus for some natural future event, we'll miss out on establishing His kingdom on the earth now! Now is the day of salvation! Now is high time to awake out of sleep: for now is our salvation nearer than (rather, except it be) when we believed![218] Our salvation is nearer now when we first believed. When we believed what? The law! Now we believe in Jesus Christ, who is grace and truth? Can you see the law coming to an end in you so that you are free to walk with the living God now? We only live in the now.

---

218   Rom. 13:11

2 Pet. 3:10–12 — *But the day of the Lord will come as a thief in the night, in which the heavens will pass away with a great noise, and the elements will melt with fervent heat; both the earth and the works that are in it will be burned up. Therefore, since all these things will be dissolved, what manner of persons ought you to be in holy conduct and godliness, looking for and hastening the coming of the day of God, because of which the heavens will be dissolved being on fire, and the elements will melt with fervent heat?*

In the natural this scripture is very dramatic and intriguing to say the least. But as stated many times, the Bible is a spiritual book that was written by the same author, the Holy Spirit, and He is speaking once again in a parable. The Holy Spirit always speaks in parables or types and shadows so that the Christ hidden in them may be revealed to those who seek Him with all their heart. Drama seekers will find drama. Destruction seekers will find destruction. Hell minded people will find hell. But Christ seekers will find Christ and see all those other things as foolishness.

Here is an example of the truth concerning 2 Pet. 3:10–12. Now, the day of the Lord always speaks of His coming, or appearing, or revealing. He was revealed to me in 1982 when I was in the dark. He came to me as the light of a new day. My whole life was in the darkness called night. He then stole or took my sins away. The old Adamic thinking began to pass away and with it also went the atmosphere that I once dwelled in as Adam. It all happened so fast and with such great power, that my wife and my mother, as well as the rest of our family, thought I was out of my tree. My old way of thinking and physical life was melting away very quickly by the fervent heat of the fire of God's love and presence. All the things that I thought was so dear to me were being dissolved, melting away. Such a dramatic change had taken place in my heaven (soul, mind, will, emotions, and conscience) and the elements of my earth (physical expression or fruit) that my mom (an unbeliever at that time) thought I was in a cult. She told Cindy (my wife) that it wouldn't last. No one in our family has ever become religious. But my wife felt that this might be permanent. As a result of the new heaven and the new earth being so much better, Cindy, one brother, and my mother all believed on the Lord Jesus.

With a big crash I died and the noise of it reached into all those around me. The Church greeted me, but my friends slowly disappeared. My order of life melted away and was set on fire by the presence of God. He is a consuming fire that burned up everything that came between me and Him. Both the earthy man named Adam and his works are being burned up by the revelation of Jesus Christ. If you read this and you're thinking; I'm way out on a limb somewhere and you like the natural interpretations of false prophecies better, then you don't love the gospel. You probably have a flare or spark for the theatrical and enjoy hearing of the destruction of earth and all of its people while you're safe in heaven. A little selfish isn't it? It would do us well if we remember that the Lamb died for the sins of those same people that doomsday prophets so gladly speak of their destruction. Maybe if we clarify some meanings of some words it might become more clear.

'Heavens' is a Greek word meaning air or the abode of God, the unseen realm as Jesus describe the wind as being unseen. God actually dwells in all three heavens that the Bible talks about in this unseen manner. If you remember earlier in this book, the highest abode is the Spirit realm called heaven. The next highest place He dwells is in the psychic realm or mental realm called the second heaven. His thoughts are higher than our thoughts. But now that we are born again, we have the mind of Christ in us given to us by His Spirit. His thoughts become our thoughts as His living word comes to us. This is when the second heaven is joined together with the third heaven where God dwells. He knows the thoughts and intents of the heart so that He might join the two together. When this happens the two become one flesh or the two become one in a flesh body, which is the first heaven. Why is the body a part of the first heaven if heaven is supposed to be unseen? The atmosphere in which the body lives in is the air that it breaths. If you take the body out of that environment, it will die. So the body, though seen, is one with its environment, the air.

The third heaven is where God manifests Himself in the earth, earth's atmosphere, or the physical realm. He is not manifest through everything because not all the things of this world are of Him. But He is everywhere present so that He can be known everywhere. If I make my bed in hell, behold, He is there.[219] That's right, I can go to hell and He is there with me. I don't know it until He reveals Himself to me, then He takes me out of that darkness. So when the Holy Spirit said the heavens (plural) shall pass away with a great noise, He was talking about two of the three we just mentioned. One is the psychic realm in which our old Adamic thinking is passing away. The other is the atmosphere or attitude of the physical Adam having passed away (died). Now we dwell in a new heaven and a new earth where God now dwells in and fills them both with His glory.[220]

A new thought process in which Christ is the author gives us higher thoughts and a new atmosphere to dwell in. Adam, the old earth, has been burned up with all his works, but a new earth (new creation) has been made by God. This new creation gives off the aroma of life to others who believe, but the aroma of death (absence or burial of Adam) to those who do not yet believe. Vs. 12 speaks of the heavens that will be dissolved being on fire... Not the natural physical heavens, but that which we just mentioned. Hasn't your mind ever been set on fire by God? Have not the works of the old sinful Adam been burned up?

Elements is from a Greek word meaning an orderly fundamental initial arrangement. The old fundamental order of your life was set

219   Psa. 139:8
220   Rev. 21:1

on fire by God and destroyed. He consumed it with the fire of His presence at the revelation of Jesus Christ. The words fervent heat is the Greek word meaning to set on fire with a glowing intense heat. That old fundamental order was the old order of the law that I and all of us were under. Peter being a strong Jew and having trouble getting passed the law himself, as Paul noted, was inspired by the Holy Spirit to write these things not only for us but for his fellow Jews. The old order of the Jewish customs and observing the laws with its sacrifices shall be burned with fervent heat at the appearing of Jesus Christ. It has happened to many Jews since Peter's writings and we pray that all might see His appearing soon because there is no hope in the law. It is finished!

So the old heaven and earth and its elements where Adam dwelled in a carnal state of existing under the law is burned up. And now a new heaven and a new earth is formed having new elements wherein the new man, the Christ man, born of the third heaven, <u>now</u> reigns in life with one Christ Jesus. The old is finished, has come to an end, and the new has come. This is the life the Father has freely given us now to manifest His goodness of the higher order of the Spirit into the earth so that the whole world, with its image of Adam, might be burned up and the law taken away. The work of it was finished on the cross with the death, burial, and resurrection of Jesus Christ. It is finished! This is seeing from heaven's perspective.

Chapter 2

JESUS FINISHED WHAT HE CAME TO DO

Jesus finished what He came to do. Another way of saying it is: Jesus finished or completed the purpose and course the Father had given Him.

> **Jn. 6:38, 39 — *For I have come down from heaven, not to do My own will, but the will of Him who sent Me. This is the will of the Father who sent Me, that of all He has given Me I should lose nothing, but should raise it up at the last day.***

To do the will of the Father is to do His word, His instructions, His desires, and follow through with His leading. This verse is not talking about losing none of us, but the word 'it' is used referring to the will of the Father. Jesus failed not at fulfilling one of Father's words. All that the Father gave Him to do, He did without faltering one time. He completed or finished all that He came to do, and that was to do the will of the Father.

This can also be seen as the greatest and most peaceful place an individual can personally experience before they depart as well. Paul said he had finished his course. Others I have known had the same witness within themselves before they departed. But don't be deceived into thinking that your course is how much you accomplish in this life for Jesus. It is once again not our works and accomplishments in this life, but His works accomplished in us and through us that is the course we are all on. How we finish our course is allowing what Jesus has finished to do a finished work in us. (Selah) This is where we recognize what He has done in us; and therefore, we become adorned as His Bride and freely manifest His works. We now recognize His many comings or His appearing to us as He speaks with us and leadings us. We also know that He equips us to do all those things as we walk with Him in doing them. Then it becomes Christ in us that does those things and none of them are of ourselves alone.

As we near the end of our walk with God in this earth life, we have a witness in us that testifies, "Well done My good and faithful servant."[221] Not because we are looking at our works, but we are looking at Him and what He has done in us and how we have allowed our Lord to make changes in our thinking and actions along the way. God recognizes that same glory that is in His Son as being in you; and that is why our Father is able to glorify us like He did Jesus. To and from God is all the glory! We are not self-centered glory seekers, but the Bible clearly says we are being changed from glory to glory. God glorified the name of Jesus above every name. And Jesus gave us His name. Imagine that for a minute. Jesus gave us His name that is above every name, not just to use against His enemies, but that we might be glorified with Him. That's not prideful, that's humbling. He is so, so, so good!

The only way God can do anything through us is to first reveal the work in us, which is an unveiling of His finished work in us, that causes us to see that we are complete in Him. Even if we don't do one good work that we can recall, but have allowed His good life and work to be done in us, we are walking out the course of our life as finished, and we

---

221   Mat. 25:21

now bear that same witness within ourselves. Oh, what great peace there is in that! So, don't measure your course by what you have done and are doing but by seeing what He has done in you. That is the goal or plan of God for you, you seeing the Christ in you who completes you. The manifestation of that Christ in you will then be an immeasurable flow out of you that will produce corresponding action of His good works.

There are natural things in this life that God has given us to do, but they don't count for anything if they aren't done in Christ by His Spirit. It is out of union with Him while doing them that makes this life so good and rewarding. We become doers of His works and greater works as our life preaches His life of grace dwelling in us. What a deal! It's not what we do <u>for</u> Christ that counts but what we do as one in Him. Being filled with His life produces works from an overflow of Him so that it is Him that does the works and not we by ourselves. Really, it is doing all things as Christ. How so? We lose our life in which we had identified ourselves as Adam, and now we find our new creation life hidden in Him. Truly, for real, honestly, you can lose yourself in Christ and become one with Him. He fully reconciled us and made us one with Him. Our identity is lost in His life.

Enoch walked with God and was no more. Enoch lost his separate Adamic identity and found his true identity as one with God. It is His Holy Spirit that He graciously gave us and has declared that we are His! He bought us and we do not belong to ourselves. We are His! We are one! We are of his stock, or seed, or breed of new creation. This gives us the right motive and divine expression as Jesus so expressed the Father in the earth. And as He is, so are we! This causes us to see ourselves the same way that God has seen us all along, AS FINISHED! This is heaven's view of you.

Jesus came to bring heaven to earth. His message was 'The kingdom of heaven is at hand.' Jesus finished that work. His death for the sins of the whole world assured us of heaven staying on earth and being at hand ready to manifest. The very fullness of the glory of God can now dwell in flesh. Where before, what was sinful flesh could not stand in the presence of God. But now, that sinful flesh of ours died on the cross and when we saw it, we acknowledge it and joined ourselves to it. We no longer have a flesh of sin, but of righteousness. This new order of life enables us to stand in the midst of the fullness of the glory of God with boldness and full assurance.

Did you know that Jesus never preached in order to try to get people into heaven? Never. He preached in order to get heaven into people. It wasn't an assured afterlife that Jesus was seeking to accomplish, but an assured now life which in turn assures our future one day at a time. Jesus preached the kingdom of heaven is at hand because it was so. It was so then, and it is so now! He did not preach a message of someday. The whole kingdom of heaven is here right now! Heaven hasn't moved out somewhere with earth being left for destruction. Never! Heaven came with Jesus, the Lamb of God, and heaven is staying because of the death of the Lamb and the resurrection of Jesus Christ. We cannot change that. And no matter how bad the world gets, it cannot change that. Heaven is always available because Jesus made it so. Jesus did an eternal work and not a temporal work of saving the world! Heaven is all around us as well as in us. But we cannot look at the world in hope of seeing heaven. It is when we look by faith and see Christ that we can see heaven in this world through this new life. Jesus finished the work of heaven's coming and remaining on earth.

Jesus finished His course and once again in **Luke 24:44** — *Then He said to them, "These are the words which I spoke to you while I was still with you, that all things must be fulfilled which were written in the Law of Moses and the Prophets and the Psalms concerning Me."*

Not only the law, but also what the Prophets had spoken and was written in the Psalms concerning Jesus, He fulfilled. If Jesus didn't fulfill every jot and tittle of the law and of the prophecies and Psalms concerning Him, then He is a liar. But the Son of God and Savior of the World is not a liar. He was without sin. And if anyone says that there are scriptures that Jesus has yet to fulfill when He comes back, then they are lying as well. That might be kind of blunt, but I choose to believe the word of God over any man's private interpretation.[222] Every scripture that speaks of Jesus and what He is to accomplish is finished by His life, His death, His burial, and His resurrection.

If we are truly only looking at Him and not our own flesh, opinions, or at what the world is saying, we can see that He has already finished all things. What appears as not finished in the world will be finished and made new through His body of believers as they make disciples and take dominion over their earth. Jesus isn't coming back to finish what He gave us to finish. We are working from a finished position in Christ that will carry on 'till all His enemies are made His footstool.

Remember, His enemies are not people, nor is it some spiritual entity called a devil that seems to be everywhere present. The enemy is the carnal mind of Adam that is being deceived. That's the work of the deceiver that is called the devil. He would have us to eat of the dust that he eats of so we take on the face of the fallen earth. But Jesus gave us His flesh to eat and His blood to drink. That is how we work from a finished position.

"If Jesus finished it, then how come I have to do anything to finish what He started?" Good question. What Jesus finished brought an end to the reign of Adam so the new species of being that you are, the Christ man, could reign in this life through you. The reigning is something we do with Him from a finished position. Jesus set us up perfectly so we could reign through His abiding life. He gives us the pleasure of reigning with Him in this world. This is how the Father is making His enemies His footstool.

For example, say Jim's body is sick. From a finished work position he knows that he is already healed but the body is sending signals that

222   2 Pet. 1:20

it is sick. The body has a tendency to try to take on the form of its surroundings. But knowing what Jesus finished on the cross declares an eternal word; whereas the body is subject to change because it is temporal. Instead of fighting the sick from an unfinished work and trying to get better, Jim knows that he is already healed and his body is try to make a place for the deception (devil) that he isn't healed. So, by the Holy Spirit Jim declares that he is the healed and that his body must take on that form of life. He has now exercised his reign over the earth (his body) with Christ.

Any crisis that speaks destruction is speaking things contrary to the word of God and contrary to the kingdom of heaven that is at hand. All these things have voices in the world. These are all enemies of God because they are contrary to the knowledge of God and how He created all things in the beginning. This is why Jesus went around doing good. These are the same voices that met Jesus in the wilderness that tried to get Him to bow. These are the same voices that sometimes have gotten us to bow. But we can still those voices and cause them to leave us if we will speak what is written on our hearts. It is out of the abundance of the heart that our mouth speaks. Fill it with life and we will speak life. We just as well speak life from heaven rather than the death that the voices in the world are speaking.

He has totally equipped us to manifest His reconciliation of the whole world. If the fivefold ministry would do what they have been instructed to do, then the body of Christ would know what they are equipped with to do the work of the ministry. We have the total package of His finished work abiding in us through His abiding life. But that doesn't mean we are all walking in that finished work. It is however, freely available to us. Just because we might not be walking in the fullness of Christ all the time doesn't mean we should take anything away from what Jesus has accomplished and freely given us. We are just beginning to live in the new heaven and new earth for the old is being burned up!

**Mat. 5:18 — *For assuredly, I say to you, till heaven
and earth pass away, one jot or one tittle will by no
means pass from the law till all is fulfilled.***
**Mat. 5:18 – Gspd — *I tell you the truth, as long as
heaven and earth endure, not one dotting of an i or
crossing of a t will be dropped from the law.***

The law will continue to the fullest and strictest degree until heaven
and earth perish. This of course is not talking about the physical heaven
and earth. It is the heaven, atmosphere, or dwelling place of the old man
Adam that is face to face with the fallen earth that has to pass away
before the law can pass away. When we see the death of Jesus on the
cross as our death, which is the death of the man of sin, then the law
will go away with that man. That Adam ate of the tree that produced
laws by the knowledge of good and evil. That is how Adam lived once
he started down that road. At the end of that road is death because no
one is justified by the law.[223]

To the unbeliever the law hasn't passed away; they are still under
the law. That cannot change until that heaven and earth is taken away.
That old heaven and earth still exists until they see Jesus' death as their
death on the cross. That is the taking away of Adam, the human that
created the now existing fallen condition of this present heaven and
earth. Jesus has already finished that work of taking away Adam with
the old heaven and earth by His death on the cross. But people must
see it by faith in the gospel we preach.

Once they see their death on the cross, then the law passes away
with that old life style of Adam because that is how Adam lived. Now a
new man is raised and is free from the law. He is free to live according
to resurrection life. The preaching of the cross is still the message for all
unbelievers and also the young or immature believers. The preaching
of the cross is not about you crucifying yourself or your trying to stop

223   Acts 13:39

sinning. That is still the ways of Adam trying to please God by what he can do. The preaching of the cross is about Jesus' death and how he brought about our death, not us bringing about our own death. Jesus finished our death on the cross. Only as we are joined together with Him on the cross are we truly and fully crucified as He was crucified. This brings a complete death to that heaven and earth that Adam was able to live in. That was the environment that Adam breathed. The law had the breath of death in it; for the letter of the law kills.[224] The death of Jesus on the cross was our death and our deliverance from the law.

> **Rom. 7:6 — *But now we have been delivered from the law, having died to what we were held by, so that we should serve in newness of the Spirit and not in the oldness of the letter.***
> **Rhm — *But now we have received full release from the law by dying [in that] wherein we used to be held fast; so that we serve not under the old written code but in the new life of the Spirit.***

Our dying with Christ on the cross gave us full release from the law. Now we live according to newness of the Spirit of life we have in Christ. That newness of life is His resurrection life now that eternally abides in us. We cannot experience resurrection life if we are still trying to improve the old Adam by observing religious rules of do's and don'ts. We must see that life style as crucified because that was the way of Adam and he died on the cross.

The same thing goes for His resurrection. We cannot produce His resurrection life by trying to be a better Christian. Only as we are joined together with His resurrection are we truly and fully risen with Christ. It is His life in us that produces the true Christian. A false Christian is one that still has laws, rules, and guide lines to follow so they can

---

224   2 Cor. 3:6

appear to be Christian. But inwardly they are dead because of the law that exists produces death. In place of the life of Christ and His living word, which is the life of the new man, they have more laws because they do not yet see that way of the life of Adam as crucified. A real Christian abides in His life as their life and His living word abides in them. There are no more laws, rules, or preset guide lines to lead us. Christ is all and in all.[225]

In reality, Jesus fulfilled the law by dying on the cross. What is the end of the law? Death! The law saved no one. All die being under the law; so the fullness of the law brings death.

2 Cor. 3:6 – Lam — *...for the letter of the law punishes with death...*

Was Jesus punished on the cross with death? Yes, of course, we all know this to be true. Then it was the law that placed Him on the cross so that the law was fulfilled by His death on the cross. This was the fulfillment of the law. Who put Jesus on the cross? The Scribes and Pharisees cast their false accusations at Him and made Him stand on trial. They presented their religious laws and then announced judgment against Him so that He would be crucified. The law and the people bound to that law as one condemned Him to the cross. So the law was fulfilled by His death on the cross.

But this time it was the death of an innocent Lamb; so that law could not hold Him at the place of death. The law was not His life, but the life of the Spirit of God was His light. So while in the darkness of the tomb, the light of His life filled that place, even to all those who were in their tombs. That light and life manifest something that had never been seen before, a life separate from the law. What was seen from that place of the grave was the way of the law of commandments that Adam lived by was still hanging on the cross as dead. But the light of a

---

225   1 Cor. 15:28

new life was springing forth from the grave. This one was different! He had not died like all the others before Him. He was free from the law even though He was nailed to the cross by the law.

The light of His life opened the graves of the dead. They were held in their graves by the law that they died with. The law held them in that place of death. But now the graves have been opened by the power of a new resurrection life free from the law. His death freed all who had died by the law. And many bodies of the saints (religiously blameless) who had fallen asleep (died) were raised; and coming out of the graves after His resurrection, they went into the holy city and appeared to many.[226]

Did you notice that the religiously blameless were still in their graves. Their religious observations gained them no power to escape the grave, which is often translated hell, sheol in the Old Testament. The reason hell and the grave are so much the same is that the law had no light and life of the Spirit. Just like in a grave there is no light and no resurrection life to get them out. Until now! Jesus finished the law by bringing it to an end!

Hos 13:14 — *"I will ransom them from the power of the grave; I will redeem them from death. O death, where is your punishment? O grave, where is your sting?*

There is now no need for Jesus to return in order to save, deliver, or make it all better. It was the law that held us all in bondage and His death took care of that. Now we have the power of His resurrection life living in us. The only way it could get any better than that is by making more disciples so more will be free to let the light of His life shine with us.

Jesus' coming back again isn't going to fulfill anymore of the scriptures that are written concerning Him. I know that statement still might throw

---

226   Mat. 27:52, 53

some into a tailspin. Religious teachings had us confused with untruth to begin with. I mean, if you grew up thinking 1+1=3 because your parents told you that, (because they learned it from their parents who heard it from their parents,) wouldn't it be a shock to you to find out that 1+1=2? What had been handed down from generation to generation was wrong. Well, should this present generation go on believing 1+1=3 just because that's what so many generations before them believed? Or should they study for themselves and in finding out the truth that changes their thinking so the next generation is raised up in the truth?

Maybe, just maybe, this church generation today wants only the truth because they have a strong desire to walk in the fullness of Christ. If we don't see our Church walking in it, then it's time to move over 'cause we're movin' on! So when the truth comes, then we are set free from such religion and confusion. There is great rejoicing in knowing the truth! It is when the body of Christ sees and believes that they are already made complete in Him by the blood of Jesus with nothing lacking, that the world can be delivered by them who is His body. Looking for His second coming in His own individual resurrected body can blind the body of Christ to the fact that He has already returned in bodily form by dwelling in you! There is no difference! Christ in you is supposed to be your hope of glory, not a second coming where we are told to look for His individual physical body.

Let's think for a moment. If Jesus was to appear on earth in his individual resurrected body, what would change? Do you really think the entire world will bow their knee because He claims to be the Savior of the world? As far as the world is concerned, I don't think they would treat Him any differently than they did the first time He came. We've already established the fact that He would not rule the earth by force. That is not the nature of God. He is love! So, what would be different? Would all of us 'Christians' run over here or over there just to get a glimpse of Him so we will put our trust in God limited to one flesh body again? Jesus said in

Jn. 16:23 — *"And in that day you will not ask Me nothing. Most assuredly, I say to you, whatever you will ask the Father in My name He will give you.*

So, if He was to return, we're still supposed to ask the Father in His name. Nothing has changed. He said Himself in

Mk. 13:21 — *"Then if anyone says to you, 'Look, here is the Christ!' or, 'Look, He is there!' do not believe it."*

So if He returns as the 'Christ', He told us not to believe it! Why would Jesus tell us such a thing if He was planning on coming back when the world doesn't yet recognize that the Christ dwells in the Church? The whole point of Jesus saying such a thing was so we don't get off into thinking that the Christ is anywhere else but in you!

Jn. 12:34 — *The people answered Him, We have heard from the law that the Christ remains forever;*

They had heard the law correctly from Mic. 4:7. So, answer them! If Jesus the Christ dies as He said He would, then how can the Christ remain forever? The man Jesus is not the limitation of Christ. Christ is the anointing, the presence of God, the Holy Spirit, the life of God, the glory of God, the Spirit of wisdom, knowledge, and understanding, and the list goes on and on. If the people were to think that the Christ is only contained in the man Jesus, then their question was legit, and Jesus could not be the Christ because He was going to die. But Jesus knew the Christ was to also come into a body that His death, burial, and resurrection was about to prepare, a body of believers! Will the return of Jesus get more accomplished in this world than a billion embodiments of Christ that are now presently scattered throughout the world? If they have to touch Him and see His scars personally before they will believe, will they not once again be totally dependent on one Man?

The whole point of Jesus' coming was to restore us in perfect union with the Father. Mission accomplished! Why would anyone want to place their trust in the individual physical Jesus rather than in the life of Christ in them? Is not the life of Christ in you the presence of the Almighty manifest directly to you without any time of separation? That cannot happen if your trust is in an individual physical Jesus returning. Did not Jesus tell Mary to let go (of my physical body) so that I might ascend to the Father. Then I will send the Comforter, the Holy Spirit, the Christ to dwell in you. So, let go Church!

I feel that maybe some of the Church is where John the Baptist was. While in prison, John was wondering if Jesus was the Coming One, meaning the Christ that was to come. So, he sent men to ask Jesus if He was the Christ? Jesus responded with,

> **Mat. 11:4–6 — *"Go and tell John the things which you hear and see: "The blind receive their sight and the lame walk; the lepers are cleansed and the deaf hear; the dead are raised up and the poor have the gospel preached to them. "And blessed is he who is not offended because of Me."***

John questioned if the Christ was really in Jesus. Why? Being in prison, He couldn't see what God, the man Jesus, was doing outside his cell. He was isolated from what God was doing through one man and therefore he began to doubt. It's time for the Church to come out of their cell and see what the Christ in you will do! Is the Christ in you? As long as you remain imprisoned by religion, looking for the Christ to appear in another form or another body, you will remain a doubter that Christ is already here and abiding in fullness in you! The Spirit of Christ is bidding you to come out from among them and be the Christ man that God fully intends for you to be. Sometimes you just have to come out from among the religious so you can see the real Christ that abides in you. No, you will never be Jesus the Christ, but you already are hidden in Him as one of the same! Know who you are and stop looking at your flesh, thus denying the Christ in you. Clothe yourself with the incorruptible and with immortality, put on Christ, put on the new man! This is the equipping of the saints to do the work of the ministry.

As far as the believers are concerned, Jesus has already come again to take up residence in them, and they are that body of Christ manifest in the earth. This is not saying that He will not come again or appear again. To those who have not yet believed, He has not yet came once let alone again. But He will come to them again the very moment they are awakened out of sleep.

We should always look for His coming to us individually and through His body now in the earth. Why look and wait for an event in time with others declaring He is over there or over here when you already have the most important event that has ever happened to you in His coming and appearing in you? Why put your hope in an individual to appear to you in flesh as the Lord apart from His body called the Church and the Bride, when He has already appeared to you and you already believe? "Blessed are those who have not seen and yet believe."[227] Why do you want to see? Do you not believe?

Again, didn't Jesus warn us not to look for the Christ when people say that the Christ is over there or over here? Don't believe it when they say such things because it causes us to look elsewhere when He dwells in you. If that were our hope, He would have told us so. And if that is your hope, then your hope is in the wrong place. Christ in you is **your** hope of glory,[228] not His appearing in flesh apart from His body that now dwells on earth as His body. The Bride is the Christ that is in the earth today.

---

227   Jn. 20:29
228   Col. 1:27

The Church is becoming His Bride when they mature from such things. In that marriage, they are become one. I guess that would make the Bride one with Christ, as Jesus is one with the Father and the Holy Spirit, so is the Bride. Does that offend you? It won't if you see one another the same way God sees us. And He sees us through the finished work of Jesus Christ, perfect and fully supplied lacking nothing. In this case, we ought to greet one another with a holy kiss! It's Christ we see walking towards us, not some lower class being of flesh only. If the Bridegroom has come in you, then the Bride is here with Him and they are behind a closed door. That is Christ in you and your spirit is seeing Him face to face. They are one. You and Christ are one!

> **Acts 1:9–11 — *Now when He had spoken these things, while they watched, He was taken up; and a cloud received Him out of their sight. And while they looked steadfastly toward heaven as He went up, behold, two men stood by them in white apparel, who also said, "Men of Galilee, why do you stand gazing up into heaven: This same Jesus, who was taken up from you into heaven, will so come in like manner as you saw Him go into heaven."***

Most of us have been told that Jesus will come down out of heaven some day when He returns. Nobody has seen it yet, but that is our hope we are told. I'd say that's a pretty bleak hope if billions of people have come and gone hoping for it, and it didn't happen. How disheartening to think that God disappointed so many people. And now, we the living are still hoping for that same event. Odds are it ain't gonna happen in your lifetime either. "See, you're trying to destroy my hope, Randy!" No, I want to declare to you a more sure hope. The hope that comes from Christ already being in you.

This scripture doesn't say that the same way that Jesus ascended into heaven He will descend from heaven again someday as we have probably heard it said. It plainly says that He will in like manner or the same way that He ascended into heaven by going into a cloud He will come to you in the same way. The same way is ascending into a cloud, not descending out of heaven and directly to earth, nor does it say that He will descend into a cloud from heaven. The next time we see Him, He'll be ascending into a cloud it says.

The angels, two being the witness of two or more, spoke by the Spirit of God and were speaking spiritual words. Christ did not fall on any of us. He arose on the inside of us when we were born again or awakened to His presence. We saw him for the first time when we saw Him ascend into a cloud, which is always in reference to a witness. We are clouds with water and when we speak by the Holy Spirit; that is Christ ascending into that cloud. It was when someone spoke to us the things of God that Christ ascended into that cloud that rained His presence on us as he spoke. We didn't know it, but Jesus came to us in the same manner of ascension. He rose up in you and made you a rain cloud. You are a witness filled with His life-giving Spirit. Before you believed, you were a cloud without water, a witness without the life of God. But now you are full of living water! We are much more in oneness than we may have ever imagined!

You have the risen Christ dwelling in you. You are the cloud from heaven every time you speak and do by the Spirit of Christ in you! If we truly do as the Bible tells us to do and not look at anyone after the flesh, what else can be seen? Nothing but Christ in you! So, Jesus is not ever descending anymore. He already did that once and for all when He came as the Lamb. He is only ascending into the body that the Father has given Him, which is you and me! Don't miss the real for some future event! Look at the body of Christ, and see Him plainly, see Him face to face. Yes, you have to look past the flesh, but they are and you are the resurrected body of Jesus Christ now in the earth!

1 Cor. 11:29–31 — *For he who eats and drinks in an unworthy manner eats and drinks judgment to himself, not discerning the Lord's body. For this reason many are weak and sick among you, and many sleep. For if we would judge ourselves, we would not be judged.*

The reason so much of the Church is so weak and sickly and dying too early is because we are not discerning the Lord's body correctly. The Lord's body includes all the believers. He is the head and we are His body of believers. To discern means to separate thoroughly and to withdraw from. We must separate thoroughly that the body of Christ is nothing like the body of Adam that is in the world. We must see each other as Christ being in a flesh body. The fullness of Christ dwells in each and every one of us. We must withdraw from that body the Christ in us all. There is life, and power, and glory, and love that abounds without end in every believer. I know that takes a lot of faith to see all that in some people. If you knew me after the flesh too, you would say the same thing. But nevertheless, it is the truth! To give that kind of respect and honor to one another honors God. *The least you have done unto one of these little ones, you have done unto Me.*[229]

Judging one another after the flesh is a judgment of the law. If we see one another according to the flesh, we are under the law. If we compare ourselves with one another, we are unwise,[230] because that becomes our rule for setting our standard of life. That's the way of Adam again. The law is passing away so we cannot judge ourselves or others that way no longer since we see Adam with that law conscious life style as crucified. But it is up to us to reckon that old man of sin under the law as dead. No one can do it for you. We can only remind you of his death and keep pointing you to His resurrection life.

---

229   Mat. 25:40
230   2 Cor. 10:12

Maybe we should judge ourselves according to His righteousness which is by grace. In this case, there is no more judgment of the law that can come to us. As long as we judge ourselves according to the law, more judgment will come, and come, and keep coming until we see that the man of the law was crucified when Jesus was crucified. That law doesn't just give us a wrong lower state of mind, it's a package deal. Even if you are born again you get all of what is behind tomb number one because you have chosen to live according to the old man Adam that was crucified! You get your old judgmental attitude of sinful Adam with his self-condemnation; you get guilt back; you get sickness and an earlier death as stated in this scripture; you get a wrong or evil spirit that speaks lies and deception; you get strife and bitterness all around you and everything else that is supposed to be left in the tomb of Adam.

But seeing the life of the law as passed away with dead Adam and now seeing the newness of life in Christ leaves us with only having His righteous judgment for ourselves and others. That judgment declares us as His children and heirs to the promises! We are His body and His Bride! We are one with Christ! As He is, so are we! We have just chosen what is behind curtain number one. That curtain of the law has been ripped into and now removed by the resurrection of Christ in you! What was behind the curtain is the glory of God and all that He is, and all that He has is yours! We now have the freedom to judge ourselves and others according to that righteousness we see in Him. Here in lies the truth for the Church to be relieved of all its weakness, sickness, and premature death. At least, that's what the word of God says,[231] not I.

When my Pastor and I went to Ghana, Africa to preach where the gospel had never in that generation been preached, the people surprised us with their words and actions. Brothers went before us into the mountain villages and hang posters all over the villages that we were planning to go to. Most of the people, if not all, had never seen a white person. But what they saw in their mind's eye and in their hearts

---

231   2 Pet. 1–4, 1 Pet. 2:22–24, Mat. 8:17, 2 Cor. 8:9, Psa. 91

more than color was that men of God were coming to them to declare the works of God!

When we first arrived in a car (they had none), children were playing outside of the small concrete block school building. They were saying something in their language, and we asked the missionary, that was actually born there but had not yet preached there, what are they saying? He said the children were saying, "White man, white man." They were all excited and laughing. But when we got out of the car and was walking around the square where there is buying and selling, the people were saying something else very softly. The missionary said they were saying, "The man of God!" "The man of God!" That has a tendency to change the way you see yourself when others declare you are a man of God. This is how they saw us and because they saw us that away, they listened to us as though we were men sent to them by God that had the words eternal life.

They heard the word of God about what Jesus had done for them and then many were healed. We saw more instant healings in one meeting than we had seen in our whole life combined. Some couldn't even wait for after the man of God to stop preaching and were healed while the word was still being declared to them. They were coming forward and telling us what was wrong with them before Jesus touched them. Then they proved they were healed by showing us or doing what they were unable to do before.

But why there and not so much in America was my question? They saw us not as one from their own hometown (village), but as men of God. They saw us not by the color of our skin, but by the Spirit in which we were sent. These people knew about spiritual things that they were real because their witch doctors were the only doctors they had. So, what they mostly knew about spiritual things was of Satan. A few were demon possessed because of it, one totally. So they knew about the spirit of darkness and were aware of spiritual things. Our presence upset those witch doctors and the atmosphere in those villages that were under the dominion of darkness. One village chief told us we were upsetting the spirits. They had grown fond of these spirits because that is all they had known, until now!

There were drums from other villages going all night long trying to drive us out. There were demonic manifestations in the night that brought great fear into the villagers while we were sleeping. But every person, except for one or two witch doctors who hid behind the bushes, came out with great anticipation and excitement to hear the word of God from the men of God. Jesus was honored and He in turn honored them by saving them all and healing them. The villagers honored us because they saw past our flesh and in doing so they honored the One in us, Christ. Even some of those witch doctors came out from where they were hiding and were saved.

Only when we see that Jesus finished everything that He came to do, then can we begin to see ourselves as the product of His finished work from the inside out. We cannot judge ourselves or compare ourselves with one another, that is only comparing flesh with flesh. Neither can we judge ourselves by our failures, or sin, or even our successes. Jesus has already finished our past, present and future failures and sins by taking them all upon Himself. And our successes cannot be the determining factors of judging whether the fullness of Christ dwells in us or not. That would still leave us judging ourselves by self-appointed laws that cause us to see ourselves from a lower valley of death view and place a limit on the Christ within. For we can do nothing great or small with a lasting impression except Christ alone manifesting Himself from within us.

The heavenly view will carry away all that sells you short of the glory of God. Jesus carried them all away. Now the only thing that remains is the Christ man! All and nothing but all that is of Adam is gone by Jesus' death and burial. The old has passed away, and according to His resurrection the new that has now come is perfect. The new is the resurrected Christ in your inward man. The old heaven and the old earth that you were have been rolled up in the scroll of Jesus' death.[232]

232   Rev. 6:14

The realization of it to you appears in His burial as you see Adam dead and buried. That's the old being burned up with the fire of His presence that teaches us about our new identity. The new heaven and new earth is found in His resurrection life that dwells in you if you are born of His Spirit. We just have to only discover that pearl of great price that is hidden in the field that you are. That's all that is left to do because Jesus finished it all! Discover the Christ (ian) that you are and see yourself as one with Him. As you see yourself as His finished work in earth, you are seeing from heaven!

Chapter 3

GOD'S JUDGMENT AND WRATH

It is finished includes an end to all, all, totally all of God's wrath and judgment of sin.

Jn. 12:32 — *"And I, if I am lifted up from the earth, will draw all to Myself."*

The missing word here in some translations is italicized, which means it was added for our misunderstanding. So I left it out for that reason. Now we have to know the subject that is being spoken of in the previous verses to fill in the blank. Then we will get the true meaning of what will be drawn to Jesus on the cross.

Jn. 12:31 — *"Now is the judgment of this world; now the ruler of this world will be cast out."*

Judgment! Jesus as the brazen serpent on the cross drew to Himself all the judgment of the sins of this world; past, present and future. The judgment of the sins of Israel was poisonous serpents because the words from their mouths came from an evil, poisonous, and deceptive heart and mind that infected those around them. As a people under the law, an eye for an eye and a tooth for a tooth was their judgment. Once bitten by a poisonous serpent, they would die a painful death. But if they looked upon the brazen serpent (their just judgment) on the pole set on the hill, then they would live. So the judgment of their sins was taken away by the brazen serpent on the cross, then they were free from the poison in their body as well.

Jesus was saying the same thing here. "And I, if I am lifted up from the earth, will draw all judgment to Myself." If all judgment is drawn to Jesus on the cross, how much remains? Even if some hard hearted stubborn Israelites that were bitten didn't look at the serpent on the cross, their judgment was still placed on the serpent on the cross. But they couldn't be saved from death until they looked and saw. Their forgiveness and the end of their judgment were still presently provided for them. They were forgiven, but they didn't see it. They were healed, but they couldn't believe it because they couldn't see their own judgment as being taken away.

The law works that way. Our own conscience condemns us in our heart and soul. Then our body begins to take on that form of image that reigns over it. Condemnation is the judgment that brings a person down, sometimes to their death. It produces in us a mode of self-destruct. Having the law as one's god is bound to produce condemnation, guilt, and judgment. Now isn't it good to know that your judgment and the judgment of this world was placed on Jesus!

Seeing Jesus hung on a tree is seeing the sins and the judgment for those sins of the whole world placed on Jesus. How much judgment then still remains for the whole world? None. If there is one ounce of judgment left in God our Father towards the world, then Jesus must come back again and be crucified all over again.

Most of the world is still snake bit because of the words of their mouths and are dying. They just have not seen yet what Jesus has done to the law and their judgment; therefore, they condemn themselves and reap the judgment of the same from that law that we were all trained by in this world. God does not condemn them. He took their condemnation upon Himself. He sees them as forgiven. But they remain snake bit and deceived until the word of reconciliation comes to them. We are His ambassadors sent into the world to reveal the works of Jesus Christ on the cross.

Going one step further with this scripture in Jn. 12:32, just leave the word 'men' that's in italics out, and do not go to the previous scripture and understand in its fullness. "And I, if I am lifted up from the earth, will draw all to Myself." All what? Just all! Only all, that's all. Jesus will draw all that has come under the curse to Himself and bring it to an end. Thus making a new heaven and a new earth wherein righteousness dwells. The cross is an end to all that is cursed, and the resurrection is the beginning of all receiving newness of life. Jesus not only redeemed all mankind from the curse, but also all that was placed under man's authority at that time that Adam had dragged in under the curse. All the earth and its natural heaven or dwelling place has been redeemed from the curse. But until the sons of God (us) are manifest in our place of influence or dwelling place, the earth will remain in its present state of deception, darkness, and being under the curse of the law, even though Jesus finished that work.

The Israelite that didn't look at the serpent on the cross remained in darkness and died, not experiencing the glory of the cross. But the ones who looked and saw received the mercy of God and lived. They were changed spiritually, mentally, and physically by what they saw. We cannot help but speak what we have seen and heard. Do we see all men as well as all things drawn unto Him when He died as Adam (us) on the cross, or only a few things selected by our own opinions?

Jesus' hanging on the cross doesn't draw natural men unto Him. The word draw actually means to drag or to take for oneself. The first Adam dragged the whole world in under the curse and we had no choice about it. Could it be that the last Adam, Jesus, drug it all back out from under the curse? Jesus didn't ask us first and then invite us to join Him on the cross. You would get about as good a response as when Jesus said, "Except you eat the flesh of the Son of man, and drink his blood, you have no life in you." Naturally you are not going to get a very good response. And hanging on a cross really isn't exactly anyone's lifelong dream. So Jesus <u>dragged</u> all our sins with all its judgment and wrath to the cross in our place as Adam. All of God's wrath against the world of sin past, present, and future was laid on Jesus. The Father took it all out on His own Son, so that love is the only thing left reserved for the whole world. Do we have good news to tell the world or what?

Jesus expressed the Father as having already redeemed all things, all people, and even all the elements of the earth. All was subject to Him, and all was redeemed. The fruit of His life proved it! If only a select chosen few were redeemed, then only a few could have been healed. But Jesus healed them all! If only a select few things were redeemed, then He would not have been able to still the storm, calm the sea, multiply the bread, nor raise the dead. No, Jesus drew it all to Himself and put an end to the ruler of this world. That ruler of this world has already been cast out!

Who is the ruler of this world that has been cast out? Satan (devil) the accuser rules this world. So, how does he rule? By the law. Have you noticed that everything in this world around us is run by laws or rules? If the accuser has been cast out, then why do some still talk as though he has not been cast out? Because they do not yet see the law as nailed on the cross. The law was nailed to the cross and the judgments of the law that accuses are one. The law, the accuser, and judgment work together. You can't have one without the other. Glory to God for the end of those things in our lives!

Didn't most of us allow the devil (deceiver and accuser) to reign through us before we believed? We all did. It is the deception that keeps the body of Christ from reigning on the earth right now. So if the deceiver has been cast out, then why is it so hard for us to believe that we can live our life as one reigning with Jesus on the earth right now? Maybe it is because we were taught that that time of reigning will come in some mysterious time in the future. So the deceiver is still in the earth? Only if the Church is not founded on the Rock of knowing who Jesus Christ is and what He finished. The law deceived us and it was hung on the cross. It is by looking at the natural things of this world instead of what Jesus accomplished on the cross that we draw the wrong conclusion and therefore act like we are still under the curse and are without His authority. The true Church is only built on revelation knowledge of who Jesus Christ is and what He came to accomplish and that He did finish His work that He came to do.

"Now the ruler of this world <u>will be</u> cast out." 'Now' is the time of Jesus' crucifixion. It was at that time that Adam under the law as well as the law itself that deceived us was hung on the cross and they died; they came to their end. 'Will be' is the time that the Church wakes up to what He had accomplished by His death, burial, and resurrection. We didn't have much of a problem experiencing the devil's (deception's) reign in the here and now before we were born again. In fact, we were so deceived that we didn't even know it. But as a believer some have been told we can only reign with Him sometime in the future when we come back to earth with Him. And then in another sermon we were told to do the works of Jesus now! "Okay, now I'm confused." We all have a tendency to bring our deception on into the life of the Church with us.

But truly, the only way to do the works of Jesus is to live and reign with Him now and He made that easily available for us to do. We can and will, knowing that all of the judgment of this world has been drawn to Him on the cross. The Lamb and the King is present in us and His work has been finished. That finished work paved the way for the Church to reign from that Cornerstone position in the earth. Just like Jesus did, we are to cast out evil deceptive dominating spirits, heal the sick, open the eyes of the blind, make the lame to walk, and raise the dead from His position of having already accomplished everything that might have hindered us from reigning as kings. So let us speak of better things than earthquakes, tornadoes, hurricanes, sickness, cancer, lack, depression and other natural conditions of the fallen state of this world, knowing that all those things have been drawn to the cross. It's ALL been redeemed by the blood of the Lamb. It is finished!

If it has all been redeemed on the cross, then why are there more earthquakes, tornadoes, hurricanes, sickness and destruction in this world? If all were in agreement with the truth of Jesus Christ then there would not be any! Jesus put an end to all those things everywhere He went. Come on Church, we are the body of Christ in the earth today!

Every man, woman, and child caries authority given to them by God to have dominion over their earth. But while under the law and its deception, we had actually gave our authority to that law and its condemnation with judgment that also came with the law. That is why the people in this world still speak things that declare judgment and things concerning the curse. The world is still deceived because they have not the knowledge of Jesus Christ. So when news of these fallen things come, the people believe the evil report and speak those things rather than the good report of Jesus' finished work. They speak the same thing as the news directs them to. The news only reports natural unchanged things, not things pertaining to faith in Jesus Christ. So when they agree with the judgment of the law that has come upon them, they have just given authority for such things to happen to them and their earth. What a tragedy! And the only way it could have been avoided is by the Church speaking from the place of the Chief Cornerstone that gives them heaven's view of much better things then those. Yes, the Church that has Jesus Christ as their head is out numbered. So let's make more disciples. But changing your world doesn't take a majority vote, it just takes one Christ centered filled man.

When God told Adam and Eve to rule the earth, He meant it! So how are you going to rule your earth? Speak the truth as though you know it has been redeemed by the blood of Jesus; and you will reign with

Him over it. That doesn't mean you have to know scriptures to do that, unless your mind is trying to deceive you. You just need to know the person of the Cornerstone and who you are. But you cannot rule another one's earth against their will. Therefore, we will continue to have these things until the sons of God manifest such a truth to the world.

What if? What if the news informed the people that a hurricane is going to hit the coast. But the people only knew (identified themselves with) the good news of the life of Christ and His finished works. The people would then speak the same thing that they know to be the truth rather than the evil news report. Knowing Him, they would in turn speak to the hurricane and command it to be still. I completely, assuredly, and absolutely know that I know, that the hurricane would diminish and be no more, just like Jesus did by speaking to the storm. It would obey the people because people have been given dominion over the earth by God, their Creator. What if?

This is not something you try to do. This is something that you do because you know Him and are fully convinced that the awesome price of the Son of God hanging on the cross fully brought an end to all the judgment of the law that was against us.

> **Col. 2:14, 15 — ...*having wiped out the handwriting of requirements that was against us, which was contrary to us. And He has taken it out of the way, having nailed it to the cross. Having disarmed principalities and powers, He made a public spectacle of them, triumphing over them in it.***

I remember when we moved to Topeka, KS on the top of Burnett's Mound. That is where a devastating tornado came through and ripped a half mile path through Topeka on June 8, 1966. When I told people where we had moved, some responded with, "Oh, tornado alley." So I asked the Lord why He had moved us to that exact location. He said, "I put you there because I want to protect the people in the city." Part of the word sozo (save, salvation) means protection. This was not anything I could boost about, but He let me know that with the knowledge of Him also comes the opportunity to walk it out. The Lord knew that if any bad storm came our way, I would speak to it from the place of being hidden in Him (Jesus name) and send it packing. When we heard of storms coming with possible tornados, we responded with "It is written." We lived there thirteen years in safety.

This is an example of a small part of making a spectacle of the rulers and powers of the law and its judgment. Jesus didn't allow the judgment of the law that was against the world to destroy the world where He was. Instead of preaching and living a life of bringing judgment, which in turn brings destruction to the world, He caused the rain to fall on the just and the unjust. He went around doing good to all, which declared all are saved with the Lamb being present. None can be saved if the Lamb is not present. Is the Lamb presently dwelling in you?

Rom. 5:12–21; Vs. 19 — *Just as through one man's act of disobedience many sinned, so through one man's obedience many* (will be) *made righteous.*

In the Greek 'will be' is not there. It should be read, so through one man's obedience many made righteous. Not will be, but are made righteous already by that One, Jesus Christ. When we truly believe this as Christ so declared it by His life and action, then we will never again read about the wrath of God to come as though it is reserved for us or for anyone else. The entire wrath of God was poured out on Jesus because He was the sacrifice for the sins of not just believers, or "Christians", or church goers, but for the sins of the whole world.

So when the Bible speaks of the wrath of God being stored up because of those who have resisted the truth, it is because they continue in their sins that wrath is being stored up. Where is the wrath of God being stored up? In their own consciousness of condemnation because they are conscious of their own sin! **God isn't keeping record of it**, but that person is and they are <u>self</u>-condemned. This is how they bring judgment upon themselves. Jesus said, "But he who does not believe is condemned already."[233] The Lamb of God said this and just before He said that, He said, "For God did not send His Son into the world to condemn the world."[234] If God isn't condemning them, then who is? They are self-condemned by their own conscience, which is why the blood of Jesus is necessary for the cleansing of our sin conscience. They were bringing their own condemnation and judgment upon themselves because they were still under the law by not believing in Jesus Christ. Again, God is not judging them! At least that's what Jesus said.

But when they finally do see in this life or in the life to come that Jesus has already taken their sin and the full wrath of God was laid upon Himself through Jesus, they too will be free! Praise God! That is the truth as seen from heaven within the scriptures sent to us from heaven.

God knows He already took care of the sins of the whole world by laying it all on Jesus. But if that person doesn't know that, then they store it up for themselves in their own conscience the measure of judgment they deserve according to the law and the guilt that testifies against them. Which is why some still preach hell and damnation because they themselves still have a sin conscience always reminding others and themselves of the law of commandments. What a waste! Storing up all that wrath of God for however long; suffering guilt, condemnation, depression, and sickness as a natural part of this life under the curse when it's all been taken care of on the cross.

Rom. 15:20 — *And so I have made it my aim to preach the gospel, not where Christ was named, lest I should build on another man's foundation...*

233 Jn. 3:18
234 Jn. 3:17

Why didn't Paul want to preach where other's had preached? Did he have an attitude problem or what was his real reason? The words 'another man's' comes from the Greek words meaning different, not akin, hostile, and strange. Paul had a pure gospel that did not mix the law with the grace of God that came through Jesus Christ. Many others, especially the Jewish believers, were mixing the gospel of Jesus Christ with some of their laws, much like of what is being preached today. The true gospel cannot be laid as a foundation upon the law and neither can it be mixed. The law is the voice of a stranger. It is a different and hostile message that is not akin to Jesus Christ. How is it hostile? The law is the handwriting of requirements that speaks against us because we are unable to do all that is written in those handwritings. Because we are unable to do them completely without fault, they in turn speak condemnation, guilt, and judgment.

The natural fallen condition of this life can be replaced with the much higher zoe (life of God). On the cross, laid on Jesus was the sins of the whole world and the just judgment and wrath of God were its penalty paid in full! So how much judgment and wrath still remains for anyone? Zero, praise God! If it wasn't all placed on Jesus on the cross more than 2,000 years ago, then He will need to come back again to suffer death again for us and finish what He only started. But he did finish it, and He said He did. Then we must account it as finished in our thinking as well. Knowing this and being convinced of it, we have come to the place where we no longer have any condemnation towards anyone, not ourselves and not even those who have hurt us. We are free!

Mat. 21:44 — *And whosoever shall fall on this stone shall be broken: but on whomsoever it shall fall, it will grind him to powder.*

The one on whom the stone or law of judgment falls, it will grind him to powder. He is left worn out and with no life left having tried all his life to live by a code of ethics, or morals, or laws. With great sadness, many have lived their whole life this way and at the end of their life, they were all worn out by trying to do right and please God through observances of the law and reaping only condemnation. Wrong god! Their testimony before they leave is, "I'm tired, and I just want to go home." No condemnation, but as a believer it should be said, "I've ran my course. I've finished my race and now I'm ready to depart and go home to my Lord."

It's sad that believers get so worn out that they want to go home early. Why? It might be that they have been laboring all this time by the sweat of their brow because they are still under the law. Being busy about doing the law will just leave you all worn out. Being busy because you think the time is short and you have got to get certain things done can easily turn into a work of the flesh. God has all time and He knows the time you have and He desires that above all the things that you do for Him that you do them as Him.

Unbelievers have worked with condemnation trying to make amends for their failures and wrong doings, and it never satisfied by fully removing that guilt and condemnation. They may have labored endlessly in an effort to produce many good works and yet missed the greatest work of all, rest. To enter into the labors of the Lord is to rest while you work.

The one who falls on this stone is the one who admits he has failed and cannot keep the law. This represents the death of the works of Adam and that is good news! That one is looking for the mercy of God and salvation supplied by the grace of God. We have seen Him wounded for our sins and bruised for our punishment.[235] All His beatings, bruises, torn flesh, sicknesses, diseases, infirmities was the wrath of God against our sins that was reserved for Adam, all humanity. There now remains no more judgment for sins which is why it is Jesus the Lamb of God that is seated on the judgment seat of the Great White Throne and

235   Isa. 53:5

not the devil. So the devil cannot accuse someone for an eternity of condemnation! Praise God for the time we all stand before the Great White Throne seat of our judgment that was laid on Him, so that He declares as finished all the judgment that was against us.

It is sorrowful that some will never experience that payment of forgiveness now in this life, which is the reason for our preaching the good news today. If there still remains a thought or belief that takes away from this part of His finished work, it is heresy. When it is taught, it brings disunion. The teaching of the law, even if it only has a small portion of the law in that teaching, is heresy. A little leaven leavens the whole lump.[236]

If there is an ounce of consciousness that believes God still might have some judgment left for you, you cannot get as close to Him as He would like you to be. How close does God want us? As One! You just can't get any closer than that. But fear of judgment that is not really there will keep you at a distance. Fear of that judgment will keep the world away from such an angry god. We then fear something that does not exist because the blood of Jesus actually washed it all away. And the blood of Jesus still speaks of the forgiveness of God for all mankind.

A lie is not real, but it has the power of deception to hold those in bondage who believe it. Only the truth of God's word has the power to set us free, and that word of truth lasts forever. We have an everlasting word and a finished work that ended all judgment against us. Therefore, there is no reason to ever be afraid of our Father. Love and compassion is all that He has left for us and the world, as expressed through Jesus Christ.

Yes, God hates sin, but only because it had separated us from Him. But He has already taken care of all that sin business on the cross, and that is what God sees. He sees it as finished! And we have been given the ministry of reconciliation so that we might declare that all sin and the judgment of it as ended on the cross. What good news we have for

---

236   1 Cor. 5:6

all! The wrath and judgment of God was finished at the cross. Only love, peace, joy, health, protection, provision, and all manner of having a blessed life is all that remains as God's expression towards you.

> **Php. 2:9–11 — *Therefore God also has highly exalted Him and given Him the name which is above every name, that at the name of Jesus every knee bow, of those in heaven, and of those on earth, and of those under the earth, and every tongue confess that Jesus Christ is Lord, to the glory of God the Father.***

I supposed you noticed that the word 'should' was left out twice. That's because it is not in the original Greek scriptures. The word 'should' was once again added according to man's understanding at that time. The word 'should' leaves us with the impression that some should but won't or should but can't. It also might leave us with the impression that we should as though it is demanded by law. God didn't use the word 'should', but simply stated that Jesus has been given the highest name, and when all recognize what all He has done for them, then every knee bows and every tongue confesses Jesus as Lord. Pretty simple isn't it. It's just a spontaneous reaction that God will get every time, every time, every time someone's eyes are opened to what Jesus has done for them.

When the overwhelming love and goodness of God is revealed to them, how could they not freely with thanksgiving bow? God will never force the bowing of one's knee. He just isn't into breaking someone's knee. He doesn't have to use such a worldly lowly method for all to bow their knee. God is most awesomely good, and loving, and full of mercy, and when all see Him in that light, then all will gladly in a manner of worship bow their knee and confess Him as Lord. If something is too good to be true, but it is the truth; that would be God. Who can resist the goodness of God forever?

God hears the cries of the people that are hurting and being oppressed. He knows the world is not yet living in the fullness provided for them and He condemns not; because He sees from an everlasting point of view and not a temporal one. The work that was accomplished in Jesus' death, burial, and resurrection is an eternal work that will speak throughout all ages, world without end. And He looks from His dwelling place, heaven, and from the finished work and sees beyond what is in the natural fallen temporal condition. He therefore, keeps sending forth His word to heal and change that condition. Bad things that happen in the world are temporal, and God sees greater things than those and is more than able to change it as He works with His body in the earth.

Looking at the problem never brings the answer. The answer is seeing through the eyes of our Father. If we see as He sees, we have His faith to change things. Seeing that all past, present, and future judgment and wrath has been poured out on Jesus Christ is seeing from heaven's view. It's God's view of the world and if the world could only see as He sees, it too would be totally changed. So if the Church would first see the world this way, then the world would have the light to see it too. Now is the time for us all to see from heaven and change our world!

Chapter 4

REDEMPTION IS A FINISHED WORK

Redemption is a finished work.[237] To redeem is to purchase back with a ransom paid for something that once was owned by another.

1 Jn. 2:2 — And He Himself is the propitiation for our sins, and not for ours only but also for the whole world.

We are of God and came from Him as His child in His image. The created part of us is the man faced part. This includes our soul as well. But the spirit of man is of God and was breathed into man and not created. That spirit part of you always was, is, and shall be. The greatest image of God that we have of Himself is that which dwells in us, our spirit. It is the breath of God in you. And it is that same breath that holds all things together.[238] And it is that same breath in you that gives you the life-giving power to hold your world together! When you speak by the breath of God in you, you are imitating your Father and Creator!

---

237   Neh. 1:10, Ps. 31:7, Isa. 43:1, 44:22, Mic. 6:4, Gal. 3:13, Rev. 5:9
238   Heb. 1:3, Col. 1:17

It was through the created part of man that the devil (message of deception) deceived us, and as a result of the fall, that deception or lie became our father that trained us in this world. Now, before we came to Christ, the truth is not in our natural human knowledge and understanding. The knowledge of good and evil ruled over us having only the knowledge of it. Our thoughts and actions were based on weighing out all our options on the knowledge of good and evil that we had at that time, rather than having oneness with God and being led by the Holy Spirit. This is the separation caused by human reasoning based on the deception of the tree of the knowledge of good and evil. Even as a believer, if we reason to do this or that only based on the knowledge of good and evil without sensitivity to or awareness of the leading of God's presence, we fall under the same deception and alienate ourselves as though we are a separate individual from Christ. We are eating from the wrong tree![239]

But Jesus came from the will of our Creator God and paid the fullness of price to purchase us back from this life of deception. Adam in the beginning was without sin in the perfect image of God that God created him to be. Only one of equal or greater value could purchase us back and place us back into our original image of God. Seeing how Adam and all his descendants were in a fallen condition, they could not redeem themselves. But Jesus, the man without sin, could and did just that!

He was the second Adam without sin, and yet He also was the last Adam having taken our sin upon Himself on the cross. He is truly the first and the last.[240] The first Adam of sin became the last Adam to hang on the cross. The last man (Adam) without sin became the first of all those who believe. Now all of those who are the last to believe are become like the first, which is Christ.

If He was the last Adam, then where did Adam go? He exists no more, except in the realm of the darkness of the deception because of the

---

239   Eph. 4:18, Col. 1:21
240   Rev. 1:11,

lack of knowledge of what Jesus has done. In other words, Adam exists only in the unrenewed deceived mind that only equates its knowledge and understanding from this natural fallen earthly condition without the knowledge of God. This perception is the <u>image</u> of the beast. The beast is fleshly Adam living in darkness and speaking out of that darkness.[241]

But in truth, all mankind has been redeemed by the blood of the spotless Lamb of God. God supplied the sacrifice for the offering of **all** sin. It's a done deal, but the whole world has not yet freely received their inheritance because not all yet have believed. That is why the world still lives in destruction, but that is also why anyone in the world can be healed; for all have been reconciled through the redemptive blood of Jesus Christ.[242] Therefore all can freely partake of all that has been purchased for them at any time.

All of heaven is available to all because the redemptive purchase has been paid in full for all. But not all are saved from this false image and way of death life. If you believe in your heart the Lord Jesus Christ and confess with your mouth, you will be saved. This is not just a scripture to get people born again. This is the life of the believer speaking His fullness of redemption so that they may freely receive their inheritance. That is why Jews and Gentiles were healed when Jesus walked the earth. Only those who did not come to Him for healing, because they did not believe, were not healed. Ongoing salvation is far more than just healing. It is a life of experiencing God first hand! It is a coming out of the darkness of this world and coming into His glorious light and life. It is the death of Adam and the life of Christ experienced on an individual basis that establishes that one in perfect union with His Creator and Father. Therefore, you must believe on Jesus before you can be saved experientially. But from heaven's view, it is already finished and all are saved because all are redeemed.

---

241   Rev. 13:14–15, 15:2, 19:20
242   Hos. 7:13

Once again, no one can experience their salvation intimately or the fullness of it unless they be converted in their thinking and believe on the Lord Jesus. And that is not up to us to determine if someone believes or not. Taking on the form of our religion is what most of us look for to determine if someone believes or not. But see from God's perspective and approach someone as though they have already been redeemed and offer them the blessings of their inheritance that was purchased for them. If they refuse, then go your way. But if they freely receive, then they have just had a God encounter!

What are we redeemed and saved from? The curse that Adam was living under by only eating of the tree of the knowledge of good and evil! Redeemed from what used to be our father the devil (deception)! Redeemed from the fear of death so much so that even if we die, yet shall we live! We are redeemed from a life separate from God.

What are we redeemed and saved to? The eternal life, blessings, power, and liberty of being in Christ! Redeemed unto God! Our dwelling place of the five physical senses are no more than just an earthy experience; for our citizenship is in heaven. We were saved to live in the secret or hidden place of the presence of Almighty God while yet living on the earth! The salvation has already been supplied through the purchased price paid in full. But believing is yet necessary to bringing one into the an on-going experience.

Because the whole world has been redeemed by the blood of the Lamb of God, we are instructed to look at no man after the flesh.[243] No man includes sinners. Seeing the faults of one another is seeing each other without the application of the redemptive blood. If we, the Church, cannot see that a sinner has been redeemed before he receives Christ, how can we expect him to see it so he will? If we see all redeemed by the blood, then who can we disqualify to receive healing and all His benefits? Let's not be like the Scribes and the Pharisees. Whom did Jesus disqualify from being healed? He healed them all!

---

243   Jn. 8:15, 2 Cor. 5:16, Rom. 8:5

The Old Testament even recognizes that God has already redeemed our life from destruction and this was long before Jesus came.

Psa. 103:3 – *Who forgives all your iniquities, who heals all your diseases, who redeems your life from destruction;*

Before the foundation of the world was laid, God had already planned on sending His Son to pay our redemptive price. And when God plans something based on His own faithfulness, it is already done as far as God is concerned. We just need to agree with Him so we can walk in it. David saw grace in the eyes of God and wrote by the Holy Spirit as already seeing this work as finished, even before Christ had come. How much easier should it be to see the finished work, when we are looking back and seeing it? Naturally speaking, hind-sight is better than fore-sight. But when seeing God, there is no difference.

Enoch, whose name means 'one who knows the secrets', saw the secrets of God's plan of salvation and was no more, for God took him. Enoch learned that the secret of salvation was coming through the Lamb of God as the payment of our sins. As He walked with God, he saw the Lamb of God in the heart of God. This was the blood sacrifice that God looks for when any man attempts to approach Him or walk with Him. How can two walk together unless they agree?[244] That can only happen if you know the secret of God redeeming all mankind by His own blood. Then we can begin to realize that it is Christ in us, the hope of glory that brings into agreement or oneness. Enoch was awakened out of sleep. We all used to sleepwalk or walk in darkness without the light or awareness of God's presence. So walking with God is no more than walking with full awareness of the indwelling presence of Christ in you.

Every miracle in the Old Testament happened because the types and shadows reminded God of the real, which is Jesus Christ. Just as we

---

244   Amos 3:3

look back to see His redemption and are reconciled, they looked forward to the same redemption through types and shadows. The law demanded our own sacrifices, but it lacked the power to change the heart or root of the creature. The law cannot keep us in good standings with a Holy God. The law only made us aware of the tree of the knowledge of good and evil with all its condemnation and judgment. So, the law tutored us until we came to the knowledge of Christ.

But the sacrifice of God's Son, which was God Himself, had the power to make us new creatures all along; Christ like creatures bearing His image. Redeemed fully, realizing it, and walking in it is an individual exercise of the truth. The world is redeemed, and you are the evidence and proof of that redemption. Not only are you aware that God is among us, but that He also lives in you. You are one with God manifesting the aroma of His presence everywhere! Whether the world is aware of it or not, they are looking and longing for the true knowledge and presence of God their Creator that now lives in you. Even if they strongly deny it, they still have an empty spot not knowing The Truth, which is Christ; for they were created for the purpose of having fellowship with God as a son. They are no more than sleep walking and need to be awakened! So let those, who know they are redeemed of the Lord, say so!

> **Rom. 12:1 — *I beseech you therefore, brethren, by the mercies of God, that you present your bodies a living sacrifice, holy, acceptable to God, which is your reasonable service.***

When the Bible talks about offering our bodies as a sacrifice as in Rom. 12:1, or any sacrifice for that matter, it is not talking about our sacrifice that makes us more pleasing to God; nor does it somehow make us more loved by God; nor does our sacrifice make us more deserving to receive anything from Him. It is the sacrifice of our own body as one joined to His body that God is asking for. That in turn, will render our bodies not as vessels of unrighteousness or sin, but as instruments of righteousness. It identifies our bodies as one with His on the cross where Adam was crucified.

It is never by our own sacrifice that we are able to draw closer to God. It is never by our own discipline of our bodies that God is looking at. Why? Only by looking at Jesus and receiving from His life can we even offer our bodies as a living sacrifice. We are not following in His footsteps, we are in His footsteps. We are a living expression of Him!

Notice the Bible didn't say 'a dead sacrifice.' If we could do a sacrifice unto God by our own self, then it would be dead works done outside of the life of Christ. If that was what God wanted, then He would have asked for a dead sacrifice. No one can come to God or get closer to God except by Me, Jesus said.[245] So, our sacrifices are but a reality of the sacrifice of Christ in us which produces a sweet aroma of His resurrection life. At the same exact time a sacrifice is offered, resurrection life takes place. Therefore, in the natural, the stinky blood and nasty flesh burnt sacrifice becomes a sweet aroma in the nostrils of God because of the resurrection life that comes out of that death.

Also notice in Rom. 12:1 it says by the <u>mercies</u> of God to offer up our bodies as a living sacrifice. It is by seeing the mercy of God, that we can do this work of offering our bodies as one with Jesus Christ up to God. It is when we see Jesus lifted up as the mercy of God towards us, that we are able to lift up our own bodies on the same tree. That is how we are able to carry our cross daily, and the evidence of it is the fruit of His resurrection life manifest. No man can carry the cross of their own death, even Peter failed; and he was seeing the Father for three years. There is only one sacrifice worthy of the praise of God and that is the sacrifice of His own Son that He provided. Ours is but the corresponding action after the fact of seeing His, which is proof to all that we are one with Him.

You cannot crucify your own flesh so stop trying! Seeing Jesus crucified is our crucifixion! Seeing His giving of love is our spontaneous

---

245   Jn. 14:6

giving done in His love. None of our believing should ever be allowed to fall to the lower level of our own works trying to gain something from God or trying to obey Him. That is no more than dead works under the law. That would be the resurrection of Adam, not Christ. Adam cannot rise except in our own image and even that will fall once the truth comes. He doesn't have the power to rise on his own, so we can only falsely imagine his rising. His self-rising is his fall. Only Christ rises from the dead. So, these things are all done according to the power of His life that dwells in you and are not of your own.

We are so... redeemed that it is no longer us who lives, but Christ that lives in us. We have lost our own identity and have been given His. We no longer belong to ourselves but we are God's possession! Fully redeemed needs to be understood as more than just the price paid by Jesus Christ. It needs to be understood for what that price accomplished. We were lost in darkness but now we are found by the grace of God to be in the light of perfect union, oneness, and wholeness with our Father and Creator! This is what the finished work of redemption has done for all! And this is seeing from heaven's point of view.

Chapter 5

JESUS RECONCILED THE WHOLE WORLD

Rom. 5:10 — *For if, when we were enemies, we were reconciled to God by the death of his Son, much more, being reconciled, we shall be saved by his life.*

The word reconciled is from two Greek words meaning change and mutually or after the manner of. The word 'to' was added once again for our misunderstanding. So the scripture should be read: For if, when we were enemies, we were changed mutually or changed after the manner of God by the death of his Son, much more being changed mutually or changed after the manner of God, we shall be saved by his life. The mutual change was us being changed by His death which produced our death so that we also might become partakers of His life; for as He is so are we in this world!

We are more than just an instrument of God. We are brought into absolute oneness by His death, burial, and resurrection as our death, burial, and resurrection. We are changed by His action, not ours alone. And we have been given the ministry of reconciliation so that the whole world may know who they really are. God brought change, but they don't know it yet. So they continue to act like Adam because we were all born into this world that still manifests the fall of Adam. But they who have not yet believed continue to act like mire dust creatures instead of new creations from heaven. We don't have to make anything happen, just tell and live the results of His death, burial, and resurrection as our death, burial, and resurrection. The truth will not return void.

The preaching and teaching of such good news is the burial of Adam's thinking or the transition from darkness to light. The Adamic mind is full of darkness and the first two days of creation was all about bringing light into the darkness and separating the two. We are reconciled from darkness into light.

Jesus said we can only walk while it is day. The day speaks of the light of God that causes us to see clearly so that we do not stumble in the darkness, which is an absence of light. The first day of creation is the fact that we were without form, which means an empty wilderness. We were in ruins and darkness was on the face of the deep. Our thoughts and every intent of our heart was evil (self-induced). This is a description of me before Christ made Himself known in me. Even as a two year old, it was all about me! The first day was all of us before Christ was revealed to us.

It wasn't until the second day that God separated the waters from the waters and called that place heaven. There are the waters that are from above and there are the waters from below the firmament or expanse or development of earth. Water is a type of the spirit. So there is the Spirit that is above and the spirit that is below. There is the presence of that which is seen and the presence of that which is not seen. One is from below and the other is from above. It is at the end of the first two days of creation that the earth grew with green vegetation and began to bear fruit. So it is with our death and burial. It is when Adam is buried and is not seen no more that the fruit of a new life is raised.

Our death was produced in the darkness just as Jesus' was when the earth became dark for a span of three hours during His death. That was the hour that He spoke of when He said, "My hour has not yet come."[246]

---

246   Jn. 2:4

He was speaking of His crucifixion. One hour of One death produced three hours of darkness. The three hours of darkness produced the death of the whole of Adam's spirit, soul, and body.

The burial of Jesus was for two days, and it was during this time that Jesus descended into the lower depths, just like on the first day of creation when there was darkness on the face of the deep. It is during these two days that light comes,[247] and there is a separation because of the distinction between light and darkness. There is a separate and distinct difference between the carnal natural mind and the mind of Christ. It is not until after these two days are completed that a resurrection takes place; the resurrection of Jesus Christ and our resurrection.

That doesn't mean we have to have a totally renewed mind before we can live the resurrected life. But it does mean that some revelation of Jesus must come so that His light and life can resurrect us. One revelation of Christ can impart enough into our life, until another comes. That is living by every word that proceeds out of the mouth of God.

We cannot walk in newness of the Spirit with a carnal mind. The spirit and the mind of man must come into agreement before they can both walk together. This is having the mind of Christ.[248] The renewing of the mind are the two days where the light has come and a new heaven is produced. Where is that? In that space between the ears that was once in darkness, void, and empty of God. This heaven is that which is produced out of that light and the presence of water from above.

The waters represent a flow of a particular life or spirit that the water comes from. If the water is like the bitter waters from below that the Israelites faced in the wilderness, it is water out of the fallen world in which Adam or the image of Adam dwells. It is the bitter water of the law that brings the curse.[249] This water produces death. This water does not flow with life, but is dead, and therefore produces death.

---

247   Jn. 5:28
248   2 Cor. 2:16
249   Num. 5:19

But The Branch from the tree of Life that the Lord showed them was thrown into the dead water and that life sweetens the waters.[250] That Branch removed the death that was in it. Death was in our bitter waters, but the Branch was thrown in us and we became living water. God was trying to tell them not to drink of this bitter water of the law, for it is way of death. The law produces not the life of God, but brings those who drink it to a lower state of being than what God created us to be. So that water is corrupted or contaminated. But the water or flow that comes out of Christ that He gives us is a flow of everlasting life and manifests the life of God; thus the resurrection from the dead and a new earth that produces the good fruit at the end of the third day. We are now green with life and we bear seed after our own kind. What kind are you? The God kind with waters from above!

There is now the presence of the light of God dwelling in us. When the fourth day comes, the heavens which is first our spirit, then our soul, and lastly the physical realm are now able to divide the day from the night. It is by these heavens being lit up that separates the day from the night that all of creation came forth and is ruled by it. The world can see the difference between those who are of night and those who are of the day. The greater light of the life of Christ is the light of day. The lesser light is that of the law which rules the night. This now sets up the creation of the fifth day.

That light of Day causes the waters to abound in abundance so that it sustains every living creature. This is the living waters of life of God. Every creature was created out of the waters; thus leading up to the creation of man on the sixth day in the likeness of God so that he can supply the earth with His light and life. We now rule and reign over the earth, not with force, but with light and life that abounds with abundance through the knowledge of Christ.

Back to the two days in the grave that represents the reconciliation of our soul. There is a flow of the life of God in you that creates the

---

250   Exo. 15:23–25

firmament called Heaven! Without light and water, the word and the flow of zoe life, there can be no Heaven produced in our soul and body. So it is the light of the knowledge of Jesus Christ that divides the lower waters from the higher waters. We have been reconciled to God and God is our light and our life. Reconciliation was completed so all might come to the experience of His death, burial, and resurrection. Jesus is the light of every man that comes into the world. He is the reconciliation of the whole world! As the light of who Jesus Christ is and all that He has done comes to us, then rightly are the lower water divided from the higher waters until there is a great distance from the two.

1 Cor. 7:11 — *But even if she depart, let her remain unmarried, or be reconciled to (her) husband: and let not the husband put away (his) wife.*

This scripture being inspired of the Holy Spirit is written in the form of a parable with the Church as the wife and Christ Jesus as our Husbandman. The 'she' always represents the weaker vessel as the Church being dependent on Christ or the mind dependent on the Word for renewing. But it is never a gender issue! With God there is neither male nor female. Gender is unnoticed by God because He sees us as one body, His!

Now with the understanding we just received of the word reconciled, we can read the scripture like this: But even if she (the Church or mind) depart, let her (the Church or mind) remain unmarried, or be changed mutually after the manner of (her) husband (Christ). Reconciliation is not just bringing the two together with all our differences as we might have thought. It is the changing of the weaker one so the two are brought together as One greater being. The changed one is the mirror or image of the one who changed them. We are of His exact likeness, and therefore bear the image of Him who was raised from the dead.

When we use the word 'changed', we're not referring to Adam being changed because he's dead. The change is much greater than an improvement. The change is a complete new identity. Even the outward body begins to take on a new form or manner of living. Our flesh and blood body is of this world, but it is the means by which we manifest God in this world. Without it, we are manifest in the spirit realm only and seeing face to face all the time which is far better. But for the world's sake, it is better that we remain for as long as our course takes us and be a salt to the earth. The natural body is therefore an instrument of God.

We are reconciled or changed mutually after the manner of God! Our minds are being reconciled or changed mutually after the manner of God by the Holy Spirit teaching us and the cloud of witnesses that have rained on us with pure water. The result is that our minds or souls are brought into oneness or marriage to His life and Spirit. This is when offspring is produced, or the works of God is manifest in us and through us. This fruit is proof that Jesus has reconciled us and has given us the message that He has reconciled the whole world.

> **1 Jn. 2:2 — *And He Himself is the atonement for our sins, and not for ours only but also for the whole world.***

The word atonement or propitiation means to make amends or suffer punishment for our wrongdoing. Jesus died for the sins of the whole world. He separated us from our sins as far as the East is from the West. And if our sins are taken away, then there is nothing that separates us from our Father God! The whole world has been reconciled, but most don't know it yet!

The whole world's debt or judgment of the wrath of God was totally paid for by the blood of Jesus. He took it all upon Himself. This is why He was marred <u>more</u> than any man. He is God and took upon Himself every man's sin, even though He had never sinned. All our punishment fitting for the whole world's sin was placed on Him. Not one ounce of judgment remains left undone, or He didn't die for the sins of the whole world but only for a select few, and you're probably not in that selection. No, He died for the sins of the whole world, period. Simple isn't it? Just believe the Word.

We no longer have to try to weed out who made it into heaven and who didn't when they die. Some, with good reason, think we have a message of condemnation to those who have not believed and to those who have believed we have a message of salvation. NO! No! no! I don't know how many different ways I can say, "No!" We have only one message that comes from the ONE true God of all, and that message is Jesus died for the sins of the whole world and we come to unite you with your heavenly Father through that one Jesus Christ. Now you can freely partake of His life now in this life as well as the one to come.

But not all have believed our report and therefore cannot freely partake of His life now. Jesus' death on the earth was for the earth life so heaven might be experienced now in this earth life. But the blood sprinkled on the ark of the covenant in heaven is for heaven, and we can't change that either. It's already a done deal there as well! Very little is written about the after death life. Why? Because it's a done deal; it's been finished before the foundation of the world was laid. Jesus meant it when He said,

> **Mat. 6:34 — *"Therefore do not worry about tomorrow, for tomorrow will worry about its own things. Sufficient for the day is its own trouble*** (evil).*"**

Our future is secure in Christ Jesus. The world's future is secure in Christ Jesus. Don't worry about tomorrow. Naturally speaking, is your body dead yet? If not then that's still in our tomorrow somewhere, but don't worry about it. God will give you the grace for that day when it does come. Don't worry about tomorrow, that in itself has evil or death in it. Sufficient or enough is My grace in that day or hour to take care of the evil or trouble when it comes. "So don't be troubled by what might or might not be in your future. My grace is sufficient to take care of it with all its trouble."

You might be thinking that I'm trying to put too much into this scripture and make it say more than what it is saying. But remember, Jesus spoke in parables using natural things to compare with spiritual things. When Jesus said the day, it was a Greek word that meant day or hour. And when Jesus said, "My hour has not come yet," He was referring to His hour of the cross. It was never intended to be a literal one hour of time but the time of His suffering on the cross for us.

When Jesus spoke of the day of the Lord, He was not talking about a literal 24 hour day but the day of His appearing. His appearing brings light and life to our whole being and therefore it is called day because His appearing brings light. The sufficiency of **that** day and hour provides us with more than enough to take care of all the evil and troubles of any and all of our tomorrows. If you see this and believe it, you can experience a peaceful faith filled <u>day</u> freely partaking of Him who comes to you today. In that <u>day</u> we have peace, and we can be worry free about our tomorrows. Your tomorrows or future are already planned out with blessings by God in them. The day will be filled with knowing the thoughts and plans He has for you: which are of peace, good, blessings and not of evil, to give you a future and a hope.[251]

Again, in the real natural world you might ask, "Then why all the problems and terrible catastrophes in the world?" The earth groans waiting for the manifestation of the sons of God. Most of the Church is still having problems with the image of the beast (Adam and the tongue of the Adam filled mind) because they do not see themselves as sons of God. They do not see themselves as changed mutually after the manner or likeness of God. Only when the Church becomes the Bride of Christ, the mature sons will become adorned in His likeness. They will walk in the power of their God given authority as both the

---

251   Jer. 29:11

Lamb and the Lion working together as One in them. The foundation is already laid in every believer right now for that manifestation to happen. It is Christ in us!

But because we have not looked at or gazed at the foundation enough to understand more fully who He is and what He has accomplished on the cross, we walk as dead men or mire men of the dust realm. "Oh, we are not just little dogs under the Masters table eating a few crumbs that might fall to the floor. No, we are sons and a table has been prepared for us in the presence of our enemies! So rise up and establish the kingdom of heaven through the influence of (zoe) Life in your world: still the storms, calm the earthquakes, command the tornado to rise from the ground and dissipate!"

Don't settle for whatever will be will be. You rule with Him from a place seated on the throne in Christ Jesus! You, the body of Christ are one with Jesus Christ. Go ahead and take your world as a co-laborer with Christ! Change that which has been under the curse and declare it redeemed by the blood and speak peace, and life, and blessing into it! God gave it to you! He gave you that place called earth, and He also gave you the authority to rule over it with Him. Sure, in separation from Him you can't do anything. But why even consider that any longer? The blood of Jesus Christ has brought you near and made you His. You don't even belong to yourself. He has fully and complete reconciled you to Himself! It was His choice to do so, not yours. So why even give a moment's thought of being separate from Him? Do you want more blood or what? You are God's and you are a divine expression of Him in the earth. He loves the whole world and He made His claim to us by the work of reconciliation through Jesus Christ.

Isa. 60:1-3 — So *arise and shine; for the glory of the Lord is risen upon you. There is a darkness that still covers the earth, and deep darkness the people; but the Lord will arise over you, and His glory will be*

seen upon you. The Gentiles shall come to your light, and kings to the brightness of your rising.

This can happen to you as you take your place in Christ as a manifested son of God! Why? Because reconciliation is finished! It is based on the fact that the Messiah came to save and restore us all back to the place in the garden where Adam and Eve were first created. Not a physical location, but a spiritual position. Natural Jerusalem is no more anointed with the presence of God than any other place on earth. People may experience such a trip there as a grand spiritual experience, and I don't intend to take anything away from that. But it was only because they allowed their minds to focus on the death of Jesus long enough that they may have encountered a greater understanding and experience of His death. The same could have been achieved anywhere if we would have given the same focus on His death, burial, and resurrection. It is our understanding of Christ and His finished work that changes our view of Him and ourselves.

Reconciliation is about being restored to perfect union where we hear and know the voice of our Creator. It is being restored to full authority over all the earth and all its creatures. It is being restored to a perfect earth having a heavenly atmosphere and you are that earth! The perfect earth is not the global earth until the sons of God are first manifest throughout the whole earth, but it is <u>you</u> made in the image or exact likeness of God now. Christ made that part of the earth perfect and complete lacking nothing. And the heavenly atmosphere is the one you produce as you abide in the vine. It is a fruit from heaven or a fruit of the Spirit.

But don't think you are a restored Adam! No, you are the Christ man in the earth today! Are we not instructed to put on Christ the new man?[252] Not a new Adam, nor revised version of Adam, nor the new and improved Adam, but put on the new man made in the image of Christ.

252   Rom. 13:14, Gal. 3:27, Eph. 4:24, Col. 3:10

You are still as much a man as Jesus was a man when He walked the earth. And you are of God little children and have overcome them that are in the world just as Jesus overcame the world.[253]

Just as Jesus came from heaven, so do we come from heaven now seeing from there. Not a physical coming from heaven, but a spiritual view, or vision, or seeing from heaven that changes everything! Our physical body expresses what we have seen and heard from heaven. So, in one way, our physical body is coming from heaven as well. All things are now of God where we come from. We dwell in heavenly places in Christ Jesus and this is where we get our view, our knowledge, understanding, wisdom, life, provision, power, and everything else that pertains to life and godliness. We are in Christ and He freely supplies us with all things. For we have been reconciled to God. We were changed mutually or changed after the manner of God by the death of his Son; much more being changed mutually or changed after the manner of God shall we be saved by his life.

The whole world is reconciled but not walking in that restoration. Just as one man left us with no choice, and we were born in sin and that seed produced unrighteousness, so it is equally, that through the one man, Jesus Christ, we all have the seed of His life in us to bear the fruit of righteousness. The world who has not yet believed has the seed of Christ in them but have not yet awakened to that truth. It is when that seed hears of its own death that it begins to produce new life. Until they recognize the death of Jesus, the seed, there can be no sprouting of life from that seed, so that seed has no root and no fruit as of yet. The hope of glory for all men is Christ in all men. When they believe on Jesus Christ that seed will be awakened and a new man will arise from of the presence of God, and he is called born again, made anew, and is a man from heaven.

That new creation man can now freely partake of all that salvation through Christ provides. But even then, we will live for a while in certain

253   1 Jn. 4:4, Jn. 16:33

areas of our life as though we have not been redeemed because of the mind of Adam not yet renewed. An ongoing revelation of the person of Christ and the finished work will change that mind and bring us completely into who we really are in Christ. But notice the mind always needs an ongoing work done in it. Therefore, we put our trust in God who is able to keep us complete by speaking His life-giving word to us.

We cannot live today only by what we heard yesterday. Man does not live by day old bread alone, but by every word that comes out of the mouth of God. For our instruction, the Israelites gathered manna daily through the week. Then on the day before the Sabbath they gathered twice as much so they had enough on the Sabbath. The Sabbath was a day of the people gathering together and feasting. What we feast on today is what we have to share with others. It is out of today's union with the Lord that I am well supplied and made sufficient for the evil of today. So, no matter how much we learn today, only tomorrow's manna will be sufficient for that day.

If what the Lord is speaking to you today is more of the same thing you had yesterday, eat and be merry, it is enough! But if what He is speaking to you today is different or even new, then lend Him an ear, and listen, and see and understand. It will be life to those who find it and health to all their flesh.[254] He sent His word and healed us.[255] There is life in His word that He speaks to you directly or indirectly through another. Either way, it is the anointing of the Spirit of God that speaks with us. The Holy Spirit can even anoint the words of a donkey to deliver us and set us on the right path of thinking. This might by why some seem to be surrounded by so many donkeys. This is how we are to love one another, by speaking His word to each other; words that contain the knowledge of His reconciliation.

I have often received the words of a little child as a revelation of Jesus. The child didn't understand it the same way the anointing revealed it to

---

254   Pro. 4:22

255   Psa. 107:20

me, but the child was God's messenger. I have also heard some of the most religious speakers speak one thing meaning it one way and the Spirit of God taking those same words and meaning it another way that revealed such great truth. As being reconciled, changed mutually after the manner and likeness of God, we are hearing and seeing from heaven.

Chapter 6

THE KINGDOM OF HEAVEN IS AT HAND

The kingdom of heaven is at hand. It is finished in that Jesus came to preach the kingdom of heaven is at hand and He completed that work; not the preaching of it, but the bringing of the kingdom of heaven to the earth. The reason He preached the kingdom of heaven is at hand is because He saw it clearly was as near to Him as it is to you today. But Jesus didn't preach it until He saw it as such. Jesus manifested that kingdom into this physical realm so that the kingdom of heaven would bring the peace and good will of God into all the earth. The kingdom of heaven is just as near today as it was when Jesus walked the earth proclaiming it because He is still walking the earth today through His body.

The Lamb of God ushered in the kingdom of heaven, and because His blood was for the whole world, the kingdom of heaven is still here in fullness waiting to be received by the whole world. The blood of the Lamb closes every gap between Heaven and earth. Heaven and earth have kissed each other in Christ. Heaven and earth has now kissed each other in us. Heaven and earth are one through His body that reigns on earth. As it is in heaven, so on earth is our Lord's prayer and ours. So we ought to first see it from heaven and then walk in its fullness on earth. Does God hear you when you pray such things? Yes, so look for the answer coming from heaven's view, believe it when you hear it or see it, and walk it out in Christ. That view you then see has the power to bring itself to pass, if we will only believe it and do it! When Jesus authors it, He will also finish that view He just gave you from heaven!

The kingdom of heaven is at hand is what the Church ought to be preaching rather than doom and gloom if you don't get saved.

Mat. 24:14 — *And this gospel of the kingdom shall be preached in all the world for a witness unto all the nations; and then shall the end come.*

Jesus is not saying that there is coming an end to the world that now exists. This is of course another parable of the kingdom. But it is an end to the world that you once saw and lived in. Receiving the kingdom of heaven gives us a whole new view of how we see, hear, and understand the things going on in this world. We have a whole new perspective because all things are become new and all things are of God! Now you see greater things than those of Adam! It is an end to an Adamic image or perception of being separated from God and His kingdom; an end to your part of the world living like it is still under the curse rather than like it has been redeemed and reconciled by the blood of Jesus. This end marks our new beginning where all nations (peoples) will rule over all the earth by the love and power of our union with the God who created it all. We once manifested only what already is, the kingdom of this world; but now we manifest what is in heaven and what shall be on the earth according to the highest kingdom, the kingdom of heaven.

As one people having one mind, the mind of the Spirit, we will rule and reign with Christ in the earth. This is not a natural new order of government that forces the rule of God's laws over people like the Jews were expecting and wanting Jesus to do. The rule of the kingdom of God is an individual spiritual government established in each of us where Christ rules from within us. The kingdom of heaven must be preached and manifest through us for the whole physical earth to see and experience that kingdom.

A confidence must be built in us concerning the kingdom of heaven being fully at our hand and our Father wanting to manifest His goodness to all. Then we will truly understand that God has the rain to fall on the just and unjust alike; the rain of His love and His word with demonstrations of power to change that which is corrupted by manifesting the incorruptible. Manifesting the goodness of God and His kingdom is what will lead all the nations to repentance.

It is finished means there is nothing left for God to do to save and restore or make the kingdom of heaven appear. It is now up to us to see and hear from Him, and then believe and manifest the kingdom of heaven in the earth. He has already done everything that needs to be done. It is up to us to draw near to Him and receive whatever we have need of at this time. It is up to us to go forth in His name and do the works that He did and greater works by His abiding life.

It is imperative that we begin to see and believe that we are His finished work and bear the fruit thereof. For we lack no good thing being fully secure and equipped in Christ. Sure, we don't know everything that can be known and never ever will. But we know Him who does know everything, and He dwells in us and will make known all things to us as we have need of knowing such things. Therefore I know all things that are necessary for me to know right now. He has many things yet to show me, so I am confident He will share those things with me when I have need of them. I therefore have lack of nothing knowing that He supplies all my present need. What peace and confidence we have in Him! There is no pride in self here. There is only a confidence in the Lord through knowing Him as my Chief Cornerstone. He has supplied us with all things when He brought the kingdom of heaven with Him, and He sealed it to remain here by His death on the cross and His resurrection.

That's right, the kingdom of heaven is sealed right here. It cannot escape! It cannot disappear! Just as the Holy Spirit sealed us as God's own children, sealed us with His indwelling life, so is the kingdom of heaven sealed in us and ready to manifest in order to confirm His word spoken to us. You cannot separate the Christ from His kingdom. If we have Christ in us, then the kingdom of His domain is in us as well. How can our citizenship be in heaven if the kingdom of heaven is not at hand? It is and we are. The kingdom of heaven is at your hand!

Because of the finished work of Jesus Christ, He is the light of <u>every man</u> that comes into the world, not just those who have believed. But the darkness of this world too often is allowed to hide that light (Christ that illuminates). That's why the sharing of the true light, which is the gospel, is so important. It is the light that lights all men!

The earth groans for the manifestation of the sons of God. The possibility of every person on earth being what God intended them to be is up to the body of Christ to share the true light they have. That is the equipping of the saints and the making of disciples. The true light revealed now is what is holding the earth together presently. Without the goodness of God and His love and mercy, planet earth would soon be destroyed as we know it by the false image of Adam that people have who know not the truth. But all things are held together by the power of His word,[256] and it is through His body that His word is released with power to still every storm and disaster. He holds all things together by the power of His word, and we are His body that speaks His word.

If our natural government or community or people around us seem to be in disorder and going the wrong direction, it is not going to be solved by our votes or our support dollars. It can only be solved by the good news of the finished work of Jesus being preached and believed upon. This manifests the kingdom of heaven and lights up every man so that every individual receives the knowledge of God which is the answer to all his world problems. Then the hearts of men will be changed, and then the government, and people around you will be of God.

---

256   Heb. 1:3

God will never, never, never come back to establish His government on the earth as some of us have physically imagined it to happen as a certain event in the future. His government must be established in the hearts of men first, and then it is through men that He can establish a government that is like that of His own kingdom. Then that kingdom of the earth will be the kingdom of our Lord. God doesn't run His kingdom from the outside of man by laws, rules and regulations being enforced, but by His love being established in all, and all expressing that love through service.

So how can God come back and establish His kingdom on earth any other way then how it is being established now? This is His plan. His kingdom is at hand and we know it because His peace rules in our hearts as an umpire now.[257] His kingdom is established in earth now if He now reigns in you by His love. This word of the gospel must be preached throughout the whole world so God can set up His government throughout the whole world. Any other physical established governmental order in the earth can only be run by law and order at best. God has a higher plan of how things ought to be done, and that is by His Spirit from within the hearts of all men as one with them! This will in turn create a free new species of being so that love will go unhindered. This is the government of our Lord being established by the law of the Spirit of life which brings a heavenly order to all things.

So every man has been redeemed and every man has light in them. I believe that every man born into this world has the light of the seed of righteousness because of the finished work.[258] But there is still a work in this world that is of darkness and it comes to deceive and hide the light of every man.[259] There is dual thinking that exists until that person meets Jesus at the cross and has his mind renewed. Then he sees that Adam has been crucified and the Christ, the new man, is risen. Then

---

257 Col. 3:15
258 Jn. 1:4, 9, Rom. 5:19
259 Mat. 5:15

the mind of Christ fills His mind with the living water that springs up into everlasting life.[260]

> **Rom. 5:19 — *For as by one man's disobedience many were made sinners, so also by one Man's obedience many made righteous.***

If you use the N.K.J.V., then you noticed the words 'will be' were left out. You probably guested it, those words are not in the Greek. So now we might understand it like this: Just as or in the same way sin came unto 'many' through one man, righteousness came to the same 'many' through the one man Jesus Christ. If the sin of Adam is known as the seed of sin and all were born with his sin, then the righteousness of Jesus Christ would be known as the seed of righteousness and all were born with His righteousness.

At the crucifixion of Jesus Christ, that man of Adam was done away with. Born in a flesh and blood body, the world awakened us to sin through the law; but through the gospel and the Spirit of Christ, He awakens us to righteousness. Everyone born in this world is predestined to go through the same glorious door of recognizing the death of Adam and the resurrection life of Christ as their own. Just as sin remained asleep in us until the law came into our understanding, so it is that righteousness remains asleep until our understanding is awakened from that sleep by the Light of the world, the Spirit of truth, which is the living word of God. Then the kingdom of God is manifest in us and not just around us.

As a little baby or small child, we knew no need for salvation because we had just come from God and had not experienced death or separation from God through sin that comes from eating of the tree of the knowledge of good and evil. We had no understanding of the law at that time. Even as a baby, if we sinned according to the laws of our parents; such as, "Thou

---

260   Jn. 4:14

shall not dirty thy diaper," we did not know it as sin; and therefore it was not sin unto us because we had no conscious awareness of the law. We still had uninterrupted spiritual union with Him. So the need for salvation through Jesus was not seen, or understood, or even needed until sin manifest through the knowledge of the law. We already had fellowship with God and that without much knowledge, but only having an inward knowing and presence which is Spirit to spirit.

God is a Spirit of love, peace and joy and that is how we fellowshipped with Him as a baby or young child without knowing and understanding many words to describe it. That light was later hidden under a bushel called the law. That law produced the Adam of old that has been around since the eating of the tree of the knowledge of good and evil. But the gospel of the death, burial, and resurrection of Jesus uncovered the light by the removal of Adam, the man of sinful flesh.

> **Mat. 5:15 — *"Nor do they light a lamp and put it under a basket, but on a lampstand, and it gives light to all who are in the house.***

Men lit the candle that is in us. We were then awakened or reborn anew after experiencing the death of Adam and the uncovering of Jesus Christ, the true light. Once you are lit with the life of Christ it just doesn't make any sense to cover that light back up by the law. The Christ in you, the hope of glory is now risen from the tomb of Adam. Christ was sleeping in the boat or house that you are. Now abides the kingdom of heaven in us with Christ seated on the throne of our hearts and minds where He and His living word appears to us. This new light and life gives light to all the rooms of the house. He now lights up our mind, will, emotion, conscience, and body unto righteousness. This is seeing and knowing the kingdom of heaven is at hand. It is a finished work and yet an ongoing revelation and manifestation. Knowing the kingdom of heaven is at your hand and experiencing that glorious kingdom, is seeing from heaven.

Chapter 7

THE I AM

This is both a description of who Jesus is as our Cornerstone and of His finished work. This is the perfect last chapter of this book, because the I AM brings everything we have covered so far into the now so that we are compete. We don't want to put off into the future or only see as the past what God freely has given to us for today. It is by not understanding this one thing that has thrown so many teachers and believers off course in their believing and rightly understanding the word of God. And as a result, it has caused many to stumble in their walk with God and hindered them from receiving all His benefits. One of the greatest revelations of God is that He is the **I AM**! Jesus was the manifestation of the will of God and the life of God while walking presently on the earth. Jesus said, "If you've seen Me, you've seen the Father." Jesus is Emmanuel, God with us now. And if Christ dwells in you, then **I AM** with you!

> **Heb. 3:7–12 —** *Therefore, as the Holy Spirit says: "Today, if you will hear His voice, do not harden your hearts as in the rebellion, in the day of trial in the wilderness, where your fathers tested Me, proved Me, and saw My works forty years. Therefore I was angry*

*with that generation, and said, 'They always go astray
in their heart, and they have not known My ways.' So
I swore in My wrath, 'They shall not enter My rest.'"
Beware, brethren, lest there be in any of you an evil
heart of unbelief in departing from the living God;*

One problem with the Israelites, as well as some of the Church today, was in our believing that God is the I AM. God told Moses to tell the people that I AM sent you. In other words, what you have been praying for is now coming to pass because I am with you. You prayed for deliverance and now I AM! The Israelites couldn't put off into some future time or event the fullness of their deliverance because God was revealing Himself as the I AM.

You need healing? Jesus said "I AM"! Whatever we have need of, Jesus is I AM ever present and positioned to give it to you. The kingdom of Heaven is presently here with us now so we can freely receive from the I AM right now. This is a description of who Jesus is, and the Bible should be read first from this perspective that God **is** and not God was or will be some day.

Did you notice that in verse 12, if we put off the promises of God for today (which includes what He's already finished on the cross) for another day in the future, He calls it an evil heart. The now that we only have is today, not tomorrow. Imagine that, we born again believers sometimes have an evil heart of unbelief because we put off some of His promises for another day in the future. This is important to God because He always wants to be I AM to us all, all the time. Why put off for tomorrow what God desires and has positioned Himself to freely give you today? So, today, if you will hear His voice, let us believe and receive as though He is exactly who He says He is, the I AM!

**2 Cor. 6:1, 2 — *We then, as workers together with
Him also plead with you not to receive the grace of***

God in vain. For He says: "In an acceptable time I have heard you, and in the day of salvation I have helped you." Behold, <u>now</u> is the accepted time; behold, <u>now</u> is the day of salvation.

First of all, the grace of God is available to all. Grace and truth came through Jesus Christ who also announced that this is the acceptable year of the Lord. Grace is the unearned favor of God, the ability of God, the strength of God, and the power of God working towards you, in you, and through you. God has freely given us all things that pertain to life and Godliness.[261] And on top of all that, God qualified you to receive it all by sending us His Son as the Lamb of God. Jesus demonstrated that everyone is qualified or worthy to receive from the kingdom of heaven, unless you are still looking at your own works under the law in an attempt to qualify yourself. Now is the accepted time! Why? The Lamb is presently among you now. You're accepted! The whole world is accepted! And if we do not believe and freely receive from Him, all this grace is in vain.

Look at it from God's perspective. He's our loving Father, Creator, and Maker, and He longs to help us and make this life a grand and wonderful experience for us. He knows the weakness of this frail body we have. But that is completely okay with Him because He dwells in us to empower us, protect us, lead us, provide for us, and to inspire us. That is what godly natural fathers want to do, so how much more our heavenly Father? That is His heart's desire, for we are His children. Now He offers to us anything we have need of; therefore, we lack no good thing. He absolutely delights in giving us these things which is why faith pleases God. Faith receives freely from God. These things are what He already longs to give us and has provided for us before we knew we had need of them. But it's not just about things like what we see around us. It is about seeing God even while in the midst of trouble.

---

261   2 Pet. 1:3

Being there is the greatest joy and responsibility in the raising up of our children. That is what makes this life so grand and wonderful! It's not just about getting stuff! In our thinking those things ought to be little or secondary compared to just being there in the good times and in the tough times. This is the Father's heart and His purpose of coming to us and manifesting His life in us. You can have nothing materialistic, but if you are having a move of God in your life, and His presence is filling you up, and light is coming so fast that it boggles the mind, you are gloriously blessed far above those who have it all and don't have a clue about the things of God. And yet He still wants to give to us all those other things that we desire and have need of. Another mind blower!

Receiving from God honors God and His Son. Putting off His promises for a future of, "Maybe when," or "Someday," is very disappointing to the One who is so eager to give it to us now. This is a departing from the <u>living</u> God. He is not the living God to you if He is not now willing and able to you. Now is the day of our salvation! The Greek word again for salvation is soteria, which means to rescue, safety, deliver, health, and save. It covers every area in our lives: spirit, soul and body. He truly is able to and is most desirous to make us complete spirit, soul and body.

How important is it to see Him as our I AM? The word 'behold' is used in the imperative sense which means absolutely necessary or unavoidable and of priority. So it's not behold, it's **BEHOLD! Now** is the accepted time; **BEHOLD! Now** is the day of salvation! He is the great I AM and presently with you. Beholding Him as your I AM is absolutely necessary, unavoidable, and of priority for you and for Him to express Himself to you!

Rev. 11:16, 17 — *And the twenty-four elders who sat before God on their thrones fell on their faces and worshiped God, saying: "We give You thanks,*

O Lord God almighty, The One who is and who was and who is to come..."

It is the twenty-four elders who began first saying that God is and then saying that He was. The twenty-four elders represent the twelve tribes of Israel and the twelve disciples of Jesus. Both tribes together represent the fullness of His governmental order. Their first description of Him is that He is the Lord God Almighty. The second description of Him is that He is or He is the I AM, and then the One who was.

There is one translation that omits that He is the One who is to come. Why? Let's think for a moment. To say that He is to come while you are seeing Him now and experiencing Him on the measure of the Lord God Almighty presently, is to deny Him presently. It would be a putting off into the future what is being revealed to them right now. It speaks that all He is, is not until tomorrow. He will be the Almighty someday. And if it's far enough in the future, we can now only see it as a maybe.

Well in heaven He's everything now and they see Him plainly now. In heaven you do not put off until tomorrow what God is revealing to you today. That is an impossibility because you are one with Him. He reveals Himself to us in heaven, not as a suggestion, but as the all in all eternal life, gloriously moving and making as reality all that is. Putting off into some future what God is revealing Himself to you today would make God and heaven vain, empty and useless to you today. And today is all we have right now. Our loving Father wants to make today your best day ever. But it just ain't gonna happen today if we keep putting things off into the future. So, if we see plainly from heaven now, we ought to walk in that same light now while we have the light of day.

He cannot be the God who was if He's not the God of your present first. Your past is made by what you presently see and do now. Those who don't know Jesus as the Lord I Am in their life now would have a hard time accurately recognizing Him as the Lord who was in their past. Because they give Him little place in their present for Him to show Himself strong to them, they have little memories of experiencing Him in their past. Those who know Him not now are also those who know Him not in their past. Believe Him now if you want an amazing past to see and tell. God's loves adventure. Take a look at His creation.

Only what you experience of Him today can leave you with past experiences of Him tomorrow. This lack of knowing Him as the I AM in turn creates a mentality of God putting many things off into the future as some event in time. The word of God must first be seen, understood, and interpreted from the most important place of time in one's life and that is now! The past is past and cannot be changed, but the power of the present is in our hands now. That power of the present is given to us having been made in the image of the Creator. And our future is being prepared by our walk with the Lord today. This life is lived by what is done now and experienced now. This world needs a present help in the time of trouble and not something in the sweet by and by. Jesus told us not to worry about tomorrow; the trouble of today is enough. We first have a need of discovering Christ as our sufficiency for our right now.

Then on the other hand, some might say, that what God did in healing the sick while Jesus walked the earth and in the Acts of the Holy Spirit is only to be understood as the God who was and not as I AM that same God for you today. But the whole point of scripture is to reveal to us that the same God who did those great things back then is the same God of today! Nothing has changed but you! You are living today and God is the same yesterday, today and forever! He was with them, and now (Acts is still being written) He is with them. Them in the book of Acts is us in the now! You are the 'them' of the book of Acts that's happening today!

Heb. 11:6 — *But without faith it is impossible to please Him, for he who comes to God must believe*

that He is, and that He is a rewarder of those who seek Him.

It is not faith to believe that God healed so & so in the past. We must believe that He is our Healer and their Healer today. That's the kind of faith, the only kind of faith that pleases God. Putting our hope in future events doesn't qualify as faith that pleases God. The I AM is the same yesterday, today and forever. He was the I AM of yesterday when it happened, and He is the I AM of today, and He will be the I AM of tomorrow when it comes. We have no past or future without I AM right now!

As we read scriptures, we can see the Lord God of the past and the future, but it is discovering how these same scriptures speaks to us of the Lord 'I AM' today that God wants us to see and understand. Knowing that He is the same yesterday, today, and forever places every scripture and its fullness concerning Christ into our today. I know, we like to pick out certain scriptures and take note that this one is for the future and that one is for the past and on and on we go. Once again, if He is not the Almighty of our today, He cannot be the Almighty of our past or future. So, for Him to be the same yesterday, today and forever, He has to be the same Almighty today as He was in the past and as He is in the future or that scripture is not true.

Knowing Him as the Lord God Almighty today creates greater union than that of the past or future because our present union with Him is an experience that cannot be replayed or fast-forwarded. God seeks oneness with all of us now. He desires to show Himself strong to us now in the hard times and in the good times.

Example: 1 Thess. 4:13-18 is believed by some in the Church to mean that believers will be raptured or physically taken out of the earth to meet the Lord in the air some day in the future when He comes back; well, part way back as far as the clouds anyway. Some call it their great hope. But God never called it that. The Bible says that Christ in us is our hope of glory, not leaving planet Earth. Get a spaceship if that's your hope. This whole rapture thing is against everything we know and understand God to be and what He set out to accomplish in the earth. In sending His Son, God came to earth and brought the kingdom of heaven with Him. Why do we believe against that work and the scriptures thinking that God wants to take all believers out of the world? Did God do a shoddy job of bringing the kingdom of heaven to earth? Either He did or maybe we've missed some things.

> **Jn. 17:15 — *"I do not pray that You should take them out of the world, but that You should keep them from the evil."***

We know that the evil or evil *one*, 'one' being an added word, is not the devil. The evil one is the same one that God saw before He repented and flooded the earth.

> **Gen. 6:5 — *Then the Lord saw that the wickedness of man was great in the earth, and that every intent of the thoughts of his heart was only evil continually. 6:7 — So the Lord said, "I will destroy Adam whom I have created from the face of the earth;"***

The evil or evil one is the image of Adam that man keeps seeing himself as that causes every thought of his heart to become only evil continually. It's not an imaginary spirit being called the devil! At this time men were only seeing themselves from the face of the earth/dust. Like the serpent (messenger of deception) who was cursed to eat of his same message all the days of his life, men were only eating of the same substance of the earth, deception. By this deception they continued to get worse and worse as they continued to eat. Eventually they became trapped, ensnared by what they were eating and there heart became wicked continually. They had absolutely no concept of God being the I AM.

"Now the ruler of this world will be cast out," Jesus said in Jn. 12:31. The ruler of this world <u>was</u> the devil (deception). And the only way he could rule is through deception and lies. When the truth came through Jesus Christ and the payment for our guilt and condemnation was laid on Jesus, the devil and his ruling rights were stripped completely away. It is only the lying thoughts and imaginations of people who still see themselves as Adam under the curse that are evil. They are the only evil or evil one left on earth! And Jesus prayed that the Father would not take us out of the world so that we would tell them the truth as to what has happened to Adam and that lying curse they live under. He only prayed that the Father would keep us from the evil deceptive image of Adam. It's the image of the old man that we still have that we need to be kept from, not devil monster.

Isn't it clear that we have authority to cast out demons in His name? Then why do we look for an escape hatch to get out of here? Doesn't Jesus have all authority in heaven and earth so that when we go He will work with us? Then why are some in such a hurry to get out of here? If you see yourself as weak, then getting out of here looks pretty good. As Adam or a fallen human, they are weak. But as a believer, God embodies you and the joy of the Lord is your strength. He has made you more than conquerors through Jesus Christ. You are not alone because He is Emmanuel, God with us. So why are so many looking to get out of here? They were taught natural things from a parable of the kingdom of heaven.

God is not trying to get earth or earth beings into heaven. As far as His finished work declares, they are already there! The word of God confirms it. Our citizenship is now in heaven. We are now seat Him in heavenly places. The only thing we lack is a now perspective. Make the word of God your I AM today. Declare to the Lord that He is your I AM. Then begin to read the New Testament with that understanding and the Holy Spirit will teach you marvelous things that will absolutely astound you. God truly is amazing!

He brought heaven to earth and is looking for the Sons of God to manifest His kingdom in the earth today. He wants us to restore the earth to its fullness as in the beginning. Jesus paid the full price for that to happen. He made us to rule over all the earth to ensure it does happen. How can we rule over earth now without a physical body present in the earth? How is God going to rule with us without us? Can we do it from heaven which is believed by those same people to be somewhere five miles south of Mars? Every scripture that speaks of one being taken away and another left is speaking of Adam being taken away and the Christ man remaining so the earth will become His footstool. So let's look at this scripture from heaven's perspective first and not from a self-centered opinion that still believes more in the devil than God. Why else are some looking for an escape? I mean, if there is not a devil, what are you escaping from? If there is a devil, but in reality it (he) is nothing more than lies and deception, then let's get our Head as our head so we will no longer be deceived! Why embrace such a self-centered teaching? It only has self in mind and lets the rest of the world go to hell or stay in tribulation. Sounds like the Israelites in their thinking that they were better than the rest of the Gentile unbelievers. You are special, but each and every person is special in the eyes of God and He has never determined to leave nor forsake a single one.

1 Thess. 4:15–18 — *For this we say to you by the word of the Lord, that we who are alive and remain until the coming of the Lord will by no means precede those who sleep. For the Lord Himself will descend from heaven with a shout, with the voice of an archangel, and with the trumpet of God. And the dead in Christ will rise first. Then we who are alive and remain shall be caught up together with them in the clouds*

to meet the Lord in the air. And thus we shall always be with the Lord. Therefore comfort one another with these words.

Those who sleep in Jesus are the ones who have sown the seed of God's word in the earth and have left their natural earthen body. They are our clouds of witnesses because their words still speak of the presence of The Cloud, God. Those who sleep have gone on before us. 2 Pet. 2:17 describes those who speak words of unbelief and curse what God has blessed are wells without water, clouds that are carried with a tempest... They are clouds without rain because they speak words that do not have the life of God or water. God was seen as a cloud. What came out of the cloud? The voice of God that spoke His word, living water. Jesus was a well of living water and He declared that out of our belly shall flow rivers of living water. We have that water and when we speak from that well or river, we are seen as clouds of witnesses because the water that we speak falls upon them like a rain cloud. The water from within us is brought up and out into the air like a natural cloud that releases its rain because it is full. But these clouds have already gone on before us, and their words still speak to us today.

The Lord always comes to us from a higher place or perspective than we have at that time with the purpose of bringing us to where He is, which is higher. This causes us at that time to rise up to where He is and meet Him in the clouds of those whose words still witnessing to us. He speaks loud and clear for us to hear, and He also comes with an archangel or head messenger.

In Rev. 4:1, John heard a voice like that of a trumpet. His loud clear voice is the trumpet of God. A Pastor, or teacher, or evangelist, or prophet, or apostle, or neighbor might be that head angel for us today, but what they speak carries with it the trumpet or ram's horn that gives the sound that a male sheep has been slain (Cornerstone). In other words, the trumpet of God <u>always</u> speaks from the Chief Cornerstone perspective, which declares the favor of God toward us because of the Lamb. Those who sleep in Jesus will hear it first because their dwelling place is in heaven only and are seeing constantly face to face. They are totally in the realm of the Spirit where His voice is first heard. But they too will rise higher than they were before they heard the Almighty speak.

Heaven is a continual unveiling of the glory of God and we have heaven on earth. Isn't that exciting! Then we who are alive and remain will be caught up together with them in the clouds. Where they are is not a physical location that we can go to to meet those who sleep or have died in Christ. They don't have a physical body having a physical location, but a spiritual one. So, it is a spiritual place of knowing or understanding that comes from Him so that where He is we can meet Him there, which is where those who sleep have already gone because they have already heard.

We are caught up together in the clouds of witnesses to meet Him in the air. The Lord is in the air. He is in the breath of God. He is the living word of God that comes out of His mouth. He breathed into us and we became a living soul. This is the same breath of His nostrils that gave us life and still gives us life now. So, this too is not a physical location, but a spiritual one. 'Air' should give us a clear picture that it is not a physical place that we arise to. Jesus spoke of the wind (blowing or moving air) as a parable or parallel to the Spirit. And just as it was not a physical wind that Jesus was pointing Nicodemus to, it is not a physical air that He is pointing us to arise to. The air is the breath of God or word of God that lifts us up into a more glorious dwelling place in Him. So we are not only with Jesus but with all the saints of God as one body! And thus we shall always be with the Lord in this spiritual and soulish condition that manifest in and through our body. And this is His appearing or coming unto us. Please don't miss it or disregard it as something small and unimportant when He speaks to you. His words breathed into us are our rising!

Remember Jesus said, "I go to prepare a place for you, so that where I am there you may be also."[262] We know that Jesus went to the Father,

---

262   Jn. 14:2

who is Spirit. It is a spiritual place and not a physical location. We also know that Jesus was speaking a now present tense place of where I am, and not where I am going, though both are spiritual places. Jesus only focused on telling us that where I am now, today, this moment, there you may be also. So if Jesus is speaking of a spiritual condition or dwelling place that we can go to now, why do some preach a physical place and physical escape or departure that He wants to bring us to? Jesus' dwelling with the Father while on the earth is the same condition or dwelling place He has prepared for us on the earth so that the works of Jesus may continue.

God wants us earth dwellers to be in the glorious place of the presence of God while on the earth. If He wants to go and do this, then He communicates with His body where He wants to go and what He wants to accomplish. The Head and the body are one. The Head, Christ, is not out to operate independently separate of His body. So, to bring the body to where He is, He speaks loudly through messengers (angels). That word lifts us up into heavenly places in Christ Jesus so that we may be where 'I AM' is. If you want 'I WAS', then shut your ears and stay where you are. If all you want is the 'I IS TO COME', then put everything off into the future what He is saying to you today. But remember, "Today, if you will hear His voice, do not harden your hearts as in the rebellion, in the (now) day of trial in the wilderness." The purpose of His speaking to us is for our rising. He wants us to ascend to where He is while we are on the earth. Then the people shall come to our light and the kings to the brightness of our rising.[263] The light that brightens us up on the inside causes us to rise.

Remember again in **Jn. 17:15** — *"I do <u>not</u> pray that You should take them out of the world, but that You should keep them from the evil one."*

---

263   Isa. 60:3

If Jesus, the Christ, prayed for us not to be taken out of the world, then preaching we are going to be taken out of the world must be antichrist, for it is against the will of Christ. Still, there is no condemnation to those who are in Christ. I had studied, taught, and preached that same message and God doesn't condemn me. But now I see a better and more sure word of reconciliation. It is now impossible for me to remotely speak of such a thing.

It is in this state of glorious hearing and understanding of that proclaimed word of His voice that can never be taken away from us. What Mary heard while sitting at the feet of Jesus could never be taken away from her. Thus she will always be with the Lord and as long as she is sitting at His feet she cannot be deceived. This is a present truth that offers us a glorious hope for today. Hearing His voice today is what propelled Jesus to speak and do what He did when He walked in the earth that day. He lived in a higher realm while walking the earth than just as an ordinary earth dweller not hearing His voice. His voice comes to us from many witnesses, and they are our clouds that we ascend into. Because of what they shared with us, we are enabled to go where they are and where He is. When Jesus said, "I go to prepare a place for you ...so that where I AM, there you may be also." This is not a future event, but a now present word spoken from within us, which is the place that He went to and parpared. By His messengers (angles) we can be where the I AM is today. Thus we shall always be with the Lord. That truth can never be taken away from us! He breathes on us daily!

All scripture is for us today! Yes, it was for us in the past and is for us in the future. But all scripture has been fulfilled in Christ Jesus for us to partake of today. He came to fulfill the law and the prophets. Did Jesus fail? If not, then it is fulfilled and cannot be pushed off into some future time and event. Even His coming again is put off into some future event in our thinking so that we either miss the comings of the Lord when He speaks to us now. Either that or the glory of His present revealing is slighted or thought of as no big deal because our minds run to some future colossal cataclysmic event that leaves the earth (us) in ruins. If we respected His voice in us or His voice spoken through others as the people in Ghana, Africa did ours, we just might have the same results as they did. They were saved and healed!

"But, as long as we're out of here!" Does that sound like the cornerstone of truth to you? How selfish and self-centered! There is no love, or thought of grace, or blessings for the world with this kind of thinking. If we are the body of Christ, that mentality is sending a message to the world that God is ready to desert you and lower the hammer. It is totally contrary to God who is love and the knowledge of the Chief Cornerstone. This is forsaking the world that He died for. It is without even the slightest consideration of what the Lamb of God has done for the world. It is a law-based mentality of judgment still reserved for the rest of the world and in turn we judge ourselves as something special and better than they.

How are we so different from Israel? How are we so different from Hitler? Peter couldn't see the gospel going to the Gentiles because his Jewish background says, "We are God's chosen people and the rest of the world are but no good infidels!" What he was really saying is, "To hell with them!" But we know God straightened Peter out. To hell with the rest of the world leaves the true God out of the picture and unable to help, or deliver, or forgive, or save.

In reality, now is always the acceptable time of the year. In another thousand years it will be now. Is that now any less or more acceptable than now? Then how can we say, that God's judgment is coming after all the believers are raptured out of here? That acceptable year is not a calendar year of 365 days. If that were the case, then Jesus' preaching and teaching for three and a half years exceeded the acceptable allotted time. But He was speaking of the year of Jubilee where all things were forgiven and restored. That time still remains today because of the finished work of the Lamb that will never end. If there is no more year of Jubilee, then we are all without hope. If Jesus permanently established the year of Jubilee, and He did, then why are the doomsday prophets speaking as though the sacrifice of Jesus and His finished works are coming to an end?

Now is always favorable with God. To place an end on God's grace because of an event and to go back to judgment is to annul the works that Jesus Christ did on the cross. It is another gospel and we do not have to curse them. Their message of the law places themselves under the curse, and until they repent (change their mind) let them be accursed.[264] They truly are prophets like that of Balaam.[265] Balaam set out to curse the people that God had blessed even though God told him not to go. Hey, the money and fame with the king looked good. Balaam rode his donkey on the way to meet with the king to discuss it further. An Angel of destruction awaited him. But the donkey saved his life. The Lord spoke to Balaam and made it quite clear that your way is perverse if you curse what God has blessed.

Warning: God spoke to Peter about calling common or unclean what God has cleansed. God blessed the whole world by what the Lamb of God accomplished on the cross. God now sees them all as His because of the shed blood of His Son. They have already been redeemed. They have already been reconciled. The fullness of their judgment and our judgment was laid on Him and He cannot Himself curse what He has already blessed, because the blessing came by promise and not by their obedience. The blessing is already given by grace and not of any man's works. So, be warned false prophets of doom and gloom and hell fire, the truth is out and God will no longer tolerate ignorance,[266] for you are prophesying against those whom God has purchased with His own blood; and you are proclaiming a curse on those God has blessed! Turn to the gospel of grace and let the law with all it judgment and condemnation die on the cross where it was nailed. Then you will save yourself and your hearers!

---

264   Gal. 1:8, 9
265   Num. 22
266   Acts 17:30

How can God ignore such a glorious work when the Lamb is seated on the throne with Him? To do such a thing, He would have to dishonor Himself. It just ain't gonna happen! It looks like we are faced with a choice. Are we going to honor the Lord Jesus Christ and His works that He finished, or are we going to honor the words of natural carnal minded men who are still judging by outward appearance? Are you going to be a worshiper or a judge? Hint: Jesus didn't judge others.

God is a Spirit and will first reveal Himself from the kingdom of heaven, where He dwells on the throne. Natural interpretations of the scriptures are for natural carnal or unchanged men. CNN will not provide the right information for our modern day prophets to get it right. True prophets and their prophecies come from the Spirit of the Lord and not from putting day old news together with the Bible and comparing natural events to Spiritual things. Words of the Spirit are for those born of the Spirit or who have had a spiritual awakening. Deep calls to deep and you cannot get any shallower than the natural. The depth of your learning is shallow still speaking death compared to the life-giving Spirit and His living word.

A natural interpretation is natural and not life giving. We are led by the Spirit of God and not by natural interpretations of the Bible. The Bible is a spiritually inspired book to unveil Jesus Christ to us all and was never meant to stop at natural or surface understandings. That would be no more than looking at the Bible after the flesh, where carnal men could understand it. If that were the case, then the Bible would be a carnal book and it is not!

The Israelites knew God by His acts, but Moses knew the ways of God. One had a natural stand-offish fearful perception and expectation of God, but the other had a personal encounter with God that resonated the glory of God based on relationship even though it was the backside of God. Make the word of God a present and personal truth to you, which causes intimacy with Him now. Or make it a future natural event and remain in the natural unchanged condition you're in. If that natural future event is truth, then why hasn't it set anyone free? The natural will draw crowds, just look at football stadiums today. I thoroughly enjoy watching football, but the best entertainment of this world is nothing compared to encountering our awesome and Almighty God!

He sent His word and healed us is a spiritual word and has the power to change the natural. But the natural has no power to change the heart of man. All things were created from the realm of the Spirit and all things are held together by the same Spirit. The Bible is a word of the Spirit given to lift us up into the greatest dimension of life, the dwelling place of God, the Most Holy Place. And if God can have our now, our past will leave a trail of surely goodness and mercy following us all the days of our lives. And if God can have our now, then our future will be filled with the I AM when it comes, and we will experience all His plans of good and blessings that He has prepared for us.

If God has only plans of good and blessing for us as stated in Jer. 29:11, then where does hell fit those plans? That no good news gospel (oxymoron) isn't any different than any other religion out there. But true Christianity should be preaching that He did it for all and all are made worthy to receive the blessings of the kingdom of heaven that is now at hand! Did God really mean it when He said:

> **Php. 2:10, 11 (Amp.) — *That in (at) the name of Jesus every knee should (must) bow, in heaven and on the earth and under the earth, and every tongue [frankly and openly] confess and acknowledge that Jesus Christ is Lord, to the glory of God the Father?***

If He didn't mean it, He wouldn't have said it. But do we really believe it? This scripture is possible because the finished work of Jesus cannot be changed or cancelled out. It affected all three heavens that we know: the spirit realm, the soul realm (mind or physic realm) and the physical realm. It is only by a present truth of Christ revealed to someone that can cause any and every knee to bow. Some have preached that those who didn't believe on Earth will bow in hell! That's not bowing, that's breaking their knee. That's a forced bowing of the knee and God's just not into that kind of worship.

Those who worship Him must worship Him in spirit and in truth. There is no truth in hell, that's why it is hell. Hell has no truth, so what good is a message from hell? No one is bowing to Christ in hell. Hell is where the soul (mind, will, emotion, conscience) of Adam goes because there is no revelation of Christ at that particular time. But even...

Psa. 139:8 — *...if I make my bed in hell, behold, You are there.*

The One who is the truth also has the keys of death and of hell.[267] The keys are the truth and they are life. It is the truth that will set us all free that are in hell. "I'm not in hell," you say. But you have been and it was the truth that set you free. "I've never been in hell," another says. Everybody has been in hell. It is not a physical place, though it can be physically induced; but it is a place of the fallen soul that is of Adam. If you have never been in Adam's shoes in your mind, then you have never been to hell.

If you have never had a bad thought long enough to cause you to become angry at yourself or another, then you have never been to hell. If you have never been offended or bummed out because you were degraded or belittled by another, then you have never been to hell. If you have never been to the place where you lost all hope, even for a minute, then you have never been to hell. If you have never had a heated argument with a loved one, to only regret it later, then you have never been to hell. Is the definition of hell clear yet?

But each and every time you have been delivered out of it and it wasn't by your own strength or will power. Jesus is the only one who has

---

267   Rev. 1:18

the keys that delivers us out of those places, those attitude, those dark thoughts, those hateful places. Even if you make your bed there, He is going to meet you there and pick you up and carry you out because He loves you and He just can't stand it when your soul is not one with Him. He loves the whole you and will tear down every wall that separates.

> **Psalm 86:13 — *For great is your mercy toward me, and you have delivered my soul from the depths of hell.* Pro. 23:14 - *You shall beat him with a rod, and deliver his soul from hell.***

These were not written by men who have died and crossed over to the other side, only to find themselves in hell. What is delivered out of hell? The soul, which includes the mind, will, emotions and conscience of man. The word hell is the Heb. word sheol, which means the dead or grave. This of course is not a physical death or a physical grave. If it were, then these scriptures would not have been written because David would have died in that hell or grave. It was the soul that was delivered, not the body.

How does one's soul descend to the depths of hell? Just keep eating of the tree of the knowledge of good and evil and it will soon find itself in hell. Why? The day you eat of it, you shall surely (die) die. But our faithful God keeps throwing in the olive branch; which is the living word (Jesus Christ) who sweetens up our thinking and the next thing you know, we're free! Free from what? Hell, the place where the dead hang out, where there is no revelation of Jesus Christ, where there are lies and deception all around. Sometimes it is our religious deceptions that put us in the grave, tormented with the thoughts of so many people dying and going to hell forever and ever without end. But the truth can deliver us and keep us from ever going there again if we will believe the truth.

Saul whose name was changed to Paul had the hardest of all hearts, and he bowed his knee, not by force, but willingly when the light dawned on him. And by his own words and anointed by the Spirit of God, this same man said <u>every</u> knee and tongue will give honor and glory to God. He had this understanding that if Jesus Christ can save me, who was the chief of all sinners,[268] then He will save all. Isn't it wonderful?

Then where does eternal hell without any remedy for the lost fit in this scripture and our foundation of Jesus Christ as our Chief Cornerstone? Looking from heaven's point of view by understanding the Chief Cornerstone, you tell me. Is He the Lamb of God here but in the Spirit realm one who condemns to an eternity of hell, even though He said, "I did not come to condemn?" Can the same soul that was delivered out of hell on earth find that it cannot be delivered out of hell in the Spirit realm where Jesus is clearly seen? Can the natural unchanged or unrepentant physical mind stop a spiritual revelation of Jesus Christ on the other side after this life? Did Jesus change His identity in heaven, or is He the same there as He is here? Is He love here, but on the other side one who is filled with anger and gets his kicks out of declaring people guilty and rendering the judgment of hell without end?

Eternal hell is just one point where our belief system doesn't fit in the foundation but takes away from the truth that sets us free and keeps us free. It causes a separation rather than a reconciliation of oneness. This Western style of religious understanding of hell completely leaves out the great I AM as the Lamb. It seems to me, where the scripture says, "He is a very present help in the time of trouble,"[269] would have its greatest affect when someone found themselves in hell, not in heaven. If the soul is troubled, wouldn't that be hell. It sure isn't the peace of God.

The subject of hell can be a sore spot with many people, so we need to first be assured we really believe in the foundation laid as only being Jesus Christ. Just for fun though, ask yourself this. I have Jesus Christ and I have hell, so where's the union or oneness of Christ and hell? Are

268   1 Tim. 1:15
269   Psa. 46:1, 41:1

they the same thing? I thought hell was the absence of Christ? Then why is the subject of hell even mentioned to unbelievers as though it is a part of our foundation of the good news gospel? Aren't we supposed to preach the good news? I know, we have preached hell to warn them to repent or they'll go there. But without God in their soul, they often find themselves in hell and their body experiences it as well. So how is the gospel of hell going to help?

Could it be that over a hundred years ago, the church clergy, decided that is was best to preach a hell, not because it was the truth, but that it actually scared people into attending church, which drove up church attendance as well as more money? I would just as soon people stay away from church meetings if that is what they are going to hear. Church meeting can't help anyone if there is no revelation of Jesus Christ. And a mixture of grace and the law doesn't help people either. It only brings confusion. Well, before I went to church I may have been confused, but I didn't know it. Then after I started attending church, I got more confused and I knew it. I also received some truth too, but I also got some laws that I never had before I became a believer.

A message about hell cannot deliver anyone out of hell. Only a message from heaven about what Jesus accomplished for them can deliver them from hell. And if the truth can deliver us from hell on earth in this form of life, is it powerless to deliver those who have not yet believed after death of the natural body? To be absent from the body is to be present with the Lord, not just for believers only, but for all that came from God. And it just so happens that everyone did come from God, whether they act like it or not. Here we are, absent from the body, yet we believe that we can somehow carry our natural sins committed in our natural body into the spiritual realm without a natural body. That sounds far more impossible than it does to believe that the same Jesus that saves here can also save there.

Only the condemnation we carry in this life is carried with us after the natural body dies. That's why some are tormented. It is the guilt and condemnation they still have in their soul, because they have not yet believed that the law with its condemnation has already been taken away. Is He the I AM here and the TOO LATE there? Is He the all possible God here and on the other side the impossible God there? If the condemnation that is carried into the Spirit realm is greater than the blood carried into the Spirit realm, then I don't want to go there. What joy is there in seeing others suffer self-condemnation? It has to be self-condemnation because we know Jesus doesn't condemn. Is God bigger than self? Much! Then is God bigger than self-condemnation? Much again!

What if Jesus actually used the keys of death and hell instead of putting them in His pocket and forgetting He had them? What if it dawned on Him that He had the keys to bail them out or pay the ransom of those who went to hell? Is it possible that our Lord and Savior is able to deliver out of hell all those who went there? He delivered you out of hell on earth didn't He? He being the I AM is the Chief Cornerstone of all our beliefs. If it is not, then confusion will be our cornerstone and sand our foundation.

In the Hebrew the word foundation is yasad (yaw-sad'). It means to set or set down together; that is, He settles us by consulting with us. The Holy Spirit has been given to us to reveal Christ Jesus to us, individually. Everyone has been taught things that weren't quite correct, and that's going to happen because we all came from an Adam mind set. Some of us might be more confused than others. I have taught things in the past that I now know were not the truth now. So I don't teach them anymore. I trust the Lord will show them the truth as He has me and will continue to show us more truth.

So, why all the confusion? I didn't, and nobody else, took the time to first lay a proper foundation and then look at everything in the Word of God from that perspective and only from that view. I was told to read my Bible everyday. So the first year, I read through the whole Bible. The only problem was, I was reading and understanding from an unrenewed mind of Adam. So I saw mostly from Adam's perspective. I'd talk to my Pastor about some things that I thought I understood and found out I really didn't understand yet. Why? No foundation to start understanding correctly. Then if I did understand correctly, I was told I was wrong because they had more religion than me. So, I believed their religion because I trusted man more than the Christ in me. Why? No foundation laid in me to trust.

We have all been drawn away from the truth by well-meaning preachers and teachers that were confused and didn't know it. But boy could they preach like it was true! They had me convinced and I helped others to be convinced too. We all got carried away with the deception. We experienced preachers have a knack of being able to teach and preach under the anointing, and then say some things that aren't quite right, but say it with the same force and energy as though it was God and God anointed. But when we begin to catch ourselves saying things that are not correct, it is best to stop and confess so no damage is done.

It was our opinion coming from the weaker vessel of the natural unrenewed mind called the woman that spoke, and not the man of the house (Christ). Don't let a woman (natural carnal mind) teach in Church![270] Don't let the natural unrenewed mind speak in Church! Even if we have a renewed mind, we are still not supposed to speak from it. The anointing of the Spirit of God doesn't come from a renewed mind, it comes from the spirit of the new man.

It is when we say things that aren't true with the same tone and emphasis on it as we do the real anointed truth that his type of presentation can even confuse the more mature believers into believing something that is not the truth. The woman, natural mind, can be very persuasive. And what we believe to be the truth is the perspection we have as we read our Bible. That's why it is so important that we understand the Chief Cornerstone and look at all scripture from that perspective only. Then, He who is the Chief Cornerstone becomes the

---

270   1 Tim. 2:12

author and finisher of our faith and not some tradition handed down to us by religion.

Example: 99.999% of American believers today were either born again knowing that if they didn't receive Jesus Christ as Lord, they would go to hell forever without end, or they quickly found out later and believed it. Unknown to us, this formed our foundation for our reading and interpreting the Bible. And it is from this position that most of us still read the Bible. So, we read the Bible with a mixture of grace (Jesus saves) and judgment (Jesus condemns to hell) which are totally contrary to one another. The one has the perception that comes from heaven and the other sees only from the law, natural, or Adam's perspective. You cannot have both and please God. Nothing but faith in God's grace that comes to us through Jesus Christ pleases God, because that's who God is.

Grace is the hotness of God and judgment is the coldness of the law. The mixture produces lukewarmness that leaves a bad taste in God's mouth and understandably so; for He is seeing the Lamb of God sitting on the throne with Him. Most of my life as a believer, I read the Old Testament seeing God's judgment with condemnation and little or no grace. So, I used to think I'd better straighten up and obey some good Christian laws, or I might fall and get judged, which was really a certainty every time I looked at myself from the perspective of the law. But, if I confess my sins enough (still under the law of my works), I can get cleansed and forgiven. So my belief system or foundation led me back under the law, that if I do this and don't do that, and if I confess enough, and if I repent with tears, then that must be the life of the believer. And we seek to give this kind of life to others? This is heresy. Another word for heresy is 'itself'. It leaves you looking at yourself and working by yourself, and not seeing Christ only. That kind of believing is mixed up and confusing.

God isolated us for awhile in our little house church and unbeknown to me at the time, God began to redo our foundation. He was causing us to think differently from a better place and perspective than we had ever imagined. God took us back to our foundation that I thought was fine, but He refined it. God kicked over more sacred cows during those days. I lost a whole herd! And I'm not looking to get'em back either. Because I have yet to reread the whole Bible from that pure foundation of Jesus Christ and His finished work, I'm sure there are still some more cows hiding in the bushes somewhere.

For over three and a half years God began doing a fresh new work in us while in that house church, and it was like being born a new all over again! The best message God ever gave me was during that one Sunday. What Sunday? The present Sunday at that time! No kidding, I always thought that <u>this</u> Sunday, God had given me the best message I've ever heard. It was so liberating and full of grace and love. It always put Jesus Christ in a better light than I had had before that Sunday. It appeared that our Lord was getting better and better. But it was only our knowledge of Him that was getting better and clearer as the true foundation was being revealed. After about the second year, I could look back and see what God was doing. By being able to see where I was now and then looking back, I could see more clearly where God was taking us.

Here's another example of the great grace of our God from the Chief Cornerstone of the finished work.

Rom. 5:12–21; Vs. 15 — *By one man's offense many died and by one man's righteous act on the cross the free gift of grace abounded to many.*

Many is the same number that grace abounded to, as those who by the one man's offense many died. The reason many is used here and not all, even though all died, is because there were those who had **not** sinned according to the likeness of the transgression of Adam who were a type of Him who was to come. So not all transgressed, but all died, because through the one man sin entered into the world.

The sin of your father, and his father, and his father clear down to Adam was passed on to you. Did you have a choice in your being born in sin? No. No choice concerning the birth of sin. Now, did Jesus ask you first before going to the cross to die for you? No. Even before Adam sinned, God already had planned and appointed our salvation through His Son as the Lamb of God. In the same manner that you had no choice about being born in sin, you have no choice in whether you are forgiven or not, and you were made righteous. To the same 'many' that died because of one man's sin, the same 'many' were forgiven by the one man (the Lamb of God) who takes way the sin of the world, and that same many were made righteous. The only choice in the matter is whether we believe what Jesus did for us and freely receive it now, so we can enjoy our new life of righteousness and fellowship with God now. Or we can choose not to believe and live in a cursed state of existence even though we have been redeemed from it. Not cursed by God, but by having a sin conscience and unrenewed mind. Our being made righteous has nothing to do with our works or our choices. It has everything to do with what Jesus accomplished on the cross, in the grave, and in His resurrection. So, whether you believe it or not, God has already forgiven all and made all righteous. He has already loved us all and does love us all. His act alone was without our choice in the matter.

Righteousness is freely given to us and the whole world. It comes from God and not from ourselves. It is a free gift that He has already given to the whole world. God has reckoned it or counts it as done right now. But the whole world does not count it as so. So who's right? According to what God knows and sees, He's right. According to what the world knows and sees, they're right. But it is the one who sees correctly that is right. The lower view is opinionated based solely on the limit of knowledge they have. The world needs to be convinced that God has made them righteous by the sending of His Son as the Lamb. The only difference is in the Adamic mind of man that causes him to think of himself as evil continually. The light of Christ is already in him. But he needs someone to light the candle in him. He needs the stone of the law rolled away so the hidden man of Christ can come out. And when he sees it for the first time, he believes it and is awakened to it or is born again.

Jesus not only <u>was</u> the Lamb of God, but He <u>is</u> the Lamb of God and that perspective from the Cornerstone of a finished work can lead us into seeing every person as forgiven which in turn qualifies them to freely receive from the kingdom of heaven. This must have been how Jesus saw the all that He healed. If all of those who didn't come to Him would have come, then all of them would have been healed too. Why? The Lamb of God was present which qualified all. Religion will try to disqualify some if you are not one of them.

The only thing that can make one unworthy to receive is if they look at themselves rather than at what Jesus did for them. This would disqualify us all. But the Lamb of God brought the kingdom of heaven to all mankind and made it so all could freely receive of God's kingdom. It is the Father's great pleasure to give you the kingdom! So from heaven's viewpoint, all have been made qualified to freely receive from the kingdom of heaven. This is how God sees it. But this is not how the lower view of an earthly religion sees it. But what's important is how do you see it?

Vs. 20 — *But where sin abounded, grace abounded much more.*

The way most of us talk to unbelievers or talk about unbelievers, we say it this way, "Grace abounded, but sin much more abounded," as though the sin of the world is greater than the blood of the Lamb of God Himself. Hell is always in our thinking when it comes to the unbelievers. We were taught to believe that sin is greater than grace. How so? The judgment of eternal hell without end leaves us with that conclusion. But in truth, that's been finished too, but we never understood it before.

Did God create everything with an end, or full course purpose, or completion in mind except hell? We were made with a purpose to fulfill and when we run our course to the end, we have finished our course. What is the end or full course of hell? It is seeing Jesus, the truth and grace of God. Hell comes to an end when it sees Jesus. Condemnation comes to an end when it sees Jesus. Suffering in the soul comes to an end when it sees Jesus. He shall not leave my soul in hell because it saw Jesus. God comes to us while we are in hell on earth and saves us. But religion teaches us something different on the other side after death. They teach hopelessness so that they might preach fear tactics which is the opposite of love. Perfect love casts out fear.[271] Because we have heard fear preached so much, it takes perfect or complete love in our hearts and minds to finally begin to believe the truth. Once that true love is believed upon, it casts out all that fear and the false reasoning.

How can every tear be wiped away when our loved ones and friends are supposedly in hell without an end in sight? Wouldn't even heaven be tormented with such a view? Or is heaven hard hearted? We are instructed to cry with those who cry.[272] So, if we're seeing those bound in hell for ever without end, we're going to do a lot of crying. But if we see Christ with them in hell, we know that they will soon come out. No more tears,[273] but lots of rejoicing!

Does Jesus really change His character from Lamb to hangman while He sits on the Great White Throne judgment seat? If these questions leave you with wanting to know the real answers, then you are open to seeing the truth in the scriptures. But if these questions only arouse your religious anger and stubbornness to deny even these basic scriptures and their fulfillment, then you will remain unchanged until He that is perfect (in knowledge and wisdom) has come to you, and He will. Until then you will be struggling between grace and judgment. Most religious

271   1 Jn. 4:18
272   Rom. 12:15
273   Rev. 21:4

preachers don't even realize that in the same paragraph they speak of God's love and grace, and then turn right around and condemn God's children and the world as though Jesus was condemning them.

Did John the Baptist really mean in

Jn. 1:29 — *"Behold the Lamb of God who takes away the sin of the world?"*

Or did he really mean the sin of believers only are taken away? If that were the case, then many of those who didn't even know who He was, but were healed of Him, couldn't have been healed because they had not yet believed on Him. If you still see yourself as a sinner, you will see yourself as unworthy to receive anything from God, especially something as wonderful as healing. The Lamb of God walking in the earth was the forgiveness of the whole world. He saw everyone as forgiven. Only those who justified themselves by the law (mostly the religious Scribes and Pharisees) were unable to receive and walk in that forgiveness, but the power of the Lamb to forgive and heal was still there with them without their permission. They just chose not to believe and therefore saw themselves as unworthy to receive.

Here's the kicker. If you don't believe you are forgiven because you don't believe in Jesus Christ and His finished work on the cross, you cannot walk free of that sin, but you are still forgiven. That's right. Every sinner in the world is forgiven! I AM your forgiveness is a present unseen reality for the lost. The price has been paid for all the people in the whole wide world. They just don't know it! Probably because our message has been a mixed message of heaven or hell rather than, "Your sins are forgiven you, now rise up and walk" or "God has forgiven you, so what do you want the Lord to do for you now?" This is the same thing as telling them the kingdom of heaven is at hand. No one can walk upright on their feet if they don't believe their sins are forgiven them. But most people still believe judgment and condemnation awaits them because that's the message that is coming from the Church that's supposed to know God. We seem to forget that He is love, and He is forgiveness.

John 16:8–11 — *And when He has come; He will convict the world of sin, and of righteousness, and of judgment: of sin, because they do not believe in Me; of righteousness, because I go to My Father and you see Me no more; of judgment, because the ruler of this world is judged.*

Why does most of the Church today still believe the old religious teaching of men that declares that God convicts us (believers) of our sins? A mixed foundation that has left them with a sin consciousness causes a misreading and understanding of the scriptures. It causes us to error, not knowing the scriptures. We cannot properly know the scripture unless we read them from the perspective of the Most Holy Place, a place of rest in Jesus Christ. The teaching that God convicts us believers of our sins alone is enough to keep us self-conscious of our own sins. And if we believe that He convicts us of our sins, then He must be keeping records of our sins. If He is keeping records of our sins, then He must be keeping records of everyone's sins. And if that is the case, then He must be storing up wrath and judgment for us all! We are doomed for sure! The snow ball of deception just keeps getting bigger and bigger. It is widely believed among the Church because pastors, teachers, and other 'holy' men of God teach it, and who is going to question "the Pastor"? If I speak something that is not right according to the Chief Cornerstone of our foundation, I want you to question me. I want you to search the scriptures and prove me wrong; in doing so you will save both yourself and me. Thanks! I really mean it!

The preaching that God convicts us of our sins brings condemnation and guilt back into the Church that has been saved by the blood of

Jesus Christ. It declares God as our accuser rather than our Mediator. It describes God as one who looks for our faults instead of one who is without fault finding as described in Js. 1. It declares that there is no blood on the mercy seat that is in the Most Holy Place, nor in heaven for us when we sin. It is a description of the covenant under the law and not one of grace and Jesus' finished work because it has us looking at our own works. It severs any consistency we have in our walk with God knowing He is accusing and reminding us of our sins. And if He accuses us once, He'll accuse us every time we sin. So, if God's accusing me, then whose going to save me?

God is not our conscience. Our conscience is not our God. We didn't even have a conscience until we ate of the tree of the knowledge of good and evil in the garden because we only knew the life of God. That is when we gained a conscience of right and wrong, good and evil, and it was a sin conscience. But God is greater than our conscience and is able to cleanse our conscience from dead works. In other words, God has us looking at our foundation, which is Jesus Christ, and that stops us from looking at our sin. It is our own conscience that convicts us because of the presence of the tree of the knowledge of good and evil. If we had not known good or evil, then we would be unconscious or unaware of such things and only aware of God. That is how Adam was created; only aware of God. That is the same state of condition that He desires for us today.

A clean conscience before God and man is not a testimony of our good works, but a testimony of only being God conscious or God aware. Paul wasn't looking at himself and his works when he declared that his conscience was free from guilt. But that the testimony of his conscience was witnessing to him the presence of the Lord in all his conversations and acts toward them, the believers. Your conscience can bear you witness of the Holy Ghost,[274] or it can bear you witness of your sins. So, if you sense that God is convicting you of your sin, you now know it is

---

274   Rom. 9:1

not God! But it is your own conscience being made aware of sin carrying with it the remembrance of Adam because of the knowledge of the tree of good and evil. You are looking at your own works. If you eat of it, your soul will die and you begin a process of separating yourself from God; you will feel guilty and condemned, but not by God. If you eat of it not and look at your foundation, which is Christ, you will be cleansed of that sin consciousness. And that's why the Holy Spirit convicts us of our <u>righteousness</u>.

> Jn. 16:8 really says, **"When He the Holy Spirit is come, He will convict the world of sin....of sin, because they did <u>not believe</u> in Me."**

Do you believe? Yes? Then this scripture does not apply to you. Notice the only sin God is concerned about and convicts the world of is not believing on Jesus. That's it! There is no other sin that exists! But somehow, if you're a born again child of God, God convicts us of any and every sin we commit; but God only convicts the world of the one sin of not believing on the Lord. Something doesn't seem quite right with that kind of thinking. I think I'd rather be convicted of one sin, then all my sins. In this belief, I'd be better off as an unbeliever!

If you believe in Him, you cannot sin the Bible says.[275] Why? Because as far as the Lamb of God is concerned, you're forgiven and our Father doesn't hold your sin against you. He's forgotten it as quick as you committed it. It's only you who remembers it because you still have a sin conscience.

If you don't believe in Him, you are already convicted of your sin; your own conscience even condemns you. That's why Jesus said if you believe not, you are condemned already. Not a future time of condemnation, but you are presently condemned because you have not believed on the Son of God who takes away your sin and the sin of the

---

275   1 Jn. 5:18

world. You stay self-condemned because you have not believed. Even a born again believer has done that. We have self-condemned ourselves so many times because we followed the desires of our flesh or our natural intellect instead of the Holy Spirit. Now we are faced with thoughts of condemnation, but if we set our minds on things above and not on the earth, we will discover that Adam is still dead and we are hidden in Christ. Does God convict us of our sin? No, but now He convicts us of our righteousness and cleanses our conscience from sin. No more guilty, condemning feelings coming from our conscience. Glory to God!

So it's the believing part that is so important that God looks at, not the sin or the didn't sin part. It's the believing on Jesus Christ that connects us to the One who committed no sin and is able to keep us from falling. It is only when we don't believe in Him that we become vulnerable. To believe means to trust and rely on. Just because you are born again doesn't mean we always believe, trust, and fully rely on the life of Christ and His finished works. But it does mean we are born of Him, and He will come to us and remind us of our righteousness. That sure is good news to me! I need that. This is how God restores us back into fellowship without any condemnation. If He was to convict us, that would restore us back to fallen Adam. That conviction of sin is a reminder of sin. But I know that God said, "Their sins and their lawless deeds I will remember no more."[276] His indwelling presence of the Holy Spirit will lead and guide us in the truth. So the Holy Spirit never, never, never needs to convict you of your sin, because that is not the truth of the knowledge of Jesus Christ. That is knowledge without Christ which is the knowledge of Adam. You are a new creation, and God only needs to remind us of that truth. A-men.

Jn. 16:10 — "He, the Holy Spirit will convict us of righteousness, because I go to My Father and you see Me no more."

276   Heb. 10:17

We see Him no more in the flesh; we believe by faith so our righteousness is by faith in Jesus Christ and not having to see righteousness in the flesh no more. Get it? I don't even have to see my righteousness in my flesh to know that I am righteous! I am righteous because I see Him who is my righteousness. I have believed in the finished work of Jesus Christ only. Jesus Christ is my righteousness. I am reminded of that work and convicted of His righteousness, which is now my righteousness. And the way most of us have believed in the past, that's a full time job for the Holy Spirit to remind us of our righteousness because we keep reminding ourselves of our sins. But once again the Holy Spirit convicts us of righteousness which renews our minds from our old Adamic image we have of ourselves and gives us His heavenly view of ourselves. This transformation gives us the mind of Christ and having accepted this truth we can get on with life and life more abundantly. And hopefully we'll be able to go on from this foundation and do greater things when our belief system is changed so the Holy Spirit can speak greater things to us.

Jn. 16:12 — *"I still have many things to say to you, but you cannot bear them now."*

Once we get a hold of the Chief Cornerstone and He gets a hold of us, He's got many things to say to us that will totally fire us up like a refiner's fire, which will produce greater works! He must first prune the branches so they will be able to bear more fruit. What do you think the pruning is? The truth, like a two-edged sword, will cut away the dead stuff that had no ability to manifest the life and fruit of God. Now greater things said to us will produce a full grown plant that will bear much fruit. We are not the branches of a tree that loses its leaves and only bears fruit occasionally. "We are trees planted by the rivers of waters, that brings forth its fruit in its season, whose leaf also shall not wither;"[277] This tree has rivers of life and truth flowing

---

277   Psa. 1:3

to it constantly so that it produces fruit every time there is a season (expected time) for it.

Too often churches will get hung up on a particular subject, or certain doctrines, or staying within their denominational boundaries, or the non-denominational click which can build walls that will hinder more truth from coming that the Lord wants His family members to have. Often these things are used as their cornerstone for building their church. But you are not just a family member of a church group. You are a family member of the Father first and He cares whether you are being feed with well-balanced food or if it is just processed food you are getting. Individually our flesh and soul sometimes wants to feed on nothing but junk food all the time; as a result, we become spiritually unhealthy and our growth is stunted. To stay healthy, we must eat from a variety of different food groups. This kind of feasting will establish a greater, fuller understanding that will establish you in righteousness. But beware: Any teaching or preaching that has you looking at your do's and don'ts is the teaching of the law. Just spit that out in the trash because it's road kill, it's been crucified.

He has yet many things to say to us, but if we are set in our way of thinking and doing things because that's the way we have always believed or that's the way we have always done it, then we are not yet ready to hear the things that He yet wants to speak to us. Every pastor and church leader must be ready to move on from the place where they are at spiritually, mentally, and maybe even physically. But never are we supposed to build anything that is not founded on the Chief Cornerstone.

There is an endless wealth of the Lord's knowledge that He wants to share with every member of His family. God's not interested in a particular church just teaching and preaching the same message that they've always taught and staying in the same vein of understanding that they have always had. Just saying the same thing over and over again, only putting a different look on it, just isn't causing anyone to grow in the grace and knowledge of our Lord. He is much, much bigger than that.

Vs. 11 — "*The Holy Spirit will convict of judgment, because the ruler of this world is judged.*"

This judgment we are convicted of is **not** judgment against us, but the ruler of this world has been judged. The Holy Spirit convicts us of His judgment against the serpent, the devil, or the deceiver. The ruler of lies has been judged and found to be a liar. If the ruler was judged and found a liar, then the truth shall set us free. What can rightly judge a lie or deception? The truth. The Holy Spirit is also known as the Spirit of truth. The truth judged the ruler of this world. The word judged means to put asunder, break in pieces, to distinguish. Jesus Christ is the truth and He defeated the prince of this world; he is disarmed, made naked, and is without authority and dominion over us. Once again, this is not some kind of mysterious being that seems to be everywhere in the spirit. What ruled this world was the law. The whole world was under the law and most of it still is. But it has been judged as a deceiver that could not lead us to God. Trying to live by the law no longer has that position of deception to rule over us. It is only by deception that he can rule at all. The truth finds him to be a liar and leaves him powerless, and that is the conviction of judgment that the Holy Spirit convicts us with.

The only ones who believe God will convict us of His judgment against ourselves are those still under the law because they do not believe, even though they might say they do. They carry about within themselves guilt and condemnation against themselves and therefore reserve that same condemnation for others in their message. They cannot help but speak such things, because that is what is in their well of bitter water. But anyone can have a change of mind by looking steadfastly at Jesus Christ and His finished work. When this becomes our foundation and Chief Cornerstone for our life of believing, then all things will become clear, and we will be free from the ruler of this world. Glory to God!

What does this have to do with the I AM? If God hasn't already dealt with the judgment of sin and condemnation, then He cannot be the I AM to us but the 'I Will Be Some Day God'. There is nothing left of Adam and the prince of the air of this world that hasn't been dealt the blow of death and defeat. And if He has already dealt with these things, then heaven and hell are already dealt with too, not some day. The only thing lacking is not God doing more in the future but our seeing and understanding more clearly so that we may know the things that are finished and live by the power of them. This just might change your gospel to an I AM fully present with you and ready to perform my word gospel.

As far as our judgment of sin and the sin of the whole world is concerned, let's look at

Jn. 12:28–32 — *"Father, glorify Your name." Then a voice came from heaven, saying, "I have both glorified it and will glorify it again." Therefore the people who stood by and heard it said that it had thundered. Others said, "An angel has spoken to Him." Jesus answered and said, "This voice did not come because of Me, but for your sake. Now is the judgment of this world; now the ruler of this world will be cast out. "And I, if I am lifted up from the earth, will draw all to myself."*

This is how God is glorifying His own name. Now is the judgment of this world, and at the same time now is the ruler of this world cast out. When is the judgment of this present world? Was it back at the cross? It was finished at the cross, but individually we proclaim it by living free from the law's judgment and from judging others by that

SEEING FROM HEAVEN

same law. And I, if I be lifted up from the earth, will draw all judgment to myself. Do we think that God the Father has forgotten that all our sins were placed on His only begotten Son? He still bears the marks of the description of the Lamb of God in heaven. God cannot even look from His throne toward the earth and see any sin because of the blood of Jesus. So how can He convict us of our sins when He Himself removed it from us?

As long as we think for one moment that we still might have some hidden sin, He cannot be our I AM now. The cross is where all our present judgment of sin is. And that's where all our future judgment of sin is already. And that's where all the sin of the whole world is right now. Nobody but nobody has to repent before their sins are forgiven and laid on the cross. It's already done. The <u>repentance is a change of mind.</u> That change of mind is evident when the report of the good news that they are forgiven is believed and received! Oh, and by the way, what else would you like Jesus Christ to do for you now that this grace has appeared to you? Be confident that anyone who believes their sins are forgiven and they have right standing with Almighty God are ready and able to receive anything they need from the kingdom of heaven. Then give it to them with great joy because it is the Father's great pleasure to give the whole kingdom to them, not half of it, but all of it!

Our foundation, and even more so our cornerstone, is not the whole logos (written) word of God. How we read the scriptures and from what position we are standing when we read the scripture will determine whether we are rightly dividing the word of truth or not so the house (you and I) can stand upright on the foundation. All the scriptures Old Testament and New must be read and understood from the Chief Cornerstone position so the house can stand thereon. Without the cornerstone position, we will read Old and New Testament scripture from a position outside the tabernacle or from a position in the tabernacle other than the Most Holy Place as though the coming of the Savior of the world had no effect and His death, burial, and resurrection

319

accomplished nothing. So now all the scriptures contain the flavor of the Lamb of God and the King of Kings with grace and mercy and were written for our learning God.

Only from the Chief Cornerstone perspective can we approach the throne of grace which sits in the Most Holy Place. If you feel guilt or condemnation or inferiority, then you cannot approach Him. No flesh can stand in the presence of a holy God. But if your approach to Him is from the Chief Cornerstone, then you are free from those things and are approaching Him in faith with love and joy. You can now have fun, dance, turn in circles, jump up and down, and rejoice in the presence of God. In other words, just be yourself in His presence.

Example: The destruction of Sodom and Gomorra is for our instruction in righteousness as stated in 2 Tim. 3:16. It was **not** written so we might be afraid that God will do the same to us. But it was written for our learning and if what we learn from it is that God is out to kill all homosexuals, we missed the truth and are falling from grace. That is only a judgmental view from the law. And if that is the case, we have left the Cornerstone, and now we are thinking that God is seeing more sin today than in the times of Sodom and Gomorra! Then we better look out, 'cause the doomsday prophets of today would be correct.

But we can learn from a Cornerstone perspective and part of our learning is this: The fire came from heaven in judgment of their sins because they saw not the grace of God and the law judged them. But all that judgment of their sins and ours (past, present and future) fell on Jesus Christ. The payment for their sin was in their future and their sin consciousness could have been cleansed if they would have seen it. Just as our forgiveness is in our past when we saw Jesus hung on the cross, theirs was in their future.

Now the fire that comes from Heaven is that of the Holy Spirit's fire that purges us from the bondage of sin by the word of God that burns within us. His word is like a burning coal or sulfur that purges our lips. The fire from Heaven destroyed the Adam that we were and the image of him with all his sins, but out of it came one family, the body of Christ. God cannot put up with duality, Adam and Christ dwelling together. So He sends a fire to destroy the Adamic mind and his corrupted image of himself so only that which remains is of Christ.

All the Old Testament was written as types and shadows of the works of Jesus Christ to come as its fulfillment. We can find the New Testament gospel interwoven with the Old Testament types and shadows if we'll let the Chief Cornerstone live in our hearts and our thinking. Reading the Old Testament in any other light separate from the knowledge and awareness of the Chief Cornerstone will cause us to go back under the law and thus under judgment and condemnation. I AM is the truth and grace that saves. I AM is not the law that judges and condemns you. The law is weak and I AM is not weak.

Nowhere in scripture does the Bible say the blood of dead men still speaks. But the blood of the living still speaks. So if a man dies having never believed his sins are forgiven him and therefore never walks in freedom from sin, can he still speak his lies or even defend his own self-righteousness when the blood of Jesus speaks for us all? Will he not be dumbfounded and unable to speak like Zacharias was in his unbelief as he stood in the presence of the Angel of God? He was unable to speak until his tongue was loosed by the Spirit of truth. Then he was able to speak with living water flowing out of his heart.

The dead cry out for even a drop of water. Was that cry for natural water when they didn't even have a natural body? No. Dry spirits having no water in themselves cry out for the water of life, Jesus Christ. Abraham was unable to cross the gulf of disunion. But the Lamb of God descended into the very pit of hell and came out with the keys of death and hell. He is the One who is able to cross the distance and save. Where sin caused a great gulf between the two, Jesus removed by His blood and redeemed us all! He will not leave my soul in hell.[278]

---

278   Psa. 16:10, Acts 2:27

My soul as well as your soul has experienced hell, the absence of God, even after being born again of the Spirit of God. How did we descend to such a lowly place? Once again, by allowing our thoughts coming from our five senses to dictate to us until we got angry, or depressed, or bitter, or self-condemned, or fearful. That is a soul in hell. But God is always faithful to come to us and remind us of Himself and who we really are, thus delivering our soul out of hell! So, I wonder, can God do the same on the other side in the spirit realm where He is seen even more clearly?

There is only One who is worthy to open the seals of the book and that is Jesus Christ. Jesus Christ, whose blood was also sprinkled on the altar in heaven will open everyone's book. The book of many people's hearts and lives are sealed and none of us can open them. We tried to be a witness to them. We've prayed, we've preached, but nothing seems to work. Be at rest, there is One who will open the book![279] He shall show Himself to them as the Lamb of God who takes away the sin of the world. His love for them and all that He has done for them will open up their heart, and God will begin to write in that book His living word. Glory to God!

These things might give you the impression that the I AM has the present, past and future all covered. Precisely! To live everyday with the knowledge of the I AM being present with you always, is like Enoch walking with God and was no more. You will have no more consciousness of yourself as being separate from God. In that condition one cannot condemn nor be satisfied with good works. The presence of God and our fellowship is our full satisfaction. Your awareness is God centered to the degree that you are one. And out of that place you are equipped to minister without doubting anything. Where He **is**, there you are also becomes a true experience of the brightness of His shining. The revelation of Christ coming to us is the appearing of the I AM and gives us an awareness of oneness. And as He is, so are we in this world.

---

279   Rev. 5:2–5

Knowing God as the I Am, we can experience heaven now because we are seeing Him from heaven's viewpoint. The Chief Cornerstone came from heaven and He is the beginning and the end of all truth that is. Anything that is not founded on knowledge of who Jesus Christ is and what He accomplished by His death, burial, and resurrection is deception and heresy. It will bring disunion. So, take heed, take a close look to what you are building your house with. And the Lord is with you.

SUMMERY

WHO IS GOD

Chapter 1
JESUS IS THE CHIEF CORNERSTONE

The Chief Cornerstone is a person, Jesus Christ, and we are in Him. We are to see ourselves positioned in Him so that we may see as He sees all things clearly from heaven's perspective. He is the man from heaven. Just as Jesus saw all things from heaven or the Father's perspective, we can too. To position ourselves in Him is to know and understand who He is and what He finished by His death, burial, and resurrection. This allows the mind of Christ to take up residence in our thinking, where the soul and the spirit of man are one with Christ. Then you can rule over all your earth and manifest the fragrance of Christ everywhere. Understanding the Chief Cornerstone is the beginning and the end of all that is truly God because Jesus Christ is the Alpha and Omega.

Chapter 2
JESUS IS THE LAMB OF GOD

The Lamb of God is present here and in heaven. Seeing through the eyes of the Lamb of God is the forgiveness of God freely given to the whole world. Jesus saw all forgiven and manifested that forgiveness by healing all who were sick that came to Him. The Lamb of God manifest is the only requirement necessary for receiving anything from God, and the Lamb dwells in you, the believer. Our Father can see nothing on earth without seeing through the eyes of the Lamb of God. He cannot condemn because of that love and forgiveness given to the whole world; for the Father and the Son are One. Christ in you is the revelation of the Lamb of God abiding in you. We seeing all forgiven will change our approach to all and will leave us without an accusation or condemning word.

Chapter 3
JESUS IS THE KING OF KINGS

Jesus Christ is the King of kings, the Lion of the tribe of Judea. The Kingly character of our Lord reigns in conjunction with the Lamb and are never separated. A Lion without the nature of a Lamb would tear this world apart with its power and might in order to rule over it with forced control. But we find that together there is power and love ruling in the One, our Lord Jesus Christ. We also discovered that the King's greatest responsibility and desire is to protect His people and to destroy all their enemies, which is why Jesus healed the sick and cast out devils. Our enemy is never other people and neither is it unseen devils running around. But our enemy is principalities, powers, imaginations, and deception that are at work in our minds in an attempt to rule over it so that death might rule over the earth (body) as well. So in that same union of the King and the Lamb abiding and reigning in us, we have been given authority to rule with Him over all these things.

Chapter 4
GOD IS LOVE

God is love. This is the most divine attribute and nature of our God because God does not just contain love, but He is love through and through. God can do nothing outside of His love. Understanding this and dwelling in His love will cause us all to walk with Him and express that love through serving one another at the point of their need, and that includes healing the sick. Love is a divine flow of the power of the

Holy Spirit. Love is what will keep us from falling. Love, His love for us is what never stops giving us hope in this life. Following after love (zoe love) is following Christ. Love knows no end and has no limits. Love is the most powerful force in all the universe. Love is giving at the expense of self and God does that 24/7. God is love and so are you, Believer! You are born again with His overflowing love. Unless you know His continuous love for you, you cannot be born of God and neither can you know Him. There is nothing, absolutely nothing that God says or does that is outside of love. This is a good measuring stick for dividing the truth from error.

Chapter 5
GOD IS GOOD

God is good. He is never bad, nor can He do anything evil. God has no bad or evil in Him at all; therefore, He can do no evil. What is evil? Anything that is harmful or hurtful to anyone spirit, soul, or body is evil or bad. There are very few things God cannot do. But one of them is: He cannot tempt anyone with evil. Too much of the Church has an image of God watching over them with a club, and the world gets the same idea because of the Church. Some preach God causes bad things to happen to teach us a lesson. No, God is good. Jesus declared there is only One that is good and that is God. He meant that God is good through and through, over and over, time and time again and never changes from that nature. God's works of creation proves that God is good, except when He created you, and then He was very good!

Chapter 6
WHO IS GOD

The names of Jehovah are in reference not to a God whose people are under the law, but a people who are under grace. Those who are under the law are not God's people, but they belong to the god who is the law.

Those who have the Lord as their God are led by the Spirit of God, not the law. God chose a people before the law. The law brought them back under bondage even though God delivered them out of Egypt. Physical location is not bondage, but if you're serving anyone or anything other than the God of grace, you are in bondage. The law is a declaration that we are our own god because it points us to our own works separate from Him and His grace. The law was given so we might see what God is like. The law was seeing the backside of God, or His works that declared who He is. All His names are wonderful! His names are a description of the one true God and you can call Him Jesus, Lord, King, Lover, Master, Teacher, Helper, Healer, Great Physician, Advocate, Prince of Peace, Friend, Father, Brother and the list goes on and on. He will answer you by any of these names when you pray, because He is. Knowing Him as all these things to us will help keep our thinking straight, so we might freely partake of His life.

THE FINISHED WORK

Chapter 1
AN END OF THE LAW

Jesus brings all men to an end of the law. To the Scribes and Pharisees, who were religiously stooped in their laws, He gave them the perfection of the law, which is an impossibility that would eventually bring them to an end of themselves. The more law we possess, the more we see ourselves as a failure and fall short of the glory of God. Or if we think we are doing the law well, it puffs us up and we become full of pride. But when we only look at Jesus as our substitute in this life and see His works, then we see clearly that He has changed us by His death, burial, and resurrection. He qualified us to be partakers of all His blessings of the Highest kind of life, abundant life. We see today that many of us has gone back under the law as the Galatians had. Looking at and measuring ourselves by any part of any law is going backwards. Law and grace are a mixture that causes lukewarmness and God hates it because it separates you from Him. Grace makes you one with Him, where the law separates you from Him. He is a jealous God, which is why He was so dedicated in going to the cross to destroy the sin that separated us from Him and to put an end to the law. Jesus having nailed the law to the cross means there is no longer a place given where we are to look at our own works. As we do all things from the life and character of the new man born in His likeness, we have no need for the letter of the law. This is the law of the Spirit of life working in us.

Chapter 2
HE FINISHED WHAT HE CAME TO DO

Jesus finished what He came to do. He brought heaven with Him and because of His death, burial, and resurrection, which is the forgiveness of the sins of the whole world, heaven is still at hand. Heaven didn't leave when He died as some might suppose. Heaven couldn't leave because the death of the Lamb paid the full price of the whole world's sin. Jesus made it heaven on earth and heaven is presently here today. Jesus purposed to bring heaven to us, not bring us to heaven. He preached the kingdom of heaven is at hand. He never said that He had come to take you to heaven. The abiding life of Christ within is heaven in you. All we need to do is manifest His presence from within and you have heaven on earth! All the prophecies written of Him are finished. Nothing remains unfinished. We are even finished, but we might not know it and act like it if we don't dwell in the present light and life He gives us. Jesus is ascending into the cloud that you are and not descending out of heaven. This is you experiencing Christ first hand. You finishing your course is not about how much you can do for Christ, but how much you allow Christ to finished His work in you. You are that course that He came to finish or make complete. Nowhere in scripture does the Bible even talk about all the works of Enoch. But only that He walked with God and was no more. Our course is only to walk with God and whatever work He has for us to do will flow out of that union. No pressure! No confusion! So enjoy.

Chapter 3
GOD'S JUDGMENT AND WRATH

The judgment and wrath of God is finished because it was all laid on Jesus at His crucifixion. If there were any judgment of condemnation and wrath of God left for mankind, then Jesus didn't die as the Lamb of God, and it would be necessary for Him to die again. I don't care what the prophets of this world say; the only judgment God will reveal to the world is the judgment that was laid on His Son. It is because of the Adamic thinking of the world unaffected by the Church that there is so much chaos and destruction today. If we can get the true message to the world, then the world's thinking can be changed, and all his enemies will become the Lord's footstool. His enemies are our enemies and they are the deceptions we have. The wrath that is being reserved for the day of judgment is the day of His appearing to them as the Lamb who took their sins and wrath upon Himself. The unbeliever stores up for themselves in their own mind and conscience the wrath of God because they have not yet seen Him as the Lamb. Therefore, their own conscience condemns them, not God. Jesus said, "…they are condemned already." Because of the finished work of Jesus Christ on the cross, God doesn't judge or condemn anyone. Jesus came not to condemn the world, but to save it. God doesn't store up wrath. If He did, then one of the fruits of the Spirit would be wrath or anger, because as He is so are we. No, all the judgment and wrath of God against man was placed on Jesus Christ at the cross. The world doesn't know it yet, but as soon as the Church believes in the finished work of Jesus Christ, they will soon. What wonderful news we have to tell.

Chapter 4
REDEMPTION IS A FINISHED WORK

Redemption is a finished work. Without asking us, Jesus came and already laid down the greatest price for the salvation of the whole world. The world is not waiting to be redeemed from the curse; it is already redeemed. But they don't know it yet and therefore cannot walk in that light. But we are the light of the world to show forth that redemption by declaring the kingdom of heaven is at hand. Jesus not only redeemed us from the fall, but from the law. That in turn put an end to the curse of the law over the earth that we have dominion over. We just have to exercise our authority in Jesus name. Having been redeemed from being under the law, we are free to declare the works of the Lord. The blessings of the Lord are at hand! The acceptable year of the Lord is now! We overcome by the blood of the Lamb and the word of our testimony! It is the price of redemption that has redeemed the whole world from the curse. But just as Jesus had to enforce the kingdom of heaven by using His authority over all the curse, so do we. We no longer carry our own name to do such things. We are His and not our own. Our redemption gave us a new identity. The price has been fully paid by Jesus the Christ, and it is therefore a finished work.

Chapter 5
RECONCILIATION OF THE WHOLE WORLD

For if, when we were enemies, we were changed mutually or changed after the manner of God by the death of his Son, much more being changed mutually or changed after the manner of God, we shall be saved by his life. Except for us delivering the message of reconciliation, the work of reconciling the world to Himself is finished by Jesus' death, burial, and resurrection. It is our message that makes it known to all so all can receive it. It is through us that God woos or compels the world to be joined together to Him. His compassion moves us along to heal the sick, make the deaf to hear, and open the eyes of the blind, so that they may see the love of Jesus. This is the proof that He is raised from the dead and is alive in us. So, our message is one of life changing power and not just empty words. Jesus sends us forth to do the same works and greater works than He did; "For as the Father has sent Me, I send you." Let us believe God's love for the world and be moved, as He still is, by giving away freely the blessings of heaven. As it is in heaven, so be it in earth. Earth is already reconciled. Being reconciled to God is to bring people into union with the Father. We were once enemies, but His death ended all enmity. It is only the carnal unrenewed mind that is still at odds with God. The message of reconciliation brings our soul into perfect union with the mind of Christ.

Chapter 6
THE KINGDOM OF HEAVEN IS AT HAND

Our message that the kingdom of heaven is at hand has the power to reconcile the world. If we meditate on all that Jesus came to do and did, we will realize that the kingdom of heaven has always been at hand, but we were unaware of it because we were in darkness. Through prayer with the Father and learning from the Holy Spirit as His teacher, Jesus found this out and also learned exactly who He was. This enabled Him to live in heaven's kingdom as well as produce the works of that kingdom which is greater than the kingdoms of this world. All creation came out of the realm of the Spirit where the kingdom of heaven is. So that kingdom has power to change this earthly kingdom of natural things. The supernatural or spiritual realm of heaven supersedes every natural force on earth. So when the faith of God in us moves us along, all the power of heaven is available to rain blessings to reverse the curse. Noah's boat settled on the mountains of Ararat after the flood receded. We believers are to settle in those same mountains which mean the curse is reversed. We are Mt. Zion knowing and having the kingdom of heaven is for the purpose of reversing the curse. As we see more clearly from heaven's view, we will be fully assured that the kingdom of heaven is at our hand to bless the world.

Chapter 7
THE I AM

The I AM is both a description of who Jesus is as our Cornerstone and of His finished work. It is by not understanding this one thing that has caused so many teachers and believers to error in their believing and understanding the word of God. As a result, it has caused many to stumble in their walk with God and has hindered them from receiving all His benefits. One of the greatest revelations of God is that He is the **I AM!** He is an ever present (now) help in the time of trouble. Being born of God, we know God no longer by looking at His backside (works only) but face to face and heart to heart. By this we know what He is saying and doing right now. It is from this perspective and understanding that we can read our Bible and see all things are for now, rather than putting the Word in a future event in time. As God intended, the scriptures are a revelation of who Christ is right now. Christ in you is a mystery being unveiled daily as a revelation of the I AM. We saw that the future of hell had been dealt with by the appearing of the I AM. Until He appears to you, hell is very real. For hell is the absence of God in our assumption (imagination without knowledge). God is present everywhere at all times, but if we don't recognize that fact, or know Him as the I AM, it can be hell. The I AM is present to convict believers of righteousness as a reminder of who He is and who we really are presently in His sight. I AM the Lamb of God that takes away the sin of the world never changes into an, "I am the accuser." Therefore all are forgiven, but not all are walking in it or experiencing it. The I AM is also in the next life after death, and just like in this one, He is everyone's hope. If not, we are most miserable. But the revelation of Jesus Christ as the I AM leaves no one miserable, only blessed and filled with abundant life!

CONCLUSION

Hopefully after reading and studying this book you will be able by the Holy Spirit to read your Bible in a fresh new and glorious light of understanding that comes from knowing the Chief Cornerstone. If you have any doubts as to the fullness of any of these descriptions as to who the Christ is or concerning His finished work, please search Him out in prayer and in further study of His word. He is always better than what we have known Him to be in the past and in the present, not worse. If what you see Him to be seems too good to be true, it probably is true. For He is totally good and He is most awesome!

Randy Finlay grew up on the farm north of Carbondale, Kansas, where he learned to work hard and to do everything with his whole heart. Saved by God in the midst of reading the Bible, Finlay has ministered to children for over nineteen years and pastored for six. This is his first book.